KATERI

A BEACON
IN THE WILDERNESS

JACK CASEY

DIAMONDS AS BIG AS RADISHES, LLC

© 2021 by Diamonds Big as Radishes, LLC

Paperback ISBN: 978-1-7343666-0-0

Ebook ISBN: 978-1-7343666-1-7

First Edition

Cover Design by JD Smith Design

Published by Diamonds Big as Radishes, LLC
3956 Bentley Bridge Road
Raleigh, NC 27612

Cover image from bas-relief on door of St. Patrick's Cathedral, New York, John Angel, sculptor

Drawings by Father Claude Chauchetière © Archives départementales de la Gironde, H Jésuites

Kateri praying in the snow from image by Camille Drolet, S.J.

Portrait of Kateri Tekakwitha by Father Claude Chauchetière, St. Francis-Xavier Mission, Kahnawake, Monteregie Region, Quebec

Catherine tekakouita Iroquoise du Saut
S. Louis de Montreal en Canada morte
en odeur de Sainteté.

Catherine Tekakouita by Jean-Baptiste Scotin

This engraving is clearly based on the Chauchetière painting, and the caption in the original 1753 engraving stated that St. Kateri was an Iroquois and was portrayed with Iroquois features and complexion.

To my beautiful

VICTORIA

Love of my life and
Guardian of my faith

PREFACE

I attended Kateri Tekakwitha's canonization on a breezy Sunday afternoon in Rome. Twenty thousand people crammed into St. Peter's Square at the Vatican to witness the uplifting ceremony. St. Kateri's presence in my life has been profound, and I was deeply moved.

The verified miracle that propelled Kateri to sainthood 332 years after her death was the cure of five-year-old Jake Finkbonner. As a flesh-eating bacteria ravaged his face, his Native American mother prayed for Kateri to intercede and save his life. A relic of Kateri Tekakwitha stopped the spread of the deadly bacteria, allowing surgeons to repair his wounds.

In that massive crowd, I happened to sit next to Jake's grammar school nun, his scoutmaster and a few of his friends. They told me about his life in Seattle before and after the miracle. A camera projected images of Jake and his parents on a screen behind Pope Benedict XVI as he said mass. Jake's face was scarred from dozens of surgeries, but his smile was irrepressible, filled with joy and faith. Kateri Tekakwitha literally saved his life.

Who was this first Native American saint? Born into the Turtle Clan of the easternmost Mohawk village, she lost her parents and brother to a 1660 smallpox epidemic that nearly blinded her, and badly scarred her face. When Jesuit missionaries visited her village during a truce in the constant warfare between the Mohawks and the French, Tekakwitha embraced Catholicism and was baptized on Easter Sunday, 1676.

Her uncle, a Mohawk chief, hated the French for corrupting his Iroquois culture, and he persecuted Kateri for her new faith. She fled to live with other Christian natives at St. Francis Xavier Mission on the St. Lawrence River where she died during Easter week of 1680. Details of her life are scarce. If not for the mention of her in missionaries' letters and two Jesuit biographies, we would know nothing about her.

I first heard of Kateri Tekakwitha from the withered lips of an old nun when I was seven years old. I am now seventy. I've visited Kateri's birthplace in Auriesville, New York countless times, and at a second shrine upriver in Fonda, I traced the longhouses and stockade in a staked-out footprint of her village. Down a path in the woods, water still flows in the spring where she filled her water jars.

On my way home from Montreal, I often stop at her shrine in Kanawaka to light a candle and say a prayer. The portrait Father Claude Chauchetière painted of her graces the shrine's museum more than three centuries later. Kateri's remains rest in a marble sarcophagus that bears her Mohawk name, a *fleur des lis* and the turtle of her Mohawk clan etched in gold.

If the benefit of maturity is wisdom, then I believe it all comes down to faith. We are given these lives, this flesh and blood, these minds and hearts and souls along with free will to use or misuse them. While all God's children deserve our love, very few are worthy of devotion. All our lives have their struggles, and during a particularly difficult one of mine, Kateri's presence guided and helped me, so I am devoted to her.

Kateri Tekakwitha led by her quiet example and helped define Christian love, fortitude, patience, and constancy for her people. Those who knew her remarked on these qualities in the impressions the Jesuits recorded.

I painted the backdrop for this story from the old histories and from my love of this land, its mountains, lakes, and rivers. I peopled it with the men and women I met in those histories. I came to know Kateri from the existing biographies and portraits, and I strove to portray accurately the clash of cultures she witnessed and then transcended.

Long ago Kateri Tekakwitha inspired veneration with her humble, retiring ways, her strong will, and her chaste life. Over the years she has opened my eyes to the mystical and unfathomable, the hidden spiritual realms we bypass every day in pursuit of worldly things. I have come to appreciate how her purity shines like a beacon into the dark recesses of our doubts and fears.

I hope you who read this work come to know Kateri by seeing how she met the challenges and hardships of her time with love and virtue. I hope you will admire her, as I do, for questioning authority, following her heart, and living as she needed to live. And above all, I hope you learn to love her, as I do, for her unflinching goodness and faith, a timeless example for us all to follow.

JACK CASEY
Troy, NY
April 17, 2021

BOOK I
KATERI TEKAKWITHA

She dwelt among the untrodden ways
Beside the springs of Dove,
A Maid whom there were none to praise
And very few to love:

A violet by a mossy stone
Half hidden from the eye!
—Fair as a star, when only one
Is shining in the sky.

— William Wordsworth

CHAPTER ONE

ANASTASIA, A CHRISTIAN ALGONQUIN, FOSTERS A MOHAWK ORPHAN

I.

Choking yellow smoke hung in lanes of the village. Children screamed and wailed, and a steady drone of the dying rose and fell in the smoke of untended fires. A young mother wept inconsolably at her infant who would not suckle, his jaw limp in death. Hunters and warriors lay on their mats, struggling to breathe.

A smallpox epidemic was sweeping through Ossernenon, the easternmost village of the Canienga (People of the Land of Flint), Mohawks, as white men called them. The virus arrived in woolen blankets the English traded for the pelts of beaver, deer, and otter. Indigenous people had no immunity from this European disease, and there was no cure. Through heavy bearskin curtains in the smoke and stench, mosquitoes and flies swarmed around those in advanced stages, their skin peeling off in bloody shreds as they turned over. Men and women with strength enough to crawl from the bark longhouses fetched firewood and water from the encircling forest.

Tegonhat-siongo, a handsome young woman with a long black braid, entered a dim longhouse to search for her lifelong friend Kahontake (Meadow). She was born Algonquin and baptized "Anastasia" when she became a Christian. The Mohawks abducted her from Trois-Rivières six years ago along with Kahontake, who was now the wife of Tsaniton-gowa (Great Beaver). Anastasia had just returned from a month of fishing in the mountains, so her absence spared her the contagion. Seeking news of Meadow, Anastasia walked among the corpses and the almost-dead who raised hands, groaning for water. She went to the third fire pit of the longhouse, where Meadow and her family cooked and ate and slept. The fire pit was cold with ashes and charred wood.

There were swarms of flies buzzing around an elk skin robe. Anastasia pulled the robe aside and gagged to hold down her morning meal. The great chief's face, blistered and matted with bloody sores, was now a home for maggots. Next to him, wrapped in deerskin, beautiful Meadow lay in a like condition. In her arms, she held a bundle. Anastasia unwrapped it, and the corpse of a baby boy fell out. She cried out in surprise and pity. Meadow, christened Irené in the same mission class, had died without the blackrobe, without the last rites. Anastasia picked up the baby covered with boils and placed him on his mother's breast. He had died without baptism.

"Where is Ioragode (Aurora)?" Anastasia wondered. "Did she perish too?" In a shaft of light from the chimney hole, she searched among the skins and sleeping pallets. "Perhaps she escaped into the forest?"

Just then, light from the doorway lanced through the smoky gloom as four young warriors opened the curtain. They came to fetch the dead, drag them out, and bury them in a mass grave beyond the palisade. Two of them lifted corpses from the second fire pit, a mother and two babies, and the other two came toward Anastasia.

"They are dead," she said, pointing to Great Beaver, Meadow, and their little boy. One lifted the chief, and the other took up his wife and baby. The activity stirred up fleas which began to leap. Anastasia paused for one last look, and she observed a slight movement in a tangle of deerskin. She stepped over, reached down, and pulled back the skin. A little girl lay back, naked, gasping, covered in filth, her eyes half-closed, her skin encrusted with red scabs. A thick white film oozed from her eyes. Anastasia picked her up, and the child whimpered and moved.

"You live, little one!" With comforting words, she carried the child down to the river, away from the lines of men dragging corpses, away from the thick, foul smoke of bonfires where they were burning maggot- and louse-infested blankets and pelts and wicker work. On the mud bank of the river, two dozen bark canoes lay inverted in the sunlight. Weirs and nets from her fishing trip were drying in the sun. The river ran sparkling and quiet by the landing place.

Anastasia gently wiped the discharge from the infant's eyes, then dipped her in the river. The cold shock of the water brought screams of fear and pain from the little girl, startling but attesting to her will to live. Anastasia held her, rocked her for comfort, and then carried the dripping child to a decaying stump where she wiped the filth away with handfuls of moss and sawdust. Back in the water, she rinsed the child clean and dried her with her deerskin tunic.

Anastasia walked outside the palisade of tall, pointed logs and carried the naked, sobbing child to a hut of elm bank beyond the field where the "three sisters," corn, squash, and beans, ripened among charred stumps. This shack was where women stayed during menstruation, away from their men and families. Anastasia had been married briefly, but when her husband considered her barren, he divorced her. She now lived outside the village, ministering to the women who came here once a month. Anastasia wrapped the child in soft deerskin and rocked her to sleep. "I am your mama now," she whispered.

2.

A month passed. With clean air, water, and food, the child of four summers revived. Although she had been nearly blinded by the smallpox, she was soon trying to stand and walk. Her appearance was pitiful as the sores healed into scabs, encrusting her face, arms, and body. She squinted to see, her eyes almost closed, but she bore her afflictions stoically.

"Where's Mama?" she asked Anastasia one morning.

"Mama's gone away." The woman reached out and held her.

"Where?"

"She went to heaven."

"Where is heaven?"

"In the sky, up behind the clouds."

"When will she come back?"

"She won't be coming back."

"Why?"

Anastasia held her. "Mama loves you more than anything, Aurora, but she can't be with us anymore."

"Why not?" the child raised her scabbed little face.

"Because . . . because God called her home to heaven."

"And Papa?"

"He's gone away too."

"Hunting?"

"No. Papa is gone with Mama and little Aronsen. They all love you, but they had to go to heaven."

"Can I go with them?"

"No. You are my daughter now. You will live with me."

"Oh." She lay her head on Anastasia's breast. "I hear the birds. When will it be morning?"

"Soon, my little Aurora. Very soon."

As the months passed, Anastasia rejoiced for the gift of this little girl. The child's infirmities did not diminish her curiosity, and Anastasia told her stories and taught her songs, and they laughed and played together all day with the women who visited.

The child could walk, but due to her poor eyesight, she groped her way along. Anastasia made her a doll from corn husks, and Aurora held it through the night as she slept.

Anastasia kept Aurora in her hut outside the palisade during the Strawberry Moon when the village children ran into the fields and picked strawberries. Because of the epidemic, there was no festival this year. Anastasia considered she had adopted the child, but as the leaves turned colors and the cold winds blew, a messenger summoned Anastasia before the Women's Council.

The Women's Council governed the Turtle Clan, and appointed clan chiefs and war chiefs, and ruled on marriage, divorce, and the custody of children. It had voted recently to move the village to a prominent hill on the north side of the river and leave the smoldering contamination of Ossernenon behind. Crews of men went to prepare the site, to build long-houses and enclose the new village with a strong palisade. They named the place "Kanawaka" (At the Rapids). When the village was ready for occupation, the sorcerer went through the new longhouses, burning torches of tobacco weed to smudge, cleanse, and bless the air. Soon a long, slow column of survivors, carrying packs like refugees, crossed the river and wended along the bank to the new village. Anastasia was constructing a hut outside the palisade one morning when a young woman approached:

"The Council wishes that the child be given to Moneta, wife to Iowerano (Cold Wind)."

"But Moneta has no greater claim than I."

"The child is Cold Wind's niece, and his wife is barren."

"But I found her and fostered her." Anastasia held the little girl.

"You must appear at midday tomorrow," the young woman said and departed.

"What is it, Mama?" Aurora sensed something amiss.

"Everything is fine, little one."

3.

The following day just before noon, Anastasia entered the village and walked to the Council House. She bent down and pushed through a flap of bearskin into the great longhouse. The air was dim and smoky, filled with cooking, tobacco, and far less pleasant smells. The matriarchs sat in the center, cross-legged on mats. The red glow of the fire lit their wide faces, high cheekbones, and greased long black braids.

Anastasia waited until her matter was called, then she stood and walked to the mat directly opposite the three women who issued decisions. One motioned to her, "Please sit."

Anastasia sat down.

"Is it true that you rescued the daughter of the great Tsaniton-gowa?"

"It is so. Yes." Anastasia acted with respect. "Meadow, the child's mother, was my companion when People of the Land of Flint welcomed us among you six summers ago."

"You are Christian?"

"I was. Since no blackrobe is among us, I no longer practice my faith."

"But you keep your Christian name?"

"I do."

"Iowerano, brother to Tsaniton-gowa, has no children, and his wife, Moneta, is barren. Ordinarily, our blood lines proceed from mother to child, but this child's mother was Algonquin, not of our blood. Iowerano is a blood relative. It is our decree that you turn the child over to Iowerano so she may be raised in the *ohwahchira* (clan) of her blood as one of our people."

"Please hear me, wise mothers," Anastasia said. "I know I am not Mohawk. I am Algonquin, and I have practiced the Christian faith, but I saved little Aurora's life. Under my care, she has thrived. Blinded by the pox, she now sees light and shadows where before she saw only darkness. I am teaching her bead work and embroidery, and she sees well enough now to perform this work. I petition you. Please reconsider. Allow me to care for her in my cabin."

"Impossible," one of the old women growled. She was thick-faced, and her eyelids drooped. "She must learn the customs of our people, all the customs. This can only happen in the village among our people, not outside the stockade with an Algonquin."

"I could bring her within the walls," Anastasia said. "I am happy to move."

"Aurora will be raised Mohawk, not Christian." The ancient matriarch, her lined face, and long gray hair lit in shadows by the firelight, motioned with her finger to a young man. "Bring Moneta to us."

The messenger left, and soon a haughty young woman stood before them with folded arms and dark eyes flashing with annoyance. She wore a tunic of white doeskin, colorfully embroidered with dyed porcupine quills. She and Anastasia exchanged nods. Moneta detested Anastasia as she had detested Meadow when they arrived, both beautiful Algonquin women.

"It is the decree of this council, Moneta," the ancient matriarch said hoarsely, "that you will be mother to this child."

"It is true I have no children," Moneta said with a sneer, "but I have no wish for any, especially one who's blind."

"Iowerano is her father's brother."

"I cannot help that."

"We decree that Anastasia will turn the child over to you by sunset."

"I have no spare sleeping mat. I do not need another mouth to feed. I have seen the girl. She is blind and therefore useless. She is scarred and will never be marriageable, a burden always to anyone who takes her in."

"Summon Iowerano," the old woman said impatiently. The young messenger left again.

A few moments later, the chief himself entered. Iowerano was a large, imposing man, his tall rooster comb greased straight up from baldness further increased his height. He was dressed in leggings and a buckskin tunic embroidered with porcupine quills. His brown eyes were wary, fierce and he moved with arrogant confidence.

"You summoned me?"

"Your brother's daughter has survived," the matriarch whispered. "The Christian here rescued her and keeps her in a cabin near the ravine. It is the mandate of the Women's Council that she be brought back into the village and raised by you."

The chief centered himself on his muscular legs. He breathed deeply, threw out his hands, and spoke in a deep, oratorical voice: "Honored mothers of the Turtle Clan. I hear your decree. Let me answer thus. The white man's disease has killed many. The grave outside the walls of our former village, hardly covered with earth to this day, bears witness to the evil the white man spreads. Those whom he cannot kill, he sends the blackrobes to corrupt and weaken to steal our lands. We must be vigilant in our resistance. I thank you for summoning me. This child deserves to learn and live our way of life."

"I have told them . . ." Moneta stood to speak in protest.

"Silence, wife. We will accept this child into our home as we are also giving shelter to your cousin and her daughter."

"But I told them . . ."

"Silence." Cold Wind bowed to the council. "I submit to your wishes, and I welcome my niece to my fire pit."

"Very well," said the old matriarch. She nodded at Anastasia. "Bring Aurora to Cold Wind's longhouse before nightfall."

Anastasia bowed in defeat. "I will bring her here by sunset." She turned and glanced at Moneta, who was also angry with the decree. Iowerano nodded, proud of his magnanimity to the orphan. He turned, bent, and left through the flap that Anastasia held open.

Anastasia walked out of the village gate and through the humps and burnt stumps of the newly cleared fields, disconsolate from losing the child. Moneta's temper was notorious in the village, and she used Cold Wind's status as chief to shield herself from rebuke.

Anastasia felt deep sympathy for the child who was now playing in the sunlight, face up, turning her cheeks this way and that to bask in its warmth, her eyes closed against the hurtful glare.

"Little Aurora, my ray of sunshine!" she called happily. "I have good news for you."

"Tell me, Mother." She looked toward Anastasia and groped to walk toward her. Her eyes were closed against the pain of the glare.

"You have recovered so well the villagers want you to return home."

"I like it here. I will remain with you."

"I want you to stay as well . . ."

"Good. Then I will."

Anastasia gathered her up and held the scarred little girl tightly. The child rested her head on Anastasia's breast.

"You must go back, my little Aurora." She said this with great cheer, hoping the child would not react adversely.

"Why?"

"The clan mothers have decreed it."

"But why? We live here, you and I."

"Yes, we do."

"Then it's settled."

"I'm afraid not," Anastasia said. "Let us pack up your things."

"Where will I be living?"

"With your uncle Iowerano and his wife Moneta."

"I didn't think they liked me," she said without rancor. "Why do they want me to live with them now if they don't like me?"

"I cannot speak to their thinking. They have agreed to foster you, and the clan mothers have decreed it. I must deliver you to them before the sun goes down. You will be fine."

"If you say so," the child said, and she started toward her

uncle's longhouse with her hands out to encounter any obstruction.

<h2 style="text-align:center">4.</h2>

A crimson sun hung above the flowing river and the western trees as the woman and child walked, holding hands. The woman carried a bundle of bedding, the child a pack, and her corn husk doll. They walked along the ridge and through the narrow stockade gate. They passed through the lanes where dogs glowered at them and proceeded to a longhouse in the middle of the village where the great chief made his home. A spread of moose antlers hung above the door. They pushed through the heavy curtain.

Cold Wind was sitting cross-legged at the first fire pit, smoking the calumet with three other men. He nodded and grunted at Anastasia and the pock-marked child. Anastasia led the child to the next fire pit, where Moneta was stirring a kettle of *sagamite*, corn porridge flavored with bear fat and chunks of dried trout. She saw them and nodded a greeting, then wiped her hands on her apron and stood.

"So, this is the girl?"

"I call her Aurora for the light and the joy she brings."

Anastasia dropped her hand, and the little girl began to reach into the air to find her bearings in this strange place.

"Yet she is blind?" Moneta said with disgust.

"Her sight continues to improve. She can tell light from darkness."

The child was moving forward, waving her hands in empty space to encounter and guide herself in this new place.

"This girl is no bright sunrise, no aurora," Moneta said in derision. "She is blind and clumsy. I will call her 'Tekakwitha'— She Who Gropes Her Way."

"Aurora was the most delightful child before the disease."

"That matters no more. The child is scarred and blind and will require far more care than she is worth."

"Please be kind to her," Anastasia said, stroking Aurora's hair. "She is so docile and sweet."

Moneta put her hand on her hip and watched the child critically. "There is no room for sweetness in this longhouse, and as for docile, well, docile can sleep over there in the corner. Make her up a pallet and then leave us."

Anastasia led the little girl to a corner where the lashed shelves that stored baskets and bark utensils met the curved rib work of the wall. Anastasia gathered some discarded pine boughs and spread the girl's fur blanket over them. "You'll be comfortable here," Anastasia said.

"But why can't I live with you?"

"The Women's Council believes you will be safer here with your uncle and that you will learn the ways of the Mohawks."

"But my aunt doesn't want me."

"Yes, yes, she does. She loves you. It was your uncle who petitioned the Women's Council so you could join his family."

"He has never spoken to me before."

Anastasia tried valiantly to hide her sorrow too, yet the child felt her sobbing.

"Why are you crying, Mother?"

"You have suffered so much already. This fostering is needless."

"Will you visit me? May I visit you?"

"Do what your aunt tells you to do. I will visit you in the morning."

"Tekakwitha!" the aunt called. She dished a heap of the corn mush on a bark plate. "Come eat your supper."

"Goodbye, my darling Aurora." Anastasia embraced her.

"Tekakwitha!" Moneta commanded.

"Goodbye, Mother." She hugged Anastasia tightly.

"Come along," Moneta insisted. "We don't have all night."

"It is apparent I'm not invited," Anastasia said.

"We scarcely have enough for this one." Moneta rapped the wooden spoon on the kettle. "Come! Eat!"

Aurora and Anastasia embraced one last time, and then "Tekakwitha," hands out and gazing emptily forward, groped her way toward the family circle. Anastasia slunk through the doorway and out into the night.

**Mohawk Warrior detail from "The Death of General Wolfe" by
Benjamin West**

CHAPTER TWO

KRYN THE HALF-BREED RETURNS WITH
PRISONERS OF WAR

1.

With the passing of four summers, Tekakwitha's eyesight improved. Although she wore a shawl outside in the daylight to shield her eyes from the sun, in the dim longhouse, she went bareheaded. Tekakwitha now worked all day indoors, stringing wampum beads and embroidering tunics and ceremonial robes with dyed porcupine quills. Chief Iowerano had recently taken a second wife, Moneta's cousin, a widow with a daughter named Rainbow, who daily tried to lure Tekakwitha outside to play. But the orphan preferred solitude, always working near her pallet in the chief's longhouse. Moneta had come to see the high value of the scarred little girl's work as she bartered it with others. While this was a benefit, she still resented Tekakwitha's presence, a reminder of the beautiful Meadow whom Great Beaver chose over her. Moneta constantly nagged the child and dispatched her often on errands of fetching wood and water.

"If she thinks the robe that she embroidered for the chief's appearance at the Onondaga Council will excuse her from her chores, she is sadly mistaken."

What galled the woman most, though, was the child's cheerful attitude. Tekakwitha never complained and always seemed thoughtful and content. She kept to herself, creating designs that drew attention and admiration from all. With the completion of each new work, she held it close to her eyes, then set it aside so she might start another. The girl's cheerfulness was somehow a constant reminder of Moneta's inability to bear a child of her own. The girl grew even more cheerful when Kryn the "Flemish Bastard" visited.

Five summers ago, the Women's Council had elevated Iowerano to serve as a governing chief of the Turtle Clan to succeed his brother, who died from smallpox. At that same council, the women appointed Kryn a warrior chief. Although his Mohawk name was Togoniron, everyone called him "Kryn" after a Dutch fur-trader believed to be his father. Kryn was massive in size, well-proportioned and muscular. He had light skin and, unique in all the Great League, blue eyes. He also refrained from using war paint or marking his flesh with tattoos. Kryn wore his hair in a high Mohawk style, the rooster comb from the forehead back, ending in a rattail tied with a red ribbon of eel skin that swung when he walked. In summer, he dressed in a buckskin loincloth and moccasins, in winter, he wore leggings and a tunic of deerskin.

To Kryn his pale skin was a cause of shame. In this matriarchal culture, he was of Canienga blood, a member of his mother's *ohwahchira* (clan) and on behalf of his extended family, he hunted and fished to provide them food, and fashioned longhouses and canoes for them. However, the notion that his father came from a degenerate race of stocky white farmers who drank spirits and beer and ate filthy swine that rooted in sewage gave him a humility rare among the Mohawks.

Kryn often visited Iowerano to discuss weighty matters of state, particularly the likelihood of war with Algonquins, Mohicans, or the French. Tekakwitha was always thrilled by his presence at their family cooking fire. She waited on him as he sat smoking the calumet, and his twinkling blue eyes charmed her when he looked her way. His wisdom and good sense were legendary, his fidelity and courage unmatched. Indeed, for her, he represented all the attributes of the mighty Deganawida, founder of the Great League. But it was with dismay that she learned one autumn day that Kryn was returning with Algonquin prisoners he had seized while hunting. She knew Kryn was leading the prisoners back to the village to torture and sacrifice them, and this horrified her.

Excitement spread through the village as a crier announced the arrival of the prisoners. The women brought out iron rods, and knives and the children swung sticks and switches to practice for the gauntlet. It was a chilly October afternoon, the hardwoods flaming orange and crimson among the deep green of the pine. The villagers poured out of the gate and formed a line down to the ford at the riverbank. White Adder, the albino sorcerer, chanted and danced and shook tortoiseshell rattles as drummers beat a loud tattoo to incite the villagers.

Suddenly, on the facing hill, Kryn appeared. Despite the chill, his torso was naked. He wore a loincloth, leggings, and moccasins. He raised his arms and bellowed out a war cry that sent the villagers into spasms of joy, "Aiiii-yeee!" They danced and waved their spears and rods and birches high in anticipation. Kryn reached behind him and produced a tall Algonquin, his hands tied behind his back, fear and defiance mixed in the expression that peered from under his matted hair. The villagers went wild. Kryn shoved him forward, then pulled up another prisoner, a pregnant young woman. This brought shrieks of laughter from the women waiting to beat her, and the terrified Algonquin woman shrank from the impending violence. Next, Kryn brought forth an older man with a cloth around his skinny shanks. The aged man was stooped, and haggard and his hair fell limp about his despairing face. The villagers howled in derision at his age and infirmity. Kryn again raised his hands in triumph and brought forth a well-proportioned young man, naked, his hands tied in front of him. The women shrieked with laughter at his nakedness. Kryn pushed him down the hill.

"Come, Tekakwitha," Spotted Fawn urged, "let us welcome these prisoners."

"No," Tekakwitha said. "I hate the screams of pain."

"But it's fun to watch them dance when the torches burn them and knives open their skin. How can you not enjoy it?"

"I think of how I would feel if somebody did it to me."

"But it isn't being done to you!" Spotted Fawn said. She and Rainbow laughed. "You're doing it to them!" The two girls ran out to join the gauntlet, and Tekakwitha turned back, alone, to her longhouse and her work.

Dinner was postponed that night as all the village welcomed Kryn's prisoners. Iowerano returned to his fire pit to don his headdress of horned elk and eagle feathers. He did not notice the young girl in the shadows stitching quietly.

As Iowerano was leaving, Kryn entered: "Great Chief, may I ask a favor or you?"

"Of course."

"The villagers are escorting a young warrior to the platform as a holocaust to Aireskou."

"The pole and the platform are ready, and Aireskou thirsts for his blood. It will bring us good hunting and will aid us in keeping away the French."

"And yet I come to seek his release."

"But you brought him here as a prisoner!" Iowerano scoffed.

"You often speak, Great Chief, of the need to build our nation. This warrior showed outstanding courage in battle and was captured with great difficulty as he fought to the death. He is worthy of the name 'Canienga.'"

"As worthy as you?" Cold Wind sneered.

Kryn ignored the gibe. "Burning him on the platform will bring us only a temporary benefit in witnessing his courage as he dies. Adopting him into an *ohwahchira* will bring us lasting benefit. He will hunt to feed his family, and he will fight both in attack and in defense. He will breed strong sons. We have welcomed him and caressed him sufficiently with our knives. His face has not yet been painted black. Let us cut him down and adopt him."

"It has been a year and more since we have sacrificed a prisoner to Aireskou."

"Has the god asked you for this?"

"The gods do not speak to men except by signs. The sorcerer and the people require this sacrifice. I deny your request."

"Hold him for a day. Convene the council and let us put it to a vote."

"We only do that when there is some question as to the prisoner's value as a hostage. An Algonquin has no such value, and so there is no need."

"My words fall, then, on closed ears?"

"I have spoken. We are grateful to you for capturing these prisoners. Let us put this one to good use."

Kryn glared at Iowerano. He turned away, and then he saw Tekakwitha in the corner.

"Who is this?" Kryn asked.

"My foster daughter," Iowerano said.

"She is not out welcoming the prisoners?"

Tekakwitha tried to hide in the shadows.

"What is it that occupies her?" Kryn asked, walking toward her. She looked up at Kryn, then at her stepfather to see if she might speak with the great warrior.

"She's always working on something," Iowerano said with annoyance. "Let us go out and watch how well the prisoners die."

Kryn squatted on his haunches and reached for the robe she embroidered. She handed it to him, then dropped her eyes and turned her face away.

Kryn ran his thumb over the small pictograph she was sewing into the soft doeskin. A woman with wings hovered above the treetops. "Who do you picture here?"

"Sky Woman," Tekakwitha said. Shyly she squinted at him, and saw his eyes were warm and blue as a summer sky.

"So it is." He noticed another pictograph. An eagle with a wide wingspan soared over pine trees that towered over a lake. "And this?"

"The eagle who is vigilant to keep the peace of Deganawida and Hiawatha."

"Your work is excellent," Kryn said. "What is your name?"

"They call me 'Tekakwitha.'"

"Well, then, Tekakwitha, can I ask you to do work for me?"

She smiled and dropped her eyes. "Yes."

"Speak to Moneta," the chief said impatiently. "She deals in such trifles."

Just then, a scream startled them, a cry of sudden pain, ending on a note of defiance and rage.

"Come," said Iowerano, "they have reached the platform. Let us watch how heroically he will die."

"Will you embroider a ceremonial robe for me?" Kryn asked.

"Gladly," she said with modesty.

"We will talk further," Kryn said, and he touched her cheek. She looked into his eyes, and she was happy.

Kryn and Iowerano left to witness the ceremony. Tekakwitha remained behind, and as she began a new scene, she selected red quills. She sewed flames surrounding an imaginary warrior being tortured and burned as an offering to Aireskou.

All night she listened. By the dim light of embers in the fire pit, she worked the porcupine quills into the soft doeskin as the hoarse death song, ripped from the Algonquin with knives and hot irons in the flames, rose in a crescendo of defiance, edging now and then to despair. Tekakwitha had no words to describe the horror of what she heard, but alone in the longhouse, she imagined a young man, a man as brave as Kryn told, being roasted alive. Why did they kill the deer and hare and fish so mercifully but burned a man to listen to him suffer? And she suffered with him, each scream, and each defiant howl of, "Is that the worst you can do?" followed by an agonized scream. Other than the embroidery in her hands, she moved not a muscle.

2.

Morning light seeped into the longhouse. Sleeping tribespeople lay sprawled throughout the room. One by one, they had drifted in and fallen on their pallets, spent from their night of the torture ritual. Tekakwitha spread out the embroidery she had completed. Kryn had admired her work, and his praise lifted her spirits, for she loved Kryn, his fierce independence, his courage, his defiance of Iowerano. She stood and went outside to the privy ditch beyond the stockade, but she paused a moment. In the center of the village stood the remnants of the platform and the pole where the Algonquin died last night. Crows were strutting on the platform, searching for morsels of his flesh. The platform was charred and wet with the dew. The sweet, sickening aroma of burned flesh hung low like a mist. From the darkness, the villagers had summoned death for the war god Aireskou, and death had paraded, blazing, and screaming in the deepest hour of the night. The village would be quiet and sullen now for a day or two, not out of reverence, but from satiation.

Tekakwitha walked through the narrow village gate to the ditch beyond. Crows in the branches above seemed to laugh at the folly of the human sacrifice. When she adjusted her tunic and started back to the village, she heard her former name called, "Aurora!" It was Anastasia. "You stir while others sleep?"

"The night is over. The sun is rising."

"I tried not to listen," Anastasia said with disgust, "yet even in my cabin with the wind blowing across the hills, I could not escape the screams."

"May I visit you now?" the girl asked.

"Come along. We will eat."

The woman and the girl walked together through the field of

bleached corn stalks and beneath the girdled trees where crows screamed from gray, barren branches. Beyond lay the blue ribbon of the river between the green folds of the hills. Happy to be with Anastasia, Tekakwitha skipped along and greeted Anastasia's mutt, Racoon Hunter, who came to meet them. The girl played with him and nuzzled him and kissed him on his wet nose.

In the cabin, Anastasia gave her a bark bowl of porridge on which she generously ladled maple syrup and sprinkled dried strawberries. They sat cross-legged by the fire.

"My aunt never gives me strawberries."

"Then you must visit often."

"Kryn came to see my uncle last night," the girl said, hesitantly in case the subject was taboo. "He asked that a prisoner be spared and adopted, but my uncle refused. If Kryn captured the prisoner, why did he need my uncle's permission?"

"Iowerano is a powerful chief, little one. Kryn is a warrior. While the prisoner was a prize from Kryn's brave attack, Iowerano determines how the spoils and trophies are to be shared."

"But Kryn made so much sense."

"Ah, you will soon see that sense has little effect on people's actions. People act out of fear and envy and hatred far more than they act out of sense."

"Kryn praised my work, Mother. I showed him Sky Woman and Hiawatha, and he asked my uncle if I could embroider a ceremonial robe for him."

Anastasia nodded. "If we seek peace from the French, Kryn will go as an ambassador."

The girl pulled her knees up to her chin and folded her arms around her legs. "Tell me again the story of Deganawida and Hiawatha and the Great Peace."

"Ah, you will be a wise matriarch someday, for you never tire of the old legends."

"They are from a better time, before the whites arrived."

"But those times were less good in many ways, too," Anastasia said. "The five nations of our league fought constantly with each other. There was much envy and hatred and violence. No one spoke the truth. Atotarho, the most powerful chief of all, lived in the land of the Onondaga. His hair was a writhing mass of snakes. He lied, he cheated, he stole the wives of other men. He gave his word on treaties and then broke it."

"And Deganawida?"

"Ah, the Peacemaker? Yes. A Huron woman who never lay with a man bore a child whom she named 'Deganawida.' As a boy he practiced oratory on the banks of the great northern river and soon became a gifted speaker, wise and deep-thinking and able to touch people's hearts with his words.

"Deganawida was saddened by all the war and burned villages, by the scalping and death that sprang from men's passions. One night he dreamed of 'The Great Peace.' This vision brought him such comfort, he dedicated his life to achieving it. He journeyed to the land of the rising sun, everywhere encountering hunters and warriors, urging them to return to their hearth fires with his message of peace.

"Deganawida, who now called himself 'Peacemaker,' traveled to Onondaga where he met Hiawatha. He shared his plan for peace with Hiawatha, who wanted to help. He charged Hiawatha with smoothing the snakes out of Atotarho's hair. The Peacemaker then continued east through the land of the Oneida and then through our land of the Canienga and came at last to the great falls at Cohoes. There he climbed a tree and sat and waited. A band of Mohawks passing in canoes saw him and cried out they would kill him. They cut down the tree, and it fell into the river and was swept away. They thought Deganawida dead, but the next morning the Great Peacemaker was sitting by his fire. The Mohawks believed he had returned from the dead, and this power opened their ears to his message of peace. In this way, our nation, the People of the Land of Flint, became the founding nation of the league.

"Meanwhile, Hiawatha's efforts to comb the snakes from Atotarho's hair proved dangerous and unsuccessful and in anger Atotarho summoned the Thunderbird. With lightning leaping from its talons, the Thunderbird swooped down, picked up Hiawatha's daughter, and carried her away. Stricken by grief, Hiawatha left Onondaga and paddled east.

"He came at last to a lake. A great flock of ducks flew up and drew the water of the lake with them into the sky. Hiawatha walked across the lake bottom with dry feet. He gathered shells into his leather pouch. When he came to the Peacemaker's camp, Deganawida took the shells and made strings of wampum, composing the words of the 'Requickening Address.' With each string of wampum, he drew the grief from Hiawatha's heart, and they sang the Peace Hymn together.

"Together, then, Deganawida and Hiawatha came here to our Turtle Clan, the easternmost village of the easternmost nation, and taught us their rite of peace. When we accepted it, they journeyed to the land of the Oneida, who joined immediately into their league of peace. Hiawatha and the Peacemaker bypassed the Onondaga because Atotarho still ruled there, and they went to the Cayuga, who immediately accepted the peace. With three nations in the League, they went to the Onondaga at last. All embraced the peace except Atotarho. With the strength of four nations, they went at last to the Seneca, who joined and completed the League.

"The final step was to comb the snakes from Atotarho's hair. With the five nations unified in the Great League, the Peace-maker bribed Atotarho. He promised Atotarho the council fire would always remain in Onondaga if he embraced the peace and that he and his successors would always rule the League. Atotarho accepted the peace because it made him powerful. As the snakes crawled from his hair, he summoned the chiefs of every nation, fifty-one in all. The Peacemaker placed antlered crowns on the heads of all the chiefs as a sign of their authority, and they met in the first great council where Deganawida taught them the Great Law, the law we still follow today. And we lived in peace and harmony until the white man came."

"Why has he come here, the white man?"

"He comes to drive us out of this Land from Which All Rivers Flow, to seize and occupy it for himself. All rivers begin here and flow down from our land in all directions. The white man covets our land because he wishes to control our fur trade. That is why we wage war on him, strike fear into his heart about the consequences of invading our land." She stroked the little girl's braid. "Without his disease, your mother and father would still be with us, and your little brother would be alive to play with you. Instead, they are under the earth, and you cannot see well, and your aunt taunts you by calling you 'She Who Gropes Her Way.'"

"Please tell me of the symbol of the Great Peace, Mother." She dropped her head, embarrassed that the word slipped from her lips.

"'Mother' is it?" Anastasia jostled her affectionately.

"You are my mother."

"I loved your mother as my sister. We lived together on the northern river and were captured together and brought here." She hugged the child. "The symbol of the Great Peace? Hiawatha and Deganawida envisioned a lofty pine tree with five strong roots, the five nations of our league to root it into the earth. On the very top sits an eagle, ever vigilant to attack any enemy of the peace."

"Can I share a secret with you?"

Anastasia held Tekakwitha closer. "Tell me anything in your heart, little one, and I will hold it fast in mine."

"I see my uncle, Iowerano, as Atotarho, the chief with the snakes."

Anastasia laughed. "Yes, that is fitting."

"And I see Kryn as the Deganawida, the great peacemaker. When he looks at me, I know he wishes for everyone to live in peace."

"We could live so, except for the white man who knocks at the eastern gate of the Great Longhouse. Kryn feels this danger more than others because his blood is mixed. His sky-blue eyes are an accident of his breeding. He cannot deny his parentage, and so he strives to prove himself worthy of being 'Canienga.'"

"He is strong and brave, but he is also kind."

"Yes," Anastasia hugged her, "and as Kryn does, you must work harder at being Mohawk since half of you, like me, is Algonquin."

"I will watch Kryn," she said, "and imitate him."

"You make me laugh," Anastasia said. "As if you could be as great as the Great Warrior!"

"I know what I know," the girl answered, miffed at her ridicule. "And I will be what I will be."

CHAPTER THREE

CLAUDE CHAUCHETIÈRE IS ORDAINED A
JESUIT AND VOLUNTEERS FOR THE
CANADIAN MISSIONS

I.

The provincial judge was dying. His large household, recently so busy with physicians and visitors and servants on errands of dire importance, became ominously quiet. The Jesuit rector of his sons' school attended at his deathbed, heard Jehan's last confession, and gave him the last rites. Then he opened the chamber door and invited the judge's three sons in for farewells.

Father first summoned Jean, the oldest. As he whispered to Jean and clasped his forearm, Claude, the middle son, looked at the candles, the bed curtains, the crucifix, and then out the latticed window to the steeples and weathervanes of Poitiers in the spitting rain.

"Claude?" His father's voice startled him. Claude stepped forward and placed his hand in his father's. The dying man's hand was cold as clay. "You are the sensitive one," the judge whispered. "You will struggle. Your sensitive heart will be your weakness at first. But if you are strong and find your purpose, then your sensitive heart will become your strength."

"Oh, Father!" The boy was weeping.

"You must be strong, Claude." He grabbed the youth's arm with one cold hand and placed the other on the boy's forehead. Overcome with grief, Claude bowed for the benediction, then turned away. As Jacques the youngest was called, Claude rushed out of the chamber and down the hall, a great sob pressing up in his throat. He flung open the door to his chamber and threw himself on his bed. Waves of despair passed through him. The world he knew was ending.

"Dear God," he whispered, "I am in Your hands now. Make of me what You will."

As his weeping abated, he listened for an answer in the old house. He listened for the beating of the wings of the Holy Spirit. Nothing came.

Four days later the flames of twelve candles surrounded the bier in Cathédrale Saint-Pierre de Poitiers where *procureur au siege presidial* Jehan Chauchetière lay in state. Gothic vaults from the twelfth century receded into shadows, and the chanting of monks ebbed into silence. The stern lines of the judge's features found no repose even in death. In his black judicial robe and the four-cornered hat limned with scarlet, he was as severe, inscrutable, and unyielding as he had been on the bench. His fellow judges, solemn in their robes of office, paid their respects but whispered over his remains about who would replace him.

In a pew sat the three slender, pale brothers, Jean, Jacques, and Claude. At sixteen, Claude's delicate face—almond eyes, high cheekbones, and full lips—seemed feminine, framed by long dark curls. Jean the cynic whispered, "At least he died well, didn't our father?"

"He believed in justice," Claude offered.

"And he always dispensed it well," Jean smiled, "to the highest bidder."

This remark wounded Claude, more for its truth than its cruelty. The funeral mass began. During the solemn *Dies Irae*, Claude folded his hands and prayed for the soul of his father. His father's soul seemed to glow like dull marsh gas rising from the casket. Claude feared that the patriarch had too long neglected his soul in favor of ambition, and so finding its way into heaven might be difficult or impossible.

Claude had always been troubled by his father's appetite for public office, the endless plotting, the preference given to moneyed nobles and deference to ecclesiastics. His father's reputation was not for wisdom or compassion but for severity, except toward lords and their households. While the judge's harsh rulings sent poor thieves stealing bread for their families off to oars in the king's galleys, he was happy to do anything to ingratiate himself with the nobility.

The household was broken up unceremoniously. Relatives came for furniture, paintings, silver flatware, and draperies. The servants packed and left, and the notary auctioned off the empty structure. All three sons took up residence at the Jesuit college in Poitiers, where they had previously been day students, and they looked no farther to find their life's work. Stories of far-flung realms where the Jesuits held great influence opened glorious vistas to them: India, China, Japan, and the Americas. Each boy, in his way, had inherited Jehan's grandiosity. The idea of going forth as a soldier of Christ was far nobler than practicing law in the pettifogging hierarchy of this provincial capital.

The three brothers learned egalitarian principles from the Jesuits: no matter what his rank or intelligence, every man was equal in the eyes of God, and as such, possessed an equal opportunity for sin or redemption. Passionate teachers sparked a desire in them for seeking truth and finding God in all things, for treading a narrow, rocky path away from chasing money and the clashing cymbals of prestige. One by one the three young men turned to the order and were received as seminarians.

In the great seminary library, Claude pored over the Jesuits' *Relations*, letters sent by the order's missionaries in New France. Since he was a small child, the word "Canada" conjured images of forests and mountains, wild natives and brave soldiers and, above all, heroic blackrobes who went among hostile natives to preach Christ's gospel with nothing but a crucifix. In his first year at the seminary, Claude visited the deathbed of a mad old priest who personally knew the holy Isaac Jogues when in seminary together. The dying priest's lifelong wish had been to journey as Jogues had, a missionary in New France. He grasped Claude's slender wrist and twisted it. "Go out, my son, and live your life," the old priest urged with wild eyes. "Don't dream about it! Don't be trapped by your fear as I was."

Two years after his father's death, on his eighteenth birthday, Claude bowed his head and took his initial vows to serve the greater glory of God as a Jesuit. Handy with chalk and oils in drawing and painting, Claude put aside his boyhood ambition to become a famous artist in Paris. Now, asking God to reveal the purpose of his life, he bowed his adolescent will to the rigorous training of Loyola.

As a novice, Claude Chauchetière went through St. Ignatius Loyola's *Spiritual Exercises* under the strict discipline of a sponsor. He meditated on a perfect union with Christ, the splendor of the virgin birth, and the wily resourcefulness of the devil. He fasted, deprived himself of sleep, and mortified his flesh with a cat-o-nine-tails, praying to be free from temptation—

"Who art thou, O man, that darest to measure thyself against God? Thou art but flesh and full of impurities. Behold the corruption of thy nature: as dried grass ready to fall beneath the scythe. Behold thy weakness: a leaf, the sport of the wind. Behold the inconstancy of thy heart: a vapor scarcely formed, already dissipated in the air—this is thy life. A little dust and ashes; behold thy origin and thy end on earth: 'Dust and ashes.'"

During this two-year probationary period at Bordeaux, Claude Chauchetière's journal recorded a constant assessment of his unworthiness. He sketched portraits of other novices and constantly noted how weak and vacillating his vocation was compared to theirs. He feared that at any moment, he might be ejected and have nowhere to turn. He even worried that his ambition to purge all his worldly cravings was itself the work of the devil, and so he practiced unyielding humility. He volunteered for the lowest jobs; he prayed for the success of his fellows; he kept secret the one burning desire of his heart—to stand in the presence of God where his soul would fill with light and purity and divine love.

2.

At the age of twenty, Claude returned to Poitiers only to be assigned to teach elementary Latin to boys in a college at Tulle while he pursued a three-year course in philosophy. Claude hated the cramped provincialism of Tulle, the deadening ignorance of the students, the absence of any inspiration or path for transcendence, and he edged close to despair.

"Not only did I seek to detach myself from the world," he wrote of this time, "I wanted to detach myself from myself. For a long time, I was like an animal that thinks of nothing."

Still, he persevered in his studies, and received the sacraments. He conquered the drives and cravings of his young flesh and even ignored the comfort of affection in family and friends, seeking to purge from himself all that stood in the way of a perfect union with God. Then, unexpectedly, he was rewarded. God, he believed, touched him.

"On Christmas Eve in the year 1668, about nine or ten at night, I heard the bells tolling softly in light snow. I listened and enjoyed this contemplative sound until suddenly—I cannot say how—my soul was transported, swept up, higher and higher. It was a region, a province of light, pure, holy light and I wept in joyous thanksgiving as the Lord drew me upward. I followed where He led."

Clause floated on a cloud of ecstasy. The warm sky bathed his thirsty soul in a liquid light of gold and blue, and the air quivered with a single musical note which seemed to contain all music just as white light holds all colors of the rainbow.

"An odor of sanctity emanated from my body," he wrote. "I spent the night in a holy state of rapture so deeply pleasurable, I nearly missed mass Christmas morning where I was to serve on the altar. I went through the motions at mass dazed and distracted until it was time for communion. When the priest placed the host on my tongue, a glow infused my mouth and throat, and as I swallowed, I felt a sharp pain in my chest. I thought I would suffocate and faint. I followed the priest with the lamp as he gave out communion, and I stumbled through the rest of the mass. Then I groped my way back to my cell.

"As I removed my surplice, I was in a swoon, caressed by God both within and without. I knew at last God's love for me, a humble wretch. It was a love of such intensity and purity that I was ravished, breathless. My will merged in love with that of God's so no temptation or thought of disobedience seemed possible. All desire was gone. I had reached complete indifference to self, an annihilation of any portion of me that could be separate from God, and I saw at last the opening of my path."

This path, as he refined it in the coming weeks, led him out of the limestone cloisters of ritual and routine, into the wilds of New France. Long had he listened to tales of New France, the privations and horrors of the Jesuit heroes Jogues, Brebeuf, Garnier, and Chabanel. He had imagined the frozen lakes, the blizzards, the brawny natives dressed in fur, chanting and dancing in smoky superstition, erupting in violence at a wrong word. Yet cowardice soon followed on the heels of his rapture, and as he feared abandoning everything familiar to him, his soul withered.

From the height of mystical ecstasy, Claude Chauchetière immediately plunged into confusion and despair. It troubled him he could not repeat the euphoria of Christmas Eve at will, nor could he hasten his escape from the long course of study necessary before he made his final vows:

"I found myself so full of disorder as to become insupportable to myself. I was insensitive to God. I had stumbled into a labyrinth and could find no way out. I vacillated to and fro, sighing for a hidden life, alternately experiencing consolation and desolation."

He carried this desolation everywhere. It even attached to his devotions, corroding their purpose, nullifying any benefit, and he believed that his despair arose "because I had not acted according to the will of God. I had separated myself from His saving grace."

Claude returned from Tulle to Poitiers, and then he taught at Saintes. Finally, he was sent to the Atlantic port town of La Rochelle, where he fervently prayed night and day to experience again the rapture of deep communion with God. His prayers were finally answered. His second spiritual transport occurred on the feast of St. Francis Xavier, as he wrote in his journal:

"On December 3, 1671, God gradually dispersed all the clouds of my doubt. I was kneeling at the statue of St. Francis Xavier as I had since childhood and again I felt at one with God. For days this time the sensation lasted. Now and then I felt a feverish heat and I stopped breathing. I had the distinct sense that I was floating. When I awoke in the middle of the night, I felt God present at the end of my bed. I was so elevated in prayer I did not notice the passage of time. I hungered and thirst, but the thought of ordinary food disgusted me. I desired only the host and the wine transubstantiated into the body and blood of Jesus Christ. In those few days, God gave me such deep knowledge of His mysteries that all my faith seemed completely new and glistening. I saw that I must abandon myself utterly to Him. He spoke to me, and I heeded his message, 'Come to the missions.'"

Father Joseph-François Le Mercier, former superior of the Canadian missions, returned from New France the following year as Claude's seven-year course was nearing completion. Ordination was upon him, his choice must be made. He attended

Father Le Mercier's lecture, and as he listened to the haggard priest, aged and weathered by privations of the colony, Claude knew where he would do God's will:

> "I selected Canada because it was the least civilized, the most obscure place. The sacrifices were vast and the rewards small indeed. Father Le Mercier confirmed the accounts of the *Relations* that not much might be done there, the natives so decimated by disease and warfare, suspicious of our motives. There I might better serve the greater glory of God with no expectation of any reward in the regard of other men."

With the choice made, Claude now burned with happiness and impatience.

> "I had to flee from the close and heated corridors of the college to the gardens where I might cool from the fire of zeal that burned within me. I sought out Father Le Mercier for a private audience, and he was gracious enough to meet with me the day before he departed for Paris."

3.

Claude knocked lightly at the door of Father Le Mercier's apartment in the college.

"Come in, my son, come in," the elderly priest took Claude's soft hands in both of his. Claude felt their calluses and sinews. Le Mercier's skin was bronzed and weathered, with pronounced lines in his face. He had a long nose above a sharp jaw, and his eyes burned with zeal. "The prefect tells me you have volunteered for the missions of New France."

"Yes, Father."

"A noble calling! Come in, please! Sit down. I shall ring for tea."

"Please, Father, make no fuss . . ."

"We should be comfortable, eh? After so long without ameni-
ties I find them pleasing. Please indulge me." He smiled at the
younger man and directed him to a chair. It was a small, simple
apartment, whitewashed walls, and leaded glass windows overlooking a quadrangle of clipped grass and a sundial on the facing
tower. The May sun had the birds singing, and a bell tolled the
quarter-hour. Soon tea arrived, and they sat together sipping
from their cups.

"The *Relations* were accurate in their time," the priest began,
"but the colony is all changed."

"For the better, I hope?"

"Ah, the curse of civilization! The vanquishing of great forces
in man and nature that reduces everything to the commonplace."
He shook his head. "A Father Jogues in this day would be
impossible."

"Are the natives docile now?"

"Hardly," Mercier laughed. "Let us speak about the Iroquois
or, as they call themselves, the People of the Great Longhouse.
They are not one people but are in fact a confederacy of five
'nations:' the Mohawk, Oneida, Onondaga, Cayuga, and Seneca.
Many call them savages, but they are not. They may be more
primitive than we are, but they have surpassing intelligence and
deep integrity that, once turned toward the Lord, rarely wavers
or backslides. They have an enormous capacity for work. They
paddle canoes fourteen and sixteen hours a day without
complaint. They erect a hut for sleeping in less than an hour and
fashion a canoe from elm or birch bark in half a day. They are far
more courageous in battle than our finest soldiers, and they
accept the privations of their world like the stoics of ancient
Greece. Once instructed in rudimentary precepts of faith, they
evolve far beyond what our peasants here at home or the *habitans*
or *couriers de bois* of New France."

"The People of the Longhouse accept civilization?"

"After a fashion. Not often by choice."

"It is forced on them?"

"This is what is happening now, my son." Father Mercier paused for a sip of tea. "A new era commenced in 1665 when Marquis de Tracy landed at Quebec. It was grand! The lookouts hailed the fleet as it passed Isle de Orleans, and we lined the high rock to watch the ships approach. Such pomp was never seen in that land before. The Chevalier de Chaumont and a hundred young nobles disembarked from the ships in a long line, lace and ribbons fluttering in the wind, their lion's mane wigs beneath plumed hats. As they processed along the narrow streets to the rhythm of a drum, they were escorted by the regiment Carignan-Salières, lately returned from the Turkish wars. The regiment was composed of battle-hardened soldiers, and they marched in slouched hats with nodding plumes, bandoliers across their chests, and flintlock muskets over their shoulders.

"Then came the great Marquis de Tracy himself. He is one of the largest men I have ever seen! He was yellow and sallow from his illness in the fields of Turkey, yet vigorous in step, accompanied by four pages and six valets. All in all, it was a glittering pageant such as Quebec had never witnessed. As the Frenchmen shouted and the local people stared in disbelief, they threaded through the streets of the Lower Town and then climbed the steep pathway to the cliff above.

"Breathing hard but still walking vigorously, the Marquis looked askance at the dilapidated fortifications, the humble shack we called 'Castle of St. Louis' with mounting irony. He passed Bishop Laval's new seminary and reached the square between our Jesuit college and the cathedral. How the bells rang to welcome him! Bishop Laval, in crimson pontifical, surrounded by priests and our Jesuits, offered him holy water and a *prie-dieu* to kneel and pray, but the old general declined, even declined the offer of a pillow, and knelt on the bare stones. He spread his arms and intoned the *Te Deum*, and we all sang as he bellowed out the hymn."

"How I long to see this place!" Claude Chauchetière said.

The elderly priest smiled at his enthusiasm. "You can imagine our admiration for de Tracy in all his grandeur, transporting soldiers, settlers, and women to marry our young men, along with horses, cattle, and sheep to settle our colony. A few days later, Monsieur de Courcelle, new governor to the province, and Monsieur Talon, the intendant, landed with their trains of valets and followers. In all, five hundred troops from the regiment of Carignan-Salières were soon quartered. This new force was de Tracy's cocked crossbow aimed directly at the Mohawks to stop the raids and the scalpings and to bring peace to this land. You have read the *Relations* from those years?"

"Oh, yes."

"Then you know how Governor Courcelle set out in the dead of winter to chastise the Iroquois. As the cold and hunger overtook his army, he stumbled into a colony no longer Dutch but recently taken by the English under the Duke of York and Albany. Unwilling to fight the English, Courcelle retreated without firing a shot, but the Mohawks saw what the future held, and they came that summer to sue for peace. They reached terms for a treaty, but on their return home, a Mohawk killed François Chazy, the Marquis's nephew, who was out hunting. That was the end of de Tracy's patience. He sent three hundred men to retaliate, yet on the way south, they met a Mohawk called 'the Flemish Bastard,' or 'Kryn' among his people. This noble Kryn was surrendering Chazy's murderer to try and sustain the peace.

"On the final day of August, de Tracy invited the Flemish Bastard and his lieutenant Agariata to dinner. The sight of Mohawks in buckskin and feathers, and our noblemen in their finery, and the bishop in scarlet and lace made quite a pageant, and the talk was jovial. It appeared peace might prevail. But during dinner, de Tracy offered them wine. The Flemish Bastard declined it, but Agariata swallowed two or three glasses, and when the discussion turned to the murder of young Chazy, he thrust out his arm and bragged: 'This is the hand that split his skull!'

"Immediately, soldiers pounced on him. Kryn rose, no doubt thinking he was to be seized as well, but he made no protest because of Agariata's guilt and the force of arms. Our soldiers hauled Agariata into the square and threw a rope up over the limb of a tree. Calling all the Mohawks to witness as Agariata sang his death song, they kicked the barrel out from under his feet, and he sang no more."

"Did this end it?"

"No. De Tracy spoke no more about peace. He sent the Flemish Bastard home but kept two dozen Mohawks as hostages. He charged this Kryn to tell his countrymen that their nation would soon be destroyed.

"During the month of September, Quebec and Fort St. Anne on the Isle La Motte in Lake Champlain bristled with our preparations. We set out from Quebec on the day of the Exaltation of the Cross, September 14, with an army of six hundred French regulars, six hundred Canadians, and a hundred Algonquin and Huron guides, all loaded down with supplies and ammunition.

"We paddled upriver and portaged up the Richelieu and into the great lake named for Champlain. It was resplendent, my son, a paradise of color—orange and crimson and gold among the evergreen receding into the faint blues and violets of the mountains, the great rocks lapped by the lakes—a heroic vista to our heroic enterprise.

"Onward our leaders urged us, but de Tracy was afflicted with gout and had to be carried. Once, crossing a stream, his bearers stumbled and fell into the water, and they had to be rescued by a Huron. Courcelle suffered from stomach cramps and needed to be carried as well. After ten days, our food gave out, but we plunged onward through the forest. At last, a grove of chestnut trees provided us food for a sort of soup, and we ate.

"On October 1, St. Theresa's Day, as we approached the first Mohawk 'castle,' which the English call their stockades, a heavy, soaking rain set in. To keep the advantage of surprise, we marched all through the night. The wind moaned, and the cold rain pelted us. By early morning, we saw their stockade rising behind the rolling hills of bleached corn stalks. Marquis de Tracy ordered a charge *coup-de-main,* and our drums beat at a furious pace. Our soldiers rushed the gates and burst into the town with a battering ram only to discover all the inhabitants had fled. The marquis ordered us onward in pursuit.

"High on the hills, we saw Mohawk scouts here and there, and heard them firing a signal to their fellows, but they were out of range and disappeared like mist as we advanced. We marched up the river, thirteen hundred strong, and burst into the next village. This one, too, was empty and was taken as easily as the first. We heard the Mohawks yelling in the distance as they fled upriver to the next village. 'Onward!' again was the order, and to the third and then fourth town, we marched. Finding no resistance in the fourth town, we rested. An Algonquin woman, a slave who was being held prisoner, told of a final stronghold to the west. She led the way, brandishing a sword to seek her revenge.

"We marched to this fifth village, the largest of all. Strong fortifications were laid out as a quadrangle with a triple palisade, one inside the other, twenty feet high. We entered with no resistance. Bark tanks on scaffolds along the walls had been set up to douse fires if we tried to burn the great log pilings in our attack. Within the stockade, the houses were built of wood. The houses were far more solid than the bark huts of Jogues's time, some a hundred and twenty feet long with fire pits for eight or nine families. We found only two old women and a small boy in the lanes of the village, and an old man hiding under a canoe. He told us the Mohawks had assembled in this fort, determined to fight to the death, but when they saw our vast battalions marching, they exclaimed, 'The whole world is coming against us! Let us save ourselves!' and they fled.

"Marquis de Tracy ordered that a cross be erected and a flag with the royal arms hung from a pole. He drew up all the troops —in this campaign we lost only one man who drowned in the lake—and Jean-Baptiste du Bois, appointed by de Tracy, approached the cross, wielding his sword, and proclaimed, 'In the name of King Louis XIV we take possession of these lands!' and all the men waved their plumed hats and cried three times, '*Vive le Roi!*'

"That evening, we posted sentries and encamped, feasting on the stores of corn we found in underground vaults, along with smoked fish and dried venison and bear hanging in their long-houses. As the sunset on the 17th of October, our men set fire to the castle. Two Mohawk women, distraught at their loss, threw themselves into the fire. Flames rolled high against the dark sky, sparks exploding and smoke billowing into the clouds. By morning, the town was a smoldering heap of ash and cinders. Our men lined up before the cross and the royal standard, and I said mass on a field altar. After mass, we sang the *Te Deum*, and that sweet hymn echoed for the first time in this heathen land.

"We marched back down the valley, and we put the other villages and the massive stores of corn to the torch. The way back to Quebec was fraught with difficulties, swollen streams, canoes capsizing, but we had plenty of corn from the Mohawk stores, and we reached the forts on the Richelieu before the snow flew."

"That campaign brought peace at last?" Claude asked.

"Ah, yes," the priest laughed silently and shook his head, "but the English were highly insulted at our march into lands they claimed. Throughout their New England colonies, they tried to muster forces to attack us and thereby win Canada for the British crown, but they were so ill-prepared for a war that nothing came of it. Our advantage taught the Mohawks a lesson, a lesson was not lost on the other four nations of their league. After a winter spent as nomads on the hunt, the Mohawks listened attentively when Marquis de Tracy sent word: sue for peace or risk another raid.

"In April, the half-breed Kryn appeared again in Quebec along with representatives of the other four nations. Terms were negotiated. This Kryn spoke eloquently, and the Iroquois capitulated. Among the provisions of peace, they asked de Tracy to send carpenters, blacksmiths and surgeons, and de Tracy insisted they receive Jesuit missionaries in their villages. The death of young Chazy had been avenged, and the insolent Iroquois were humbled in their own country. Thus, peace was bought by the blood of young Chazy. But most importantly for us, the land where Jogues and Goupil were martyred now offered fertile ground in which to cultivate our faith."

"Nearly ten years have passed, Father. Are the Mohawk villages rebuilt? Have we missions there?"

"The People of the Longhouse still vacillate. We send priests to live among them, but with their chiefs and witch doctors stirring up resistance, we see a desire for the old ways. Our priests, while not clothed with any civil authority by the crown, serve as the governor's eyes and ears, vigilantly monitoring the peace to avoid further raids or abductions."

"My ship sails this spring, Father," Claude said. "I pray I will be assigned, like dear Father Jogues, to minister to the Mohawks."

"Other peoples of New France receive the Word more easily. The Iroquois, in particular the Mohawks, pose the greatest challenge of all. But come now, my son, all this remembering wearies me."

Father Mercier raised his hand, and the younger priest knelt to receive his blessing. "May the Lord be with you and shine every favor on your journey into that wild, primitive land."

"Thank you, Father."

CHAPTER FOUR

MARQUIS DE TRACY'S ATTACK SENDS TEKAKWITHA INTO THE MOUNTAINS

I.

When Kryn returned from the peace talks at Quebec, his brow was clouded with worry day and night. He sat at Iowerano's fire. Tekakwitha ladled porridge into his bowl, and he ate quietly, slowly chewing the food with his massive jaw. He said nothing until the plates were cleared and the calumet was lit. The girl retired to her corner to work and listen.

As Iowerano stuffed the pipe with tobacco and lit it, he complained:

"Hanging Agariata! Do they not see the retribution this rash act demands?"

"The rashness was ours," Kryn corrected him. "We should not be surprised when they respond to our provocation." He accepted the pipe and drew in the smoke, then exhaled. "We fashioned a treaty in good faith that would provide for mutual benefit as to hunting grounds and the fur trade. Onontio, the great chief de Tracy, also wanted to send the blackrobes again into our midst. Agariata recalled the box left by Ondessonk (Father Jogues) that brought the illness among us and infected our corn with worms. He spoke against receiving the blackrobes.

He was outvoted in our delegation, but he could not bury his grievance.

"As we paddled through the great lake to bring news of the peace and have our treaty ratified, we heard shots. Agariata paddled hard beyond a spit of land. We heard another shot. The French were hunting. There was no menace to us at all, but Agariata attacked and killed one of the young men, Onontio's nephew. He captured the other six whites and was transporting them here to be caressed in a way that would persuade the French to cease looking at our lands as theirs. I argued with Agariata that we could not breach the peace and that the six whites must be released. Eventually, he agreed. I was escorting the French prisoners back to Quebec when we encountered soldiers Onontio sent to chastise us. I turned our prisoners over, but they arrested me, hauled me back to Quebec, and threw me in a cell. Only when one of the whites told the great chief how I had rescued him did de Tracy summon Agariata and myself before him. He laid out a great feast for us, but Agariata drank wine and insulted Onontio in his hall by bragging that he had killed his nephew. Who acted rashly?

"Then the great chief brought all of us from the dungeons and arrayed us in the square to watch Agariata hang. Agariata sang his death song as they slipped the noose over his head and kicked out the barrel. As the body swung in the wind, de Tracy ordered the hostages back to their cells, but released me to return and tell you he will soon be marching on our villages, destroying everything in his path."

"An idle boast. We will resist him."

Kryn took a puff of the pipe and let it out slowly: "I have seen their armies, Great Chief, hundreds on hundreds of soldiers armed with muskets and swords, ready to march."

"This is our home, and we will defend it." Iowerano took a long pull of smoke and closed his eyes, defiant, arrogant, masking his fear with pride. "Let them come!"

"They will. They will burn our villages and put us to flight.

We must prepare to winter in the forest, for that will be our only option. I begin packing tomorrow."

"You desert your people in time of need?"

"I will tell anyone who asks this is the only path."

"Have you lost your courage?"

"It is not a matter of courage. It's a matter of survival."

In her corner, quietly, unobtrusively, the girl of ten summers was stringing wampum beads. Kryn's words worried her. As Kryn rose to depart, he noticed her. He stepped over to her, reached down, and hefted the wampum belt she was weaving.

"You put so much meaning into your designs."

She looked up at Kryn, so courageous, wise, and always certain of the right course. She yearned to ask him to take her hunting with his family.

"You do me great honor," she said. He put his hand to her cheek, and she raised her face and squinted to see him.

"Speak to your uncle, little one. With your clouded vision, you see more than he does. It is wise to stand and fight only when you have a chance of winning."

As Kryn left, she returned to her work. She watched Iowerano smoking, considering, and rejecting alternatives with a toss of his head. As the evening passed, he spiraled downward in his thinking until he burned with deep resentment. Moneta moved to go to bed. Iowerano left the longhouse to go to the privy ditch. When he returned, Tekakwitha stood and went to him.

"I heard, Uncle, what our war chief said."

"Yes?"

"May I go with his family on the winter hunt?"

"No."

His tone indicated any further inquiry would be useless. Still, as Tekakwitha lay her head down to sleep, she envisioned the marvels Kryn spoke about, the city high on a rock, the hundreds on hundreds of soldiers, and the retribution this army would now bring down on them, causing the Canienga to flee like a flock of birds.

2.

The weather grew mellow after the rains let up. With news of an impending attack, many families packed their hunting and fishing gear and supplies of dried corn and venison. In the next few days, dozens of families left through the village gates and wended down to the riverbank to paddle upstream into the lake country.

A week passed, then another. Up and down the valley, the leaves were turning red and orange and gold. The blue river flowed through the hills, clean and shimmering. Geese were on the wing in long V formations, and the cold night left frost on the squash and pumpkins. Suddenly one morning, a scout entered the gate and called all to rally around him.

"I saw the army of the French," he cried with wild gestures, his eyes wide with fear. "A hundred boats rowing down the lake, not canoes, but great flatboats bristling with men and arms, coming to burn us in our homes. This French army is not one that we can turn back. It will seize our land and make us captives."

Panic swept the lanes of the village. Tekakwitha watched Iowerano try to remain calm. The chief counseled others not to panic. First, he denied the report, and then he summoned the young man. Two strong warriors hauled him, struggling before the chief.

"Tell me it is not so, or I will have you bound and burned at the stake."

"I saw it! I can't deny what I saw!" The young man's eyes lurched in panic. "We cannot defend our village against them, Great Chief! We must flee!"

Iowerano exploded: "How can there be so many French?"

"In great boats, they come! My cousin, who lives near the

whites, told me. Each one of their canoes is far bigger than our village! Their great canoes have no paddles but fly across the water on white wings. When the boats arrive, a blue stream of soldiers marches through their city, each soldier with a musket, hundreds on hundreds of them."

"How can they march so many against us?"

"I have seen their flatboats loaded with men. Flee, I tell you! We must all flee!"

"Surely they will accept terms?"

"That time has passed! When Agariata struck down the great chief's kinsman, he sealed our fate." The young man looked at the warriors who had escorted him here. They made no move to restrain him. "I must go," he said and escaped.

"Anything else, chief?" the warriors asked.

It was then Iowerano's obstinacy broke.

"Tell the other longhouses we will retreat to Andagaron, and there we will make our stand with the brave Bear Clan." He struggled to his feet and called to his wives. "Moneta! Garahonto! Begin packing. You, there, Tekakwitha, roll up your blankets and pack your things. Rainbow, do the same. We're leaving!"

Tekakwitha carefully folded her beadwork and embroidery and placed it in a doeskin pack. She rolled and tied her sleeping skins and was soon ready to depart.

Moneta dished a final meal from the kettle and took it off the fire to cool. She folded the sleeping skins and bound them with a piece of rawhide. Iowerano took down the antlered bonnet that denoted his office and placed it on his head. He grabbed his musket impatiently and pushed aside the curtain to emerge squinting into the sunlight.

Tekakwitha pulled down her shawl to shade her eyes, hefted her pack and adjusted the eel skin strap around her forehead. She went outside where the villagers in various stages of agitation assembled in the village center. Iowerano called out: "We will journey to Andagaron, and there we will make our stand against the French."

Half-hearted cheers met his bravado. They turned westward and passed single file through the gate and down the pathway to the river trail.

Tekakwitha bowed her head into the weight of her pack and set her moccasins on the path. This move unsettled her. No longer might she seek shelter in the corner of the longhouse with her work. No longer would she know the familiar fire pit and her sleeping pallet. No longer could she visit Anastasia or the quiet forest or the burbling spring just down from the table-land. As uncomfortable as Moneta made her feel, she would no longer know the domesticity of this family.

In three hours, they came to Andagaron, but rather than offer them sanctuary, the Bear Clan was in turmoil, likewise preparing to flee.

"Runners have brought the news," said Mountain Cat, chief of the Bear Clan. "We cannot defend this place."

"We will pass the smaller villages then, and journey to Tionontoguen," Iowerano said. "Tionontoguen has a triple stockade and will give us the defense where we can make our stand."

They continued along the river trail, a line of refugees. They paused for the night at a small fishing village on the riverbank, and early in the morning, as mists rose from the warmer water into the cold autumn air, they continued. The small girl walked without a complaint. She ate only three strips of dried venison which Moneta doled out. It was the farthest she had ever ventured from her village. As the sun was at its highest, they rounded a corner, and high on a hill rose Tionontoguen. The great squared sides were topped with bastions. Hammer blows were heard as the Mohawks readied the fort to repel the French attack. Women carrying buckets from the river filled the bark tanks hanging from the inside walls to douse fires that attackers might ignite with flaming arrows. Their effort was helped by a cloudburst that broke as the Turtle and Bear Clans trudged up the trail to the Wolf Clan's castle.

Tekakwitha entered the busy village of Tionontoguen behind Iowerano. Everywhere men and women were working to reinforce the stockade. The heavy rain drove everyone who could find shelter indoors. Children wailed, and dogs barked as they passed through the high gates. They went directly to the center of the village, where women assigned them lodging.

With such a large influx of refugees, the longhouses were filled beyond capacity. Iowerano and his family were taken in by Gray Stag, chief of Wolf Clan, and Moneta and Tekakwitha slung a kettle above a crowded fire pit. Garahonto and Rainbow went to the next fire pit. The village was mass confusion, swarming with angry warriors and distraught women. Babies wailed, children argued, and the heavy cooking smoke, driven back down the chimney holes by the rain, intensified the unpleasantness. The worried chiefs closeted themselves in a disused sweat lodge with their bonnets and their pipes to deliberate. The three clans spent the night in excited anticipation, and in the morning, scouts ran into the village crying—

"The whole world marches against us! There is no use in making a stand! We must flee!"

Iowerano, vain as ever, grabbed the messenger. "Tell me how many they are!"

"More than all our villages of men, women, and children combined. They march to the drum, and they have passed Ossernenon and now are nearing Andagaron. They will be here tonight."

This news sent the whole village into an uproar.

"Make haste!" Iowerano cried. "We must flee into the forest!"

"Kryn warned you of this!" Moneta scolded him. "You should have listened!"

"Silence, woman!"

Tekakwitha was thrilled to hear Kryn's name. He had predicted this because he was all-wise and practical, but her uncle's stubbornness denied it all. Quickly she picked up her bundle, adjusted the eel skin strap on her forehead, and followed

Moneta. The line of refugees wended through the western gate. Having no destination, they fled upriver and fanned out into the hills.

Iowerano fumed and raged as he marched along. This invasion of the hated French! Since the time of Jogues, when the priest left his black box behind, and worms infested their corn, these whites brought nothing but difficulty into their lives.

The fleeing bands climbed into the foothills and camped. Two nights after they had departed, the eastern sky blushed and flickered with a deep, lurid red.

"They burn our villages," Iowerano spat in disgust.

"Now we must hunt like the Adirondacks," Moneta remarked, "so hungry in winter they eat their dogs and tree bark."

"We shall punish this outrage," Iowerano promised, shaking his fist at the sky.

"That I doubt," Moneta grumbled to Garahonto.

All night the fires burned against the eastern sky. In the morning, the refugees took stock of their situation. Little food remained. Two boys with the family threw up a weir in a small stream and caught brook trout, which they cooked over the fire.

"Let us go back to the village," Iowerano announced the following day.

"The village is destroyed," Moneta said. "There is no reason to visit it."

"Perhaps there will be food or tools left we can use this winter."

"All that remains there is your foolish pride."

Garahonto, his second wife, was humbler. She urged him to remain in the hills, but the following day, Iowerano and two youths and Tekakwitha returned to Tionontoguen. Other refugees had come out of the hills too and were combing the heap of ash that once was the proud village of Tionontoguen, strongest of the Mohawk towns. When Iowerano saw the great cross erected by the French, he called to others to help him, and they pulled it down, again claiming this land for their fierce war-god Aireskou.

3.

The small band wended into the mountains. The mellow weather turned biting and cold. Soft blue skies, alive with migrating geese, soon darkened and snarled with gray storms and then snow flurries. High in the mountains, along a plunging stream, they built a hut of bark and skins, large enough for a fire pit and nine sleeping pallets. Iowerano had conscripted two young hunters, White Moon and Little Wolf, and two young women, Sunflower and Fawn.

Day by day, the sun fell farther in the west, and the cold night lengthened in the howling wind. The girls, Sunflower and Fawn, were fourteen and sixteen summers respectively, and they giggled and flirted with the young hunters while Moneta heaped jealous criticism on them to Garahonto, who said only, "Leave them alone. We were young once."

Never a good hunter, Iowerano delegated the capture of meat to the young men, but they stayed in the hut until the sun was up each day and returned each night empty-handed. Fawn and Sunflower knew how to set rabbit snares, and the group subsisted on hare for a dozen nights, waiting for a deer or an elk. Tekakwitha remained in the corner of the hut working her crafts, careful not to eat much to avoid setting off Iowerano's smoldering wrath.

The darkness and cold deepened, the prospect of game lessened, and hunger and Moneta's jealousy both increased, so the mood in the hut was intolerable. Iowerano, afraid of failure in the hunt, did not venture outside. As the rabbit population gave out, they butchered one of their skinny dogs and then the other.

Two months after pulling down the cross and leaving the

smoldering heap of ashes that had been the proud village of Tionontoguen, the group lay groaning with hunger, scarcely able to get out each morning for firewood and water. Moneta boiled bark and roots and hickory nuts to make a soup, and they began chewing the rawhide and the skins of their clothing. Garahonto comforted Rainbow, who wept herself to sleep. At night Sunflower and Fawn shared their favors with the young hunters, and occasionally Garahonto coupled with Iowerano, to the stern indignation of Moneta.

One night as the wind howled and the snow blew, hunger pains seized Tekakwitha. Iowerano was busy with Garahonto, and Fawn and White Moon were groaning with pleasure. Tekak-witha could not tolerate the sound, so she arose and pulled open the flap.

"Where are you going?" Moneta asked.

"Latrine."

A stiff wind blew, and the moon, nearly full, lorded over creation with a soft blue majesty. Tekakwitha took her snow-shoes propped against the hut, fastened them to her feet, bundled herself up against the wind, and trudged off. She did not know where she was going. She only knew she needed to get away.

CHAPTER FIVE

KRYN BEGINS AND ENDS AN EAT-ALL FEAST

I.

Moonlight streamed with silvery light on the mountain peaks. Wolves and coyotes howled in the distance, and their wild calls struck fear into her heart. But she did not turn back. Tekakwitha rarely ventured out of the longhouse, and never had she gone this far alone. The work of snowshoeing warmed her, but without a path, she was moving aimlessly with no destination. In the hush of blue moonlight, she pulled back her shawl and looked out.

The landscape spread out before her was desolate. Great masses of earth and rock, covered with snow, undulated to the horizon. The moon etched the hushed, smooth mountains with crystal light. Forests reached up toward the bald peaks, and the courses of streams wended in fissures of rock. She followed the trail they had made climbing to this place fifteen days before. With regular breathing of the cold air and the exertion dulling her hunger, she was soon yawning, deeply fatigued. The pale sky arched above her, so still, so lovely and dreamlike. She longed to lay on the soft snow and sleep.

Onward she trudged, disoriented with no way to measure

time or distance, lost in the vast, bright moonscape. She worked down a path through the forest, and then she rested in the shelter of a great pine. She knew the seduction of sleep in the cold, how the temptation of sleep lulled many to a frozen death. She wanted to keep moving until the sun rose. But the shadow of the pines and the softness of the snow beckoned her to rest. She sat against the trunk of a fallen tree, and then, feeling wearier, she wrapped her cloak and shawl about her and curled up against the massive trunk.

"I'll just sleep a few moments," she told herself, and then she surrendered.

She awoke with a start. Someone was shaking her. She did not know where she was, but she was bone-weary and chattering with cold. Her insides ached with hunger.

"Aurora!" she heard, and she peered up. A rosy glow in the east lit a chapped face wrapped in a shawl, looming above her.

"Anastasia!"

"Why did you leave the hut?"

"I heard them groaning. I couldn't sleep."

"You might have frozen!"

"I hate the sound of rutting. They grunt like animals."

"Oh, little one!" Anastasia embraced her.

"How did you find me?"

"The moon was bright. I followed your tracks."

"Why are you here?"

"Kryn and I trailed a moose for a day and a half, ran it into a ravine, and killed it. We pitched our camp on the other side of this mountain. As we were transporting meat back to our lodge last night, we saw smoke from Iowerano's hut. Kryn gave meat to Moneta, and he led Iowerano and the two lads off to collect the rest of the carcass. When I heard you left, I came to bring you back."

"I will not go back there."

"You must. You'll freeze out here on your own."

"But they won't stop. Sunflower and Fawn. Not even Garahonto."

"We will spend the night with you, and perhaps tomorrow, you can return to Kryn's lodge with us."

"Yes, I want to go with you. Either you or Kryn must speak to my uncle. He will not grant the permission if I ask."

"Yes, it will be done. Let me help you up." Anastasia pulled her to her feet, and they snowshoed back to Iowerano's hut as the sun rose.

Billows of fragrant smoke rolled out of the chimney hole. The snow in front of the entrance was crimson with blood. Iowerano, Little Wolf, and White Moon walked down the path, carrying haunches of meat. Behind them came Kryn. Anastasia called to Kryn, "I found her!"

Kryn walked down to the hut. His fur coat was stained with the blood of the moose. His face was also smeared with blood, but his blue eyes danced.

"Don't go wandering away like that," he said. "We can't lose you, little one."

Moneta opened the flap to the hut, and a great fragrant cloud escaped. "I have meat cooked and ready. Come in."

"Enough," Iowerano said from inside. His commanding voice sounded as if he were the great hunter who saved the expedition. "Let us begin the Eat-All Feast."

"I have six hungry people waiting for my return," Kryn said, stooping down to enter. "I cannot stay here for an Eat-All feast."

"Nonsense. Get your people and bring them here."

"I will give you a hindquarter and the head. We can bury half of the meat in the snow where it will keep until we need it."

"No!" Iowerano said with an air of command. "We will hold the Eat-All Feast and finish the meat tonight. Get your people and bring them here. We will eat until nothing remains of your kill."

"I know the way back," one of the lads said. "I will get the others."

"No," Kryn said. "I will begin the feast, but after I eat my fill, I will be off to my camp."

"You cannot dishonor the ancient custom," Iowerano said.

"My family is hungry, and I will feed them."

Moneta had roasted a large cut of the hindquarter, and the savory aroma made their mouths water. They sat around the fire as Iowerano passed large chunks of meat to them.

"Before we eat," he said, "I will offer this first piece to our great god Aireskou who helped Kryn run this moose into a ravine." He cut off a piece of meat and tossed it into the fire, where it sizzled and burned. "May Kryn's success bring us success in the hunt as well," and he bit onto the meat and cut off a chunk with his hunting knife.

All ate. The boys ate greedily. Kryn savored his meat. Tekak-witha bit into hers and warm delicious blood flooded her mouth, awakening her sense of taste. She cut the piece with her knife.

"Now, let us cook the backstrap," said Iowerano with ceremony. He produced two long shiny red muscles and handed them to Moneta. She placed them gently on the fire, where they smoked as she turned them and were soon charred. No one spoke as they ate. Then Iowerano carved and dished out portions of the backstrap.

"Have some more!" Moneta lay another slab of meat on Tekakwitha's bark plate.

"No, Aunt. I've had enough."

Iowerano was laughing, happy in the good fortune Kryn had brought them. "Eat, Tekakwitha! Have some more. You cannot stop until we finish."

"I've had my fill," she insisted, and she groaned and turned away to sleep.

"The poor child," Anastasia said. "I found her sleeping in the snow. Let her sleep now."

"No," Iowerano insisted. "Sit up and help us finish this meat."

"I cannot," she said.

"But you must," he pulled her to a sitting position.

"We're not going to force her to eat," Kryn said. "Let the child rest."

"Tekakwitha defies me at every turn. When there is no meat, she leaves the hut and starts back to Kanawaka. Now that we have good fortune, she refuses to share it."

"She has shared it enough," Anastasia said.

"I have eaten all I can," Tekakwitha groaned. "Please! Eat what you want but let me alone."

"No!" Iowerano said. "Everyone eats until this is finished." Iowerano jerked at her coat, and she sat up. She thrust out her arms, blinked her eyes, and tried to focus. Her mouth opened and closed, opened and closed, and she scrambled on all fours to the door and then out into the sunny morning where she vomited on the bloody snow. In great surges, the bloody meat came up. Blood poured through her nose, and the sour, bitter taste of partially digested meat sickened her, caused her to heave and retch even more. Tears of shame pressed into her eyes. Within the wigwam, she heard them laughing at her.

Anastasia was at her side. "It's all right, little one. We are leaving. We've had enough, and we will take you with us."

"My uncle won't allow that."

"Kryn doesn't bow to him. Even now, he is explaining why you will be spending the rest of the winter with us. Do you have anything to pack?"

"My bedding and my work."

"Get it now before they finish talking."

"I don't want to go in there."

"Go. This will be the last time."

She pushed through the flap and was again in the dim, smoky confines that smelled of cooked meat, heated fur, and strong bodily odors of the people at the fire. She held down her gorge that threatened to come up again, and without looking at

Iowerano or Moneta or Garahonto, she packed her embroidery in a doeskin bag.

"You're leaving with Kryn?" Iowerano asked.

"If it pleases you, Uncle."

"It doesn't please me. The Eat-All Feast just began."

"Far better is it to freeze the meat," Kryn suggested. "Then you will have it in times of scarcity."

". . . you defy custom, and you defy me," Iowerano told the girl. "Nothing requires that I take you back into my household when we return to Kanawaka."

"We will discuss that later," Kryn said, and he guided the girl out of the hut with a strong hand.

Anastasia was smiling. The sun was streaming in the blue morning sky. Kryn shouldered a hindquarter of the moose. Anastasia wrapped some heavy cuts in her bag and put the eel skin strap about her forehead and began to move up the trail on snowshoes. Tekakwitha fixed on her snowshoes and her forehead strap and fell in behind her. The three of them walked up the ridge, high above the hills and the river valleys. They passed along a ridge until midday, and descended then into a sheltered valley where Kryn had made his hunting camp. He announced their arrival and summoned his family, and they came out to congratulate him. Karitha welcomed Tekakwitha to their camp and settled her inside their hut.

Karitha stoked the cooking fire and soon had cuts of the moose meat smoking. She helped an exhausted Tekakwitha to set her pallet against the wall. The girl lay down and was soon asleep while the others ate quietly with none of the anger or tension of Iowerano.

2.

In the following days, blizzards shut them in. Tekakwitha worked on her embroidery. She stitched striking pictographs with colored porcupine quills and Kryn asked her to explain them. She closed her eyes and spoke as if daydreaming:

"Cold is the moonlight on the snow. The wolf howls, and the stars echo with his outrage."

"And this one?"

"Running from hunters, the moose plunges into a ravine. The hunters cheer and dance for now there will be meat."

"And this one?"

"The chief laughs as his women eat until their bellies grow fat, and they give birth to wild little boys."

"This is work like I have never seen," Kryn observed. "Long ago, I requested from Iowerano that you prepare a ceremonial robe, but we never discussed it further."

"I remember."

"With the burning of our villages, we will soon need to make peace with the French. Their great chief Onontio will offer us terms. They have been doing that since the days of Ondessonk (Jogues)." He threw his arm affectionately about Tekakwitha. "As a display of goodwill, I will give Onontio a ceremonial robe that you embroider."

"It will be a great honor."

"I think it should be of elk skin," he rummaged among the skins that Karitha had cleaned and held up the skin of a large elk. "This one. You can begin work on this one while we hunt."

"What would Kryn like to see pictured?"

"Our three sisters—corn, squash, and beans—growing in the field. The seasons of the moon, too—the Fishing Moon, the Planting Moon, the Strawberry Moon, the Green Corn Moon. Along the bottom, the symbol of the People of the Great Longhouse, five nations with the council fire in the center, and the tree of peace, its five roots holding it firmly in the earth while an eagle watches from the highest branch."

Quietly, with deep respect and purpose, Tekakwitha took the soft skin from his hands.

"I will begin today."

Kryn then filled his pipe with tobacco and lit it with a twig from the fire. The flame illuminated his features as he pulled at the pipe to light it. Tekakwitha watched him dimly through her half-blindness. She felt immense gratitude for this man who had rescued her and now entrusted her with such an important task. She would make it more beautiful than any robe had ever been to seal the peace between the two nations, so together, they would bury the war hatchet and live as brothers and sisters forevermore.

CHAPTER SIX

KRYN CARRIES A MESSAGE OF PEACE TO THE
FRENCH AT QUEBEC

I.

The bright sun shone in a clear spring sky. Hunting parties wended down to the sparkling river valley with bundles of winter furs for trading. The former Mohawk villages were mounds of ash. After a hurried council, clan mothers of the Turtle Clan selected another site nearby for erecting a new village. This village would be called, again, Kanawaka (At the Rapids).

High on a rise, men dragged stout logs from the forest, stripped them, and set them in the ground to form a stockade. Within the large rectangle, they set tall saplings and bent them together, lashed the saplings into an arching longhouse frame, then covered the ribwork with bark.

Around the new village where they had cut the trees, women grubbed the ground with wooden hoes. They planted corn and squash and beans in humps from seeds they had carried along in their flight last fall.

Marquis de Tracy sent word that unless the Iroquois League sent delegates to Quebec soon, he would hang the hostages he had kept. Hurried preparations were made at Onondaga to assemble a delegation from the Oneida, the Cayuga, and the Seneca. The Mohawks, however, were not disposed to sue for peace. Iowerano held a warlike resentment for all the French, which had intensified with de Tracy's attack. The Bear and Wolf Clans, too, wanted war. Kryn met with Iowerano:

"Our brothers are being held in the north," Kryn said. "Unless we appear as summoned, they will be hanged."

"I cannot think of peace presently. I must supervise the building of our village and the recovery from the raid last fall. If we do not get crops in the ground, we will starve this winter."

"Someone must negotiate this peace, Great Chief. All nations but the Mohawk have sent delegations."

"Go if you wish and ask their pardon. I have a far dimmer view of the white man and his purposes here."

"We should work to live in peace with the whites."

"Easy for a man to say whose father was white. It is always on the white man's terms." Iowerano spat in disgust. "You go and open the talks. We will resolve the matter this summer."

Kryn journeyed to Quebec in April to open the peace talks on behalf of the Mohawks. Tekakwitha remained behind, embroidering the ceremonial robe that the Mohawks would give Onontio to seal the treaty's terms.

Week by week, the new village swelled as families emerged from the forests. By the Strawberry Moon (June), Kryn had returned from Quebec, and he assured everyone all the hostages would be released during the Blueberry Moon (July). By then, the Turtle Clan was living in its new village and ready to send a delegation to the Onondaga council fire to consider terms of peace.

Again, Iowerano refused to participate and deputized Kryn to represent him. Kryn paddled and portaged his canoe westward to Onondaga to discuss terms of peace with the other nations. By the time he returned, Tekakwitha had completed the robe. She had embroidered the borders with a geometric design. In the corners, she had stitched pictographs to represent the four nations of Seneca, Cayuga, Oneida, and Canienga, and a large central depiction of the council fire at Onondaga. When she held it up to show him, Kryn smiled broadly in approval: "It is magnificent, little one!" He gathered her up in his arms and held her. Unused to any embrace, Tekakwitha went limp. As he held her to his chest, she felt him laugh. It was a strange sensation feeling someone so close.

Everyone else who saw the ceremonial robe paused in wonder, but the attention embarrassed her. She had also strung a long wampum belt out of white and purple shells, taller than a man, to seal the peace with the French, and Kryn handled the belt and rehearsed a speech he would make when he presented this gift.

In a few days, with much fanfare, Kryn set out again for Quebec with a party of twelve. They walked single file overland to the lakes. When they reached the lakeshore, they found three canoes hidden in the brush, and they fashioned another one from elm bark. They glided north on the lake, then portaged a small ridge, slid across Lake Champlain, and then descended the Richelieu River. When they finally embarked on the broad St. Lawrence, they moved easily downriver with the current.

Before and behind them, flotillas of canoes descended as other nations, Algonquins, Abenaki, and the Cat Nations, sent emissaries to the French to establish a universal peace.

After three days, as they rounded a bend, the great rock of Quebec jutted up from the water. The river narrowed and ran more swiftly below it. Along the riverbank at the base of the cliff base, a village of tents was pitched, canoes with feathers flying in the wind were beached and tied to piers beneath the fort, and natives and Europeans alike traded their wares in makeshift booths. Three French shallops and a brig were anchored in the basin. High on the rock rose the log walls of the fort, which encircled the homes of the governor and the intendant.

Kryn and his party steered to shore and claimed a plot along the river for their tents and sleeping rolls. The Mohawk delegation was the final Iroquois nation to appear. They rested and then walked along the river that evening, passing by the stone warehouses built for the fur trade and visiting the booths and the habitations. They slept soundly that night. The following day, as the sun rose over the river in glorious streams of light—a harbinger of the peace—they started up the steep path to the peace council.

Fort and trading post at Quebec

The fort rose above them, a strong stockade of massive logs, with loopholes here and there through which black cannon thrust. The gate was open during this time of peace. Kryn and his Mohawks, with thin, high spikes and ridges of hair, wore loincloths, leggings, and deerskin tunics. They entered the fort gate with the Oneida, the Onondaga, the Cayuga, and Seneca.

Wooden benches were set out in the stone square before the governor's mansion and the bishop's chancery. From bastions of the fort, long pennants of blue and white and gold flew in the brisk summer wind above blue flags flapping with golden *fleur de lis*. Emissaries from the five Iroquois nations were arrayed along the south of the square. Hurons and the Algonquins and the Cat Nations were along the west. A military band marched out of the guardhouse, followed by a large entourage, and lastly walked Marquis de Tracy, a massive man, towering over Governor Courcelle and Bishop Laval.

Protocol dictated that the Iroquois speak first to present their suit for peace. Garacontie, an ancient Onondaga, head chieftain for the entire League, rose and stepped into the center:

"Great chief! We thank you for welcoming us to your fortress. Calling on the sun and the moon and the stars, on the four winds, on the trees and the grasses and the crops we plant," he turned left and then right, "on the bear and the moose and the deer of the forest, and the fish in the lakes and streams, we salute you."

Marquis de Tracy, elegant in scarlet brocade and a silver ceremonial breastplate and buckler, nodded and motioned for him to continue.

"I speak for the five nations of the People of the Great Longhouse when I say that we wish to live in peace with our white brothers. We ask that you return our brethren whom you have held as hostages for a year. In turn, we will fling the war club as far from our hand as we can, and bury the war hatchet in the earth once and for all."

The marquis nodded in satisfaction. "As you say."

"We ask, O Great Chief, that you grant us favors."

"Name them."

"Seeing how well your houses and fortifications stand, we have need of builders in wood and stone and blacksmiths to work in iron. We need surgeons to teach our people how to heal what our shamans cannot. Finally, we will accept your blackrobes to teach us the Prayer, as you insist."

All the bonneted heads of the Iroquois delegation nodded in agreement. Marquis de Tracy bowed to Bishop Laval, who in turn bowed to Father Mercier, superior of the Jesuits.

Marquis de Tracy announced: "It will be done as you wish, Great Chief. With the bonds of brotherhood, we will knit our peoples together."

When his turn to speak came, Kryn carried the robe directly up to the marquis and unrolled it to cries of pleasure from those who viewed it. Kryn then produced the wampum belt.

"In condolence for the loss of your nephew last year, we wish to make amends," Kryn said. "I come bearing these gifts to demonstrate our clean heart in fashioning a lasting peace between our peoples. Let there be no more war and no more bloodshed. May we live as brothers in this land."

Marquis de Tracy graciously accepted the robe and the belt of wampum. He clapped his hands, and the twenty-four hostages were produced. They had been washed and dressed in clean, homespun trousers and shirts. They blinked and seemed uncertain as they came into the sunlight. The Iroquois cried out in approval and stamped their applause on the ground.

"I return your brothers to you in good faith," de Tracy said. "May there be no further cause for us to raise the musket or the war hatchet against one another."

After the peace talks concluded, a detail of soldiers fired half a dozen musket blasts, and then the great booming cannon exploded, and every church bell in Quebec rang, heralding the new peace.

3.

Together the canoes moved upriver, those of the Iroquois and those of the blackrobes. At the Richelieu River, the canoes of four of the Iroquois nations continued westward, while the Mohawks and the canoe with three blackrobes went south. Kryn, his companions, and the twenty-four Mohawk hostages portaged up the rocky course of the Richelieu River. They worked together to climb around the falls and when they reached Lake Champlain at night, they camped and shared the food given them from the stores of corn at Quebec.

Kryn watched how the three blackrobes conducted themselves, gentle, polite, quiet men. They showed no aggression but rather stoicism, an indifference to fatigue and pain unusual among whites. They traveled in their canoe and slept close by each other. On rising, they read from their breviaries, walking back and forth on the shore, praying to their God as the others prepared the morning meal. Kryn knew Iowerano would be less than happy with the missionaries. Iowerano had already announced no mission would open at Kanawaka.

They paddled down through the lakes, past wooded isles, and under the brows of shaggy mountains. They paddled the canoes in the sunshine, in the rain, and through a furious summer hailstorm. A rainbow arched across the sky. The priests exclaimed that this was a sign of the covenant of God with man now manifested in nature. At the end of the lake, they paused at a cliff of flint to gather scraps to make tips for arrows and spears. Then they pressed on, down through the deep glacial valley, the same course where Jogues had first journeyed when he named this long lake "Lake of the Blessed Sacrament."

Finally, they emerged from the woods onto the river of the

Mohawks, and they followed the river to the new village of Kanawaka. Women were planting, and no one took special note of their arrival. There was no display of violence, no speeches, no gauntlet to "welcome" them. Karitha greeted the delegation at the gate to the new village, and she took Kryn aside.

"English merchants passed through on horses three days ago with barrels of brandy. They were seeking to buy our winter pelts at low prices. Iowerano led them to Tionontoguen where they will drink the brandy and conduct their trade."

"This is not good," Kryn said. "The blackrobes should not witness what becomes of a village when our people drink the whiskey, or how the English cheat us, how no one eats, how hungry children scream."

"Iowerano left instructions. He does not want the blackrobes to interrupt the drinking at Tionontoguen, so he instructed Garahonto and Tekakwitha to provide lodging and food until he returns."

"Let us take them to Iowerano's longhouse."

The families of the hostages ran out of their longhouses to welcome them home. Kryn escorted the three blackrobes, Fathers Bruyas, Frémin, and Pierron, to the chief's longhouse. Tekakwitha tended the fire where a kettle of *sagamite* simmered.

"Hello, young maiden," Father Frémin greeted her in passable Iroquois. His voice was sweet and musical. When she turned from stirring the *sagamite* and squinted at him, the priest saw her smallpox scars. She was grateful he showed no disgust.

"How do they call you?" asked Father Bruyas.

"I am called Tekakwitha. My stepmother gave me that name, 'She Who Gropes Her Way.'"

"But it is not a good name because you don't grope your way."

"A name attaches, and then it is difficult to remove."

"You are wise beyond your years," Father Frémin observed.

"Please sit," she said, and she dished out the *sagamite* and handed each priest a plate.

"This is the girl who embroidered the ceremonial robe I gave Onontio," Kryn said with pride. "And she strung the wampum beads. She is most skilled."

"We thank you for allowing us to lodge with you," Father Pierron said.

Before they ate, all three of the blackrobes knelt and, in unison, made the sign of the cross and said grace. Then they sat cross-legged and quietly ate the food Tekakwitha dipped from the kettle. As they were eating, the flap to the longhouse opened, and Anastasia entered. She saw the priests and cautiously approached.

"Good afternoon, Fathers," she said. "Welcome to our village."

"We appreciate your hospitality," Father Fremin said.

"Will you be with us long?"

"We are told," Father Bruyas said, "that your chief does not want a mission in this village. As soon as we are permitted to journey west, we will set up a mission at Tionontoguen, Father Frémin and I. Father Pierron is journeying farther west to the Oneidas."

"I am Algonquin, Christian," Anastasia said. "I was baptized at Trois-Rivières. Do you pray the rosary?"

"Yes, of course." Father Frémin opened his satchel and handed a set of rosary beads to Anastasia. She looked quizzically to determine if he was giving her the beads, and he nodded. She took the beads and held them close to her heart.

"I used to say the rosary with my mother," she explained to Tekakwitha.

"What is the rosary?"

"It is a way of praying to God the Father, to Jesus," she held up the crucifix at the bottom of the chain of beads, "and to our Mother Mary. It is like a chant." Anastasia turned back to the priest. "Can we say the rosary?"

He smiled and looked at the others. "In a little while. We

began our journey today so early we have not had time to read our daily office. We'd like to do that now."

They each went into their traveling bags and produced small black books. They leafed through their breviaries then stood.

"With your kind permission, we will go down by the river." Father Bruyas addressed this to Tekakwitha since she had prepared his meal. She nodded in agreement.

They left the hearth and the longhouse to pray. The girl turned to Anastasia. "What manner of men are these?"

"They are blackrobes. You have heard Iowerano talk about Ondessonk. He was the same. They have journeyed over the great salt sea to come among us and teach us about Jesus Christ."

"Who is Jesus Christ?"

"A torture victim. He died on a torture stake called a cross."

"Why do they teach us about a torture victim? We have had many victims here, why is he different?"

"This man was God, and like Deganawida, born of a woman who did not know man. He taught all peoples to love and to seek peace."

"How can someone be both a man and a god? And what do you mean, he taught mankind how to love? Surely there were husbands and wives and families then."

"The love he taught is a different sort of love, my dearest. It is a love expressed for everyone, and a part of that love is forgiveness. Instead of revenge, Jesus Christ taught men to offer the other cheek to someone who slaps you."

Tekakwitha scowled. "Won't the person just slap the other cheek?"

"Of course, but then you can forgive a second time."

"I don't understand," the girl said. "What did they take from the bags?"

"Prayer books."

Anastasia looked toward the door where the men had vanished, and she rummaged through one of the bags, took out another book, and opened it.

"On these pages are markings. See? These markings set forth their prayers. They review the markings as we do with designs in the wampum, and so recite prayers each day to their God."

Tekakwitha took the book and ran her hand over the smooth printed page. She felt the colored ribbons that hung as place markers. "How do they understand what the markings say?"

"They are trained. They can recall from those markings exactly what words appear there."

"Can we ever understand these words?"

"I have known some of our people who have learned to read them, but it took them a very long time and required much effort."

Anastasia put the book back into the satchel and they went outside. The three blackrobes were walking along the riverbank, reciting their daily office.

"These men," Tekakwitha said, "are so gentle."

"Their religion does not allow them to argue or fight or make war, so they are agreeable and considerate."

"And my uncle wants to keep them out of our village?"

"Yes," Anastasia said, rolling her eyes and sadly shaking her head.

When the blackrobes finished saying their office, they walked back up the hill to meet Anastasia and Tekakwitha at the gate. Together they passed into the stockade and then to Iowerano's longhouse. Once inside, they gave the girl a set of rosary beads, and they all knelt at the fire pit and recited the rosary.

4.

The blackrobes remained three days at Iowerano's longhouse. They spoke with young Tekakwitha and watched her work diligently on embroidery and wampum. She was happy to be hidden away with them in the smoky longhouse even while days were long and sunny.

On the fourth day of their stay, Iowerano returned. He was

moving more slowly than usual. He seemed depleted and humbled by his days of drunkenness. Moneta, too, was sluggish and irritable. The blackrobes presented the chief with a gift from Marquis de Tracy, a silver peace pipe from Quebec's most skilled silversmith.

"Our chief," Father Bruyas spoke, "hopes that you will consider the great peace we have established whenever you smoke this pipe."

"The Wolf and the Bear Clans will welcome you," Iowerano said dismissively. "You should leave Kanawaka tomorrow."

That night the priests packed their belongings, and Tekak-witha watched them with a sinking heart. The cruel and unpredictable Iowerano was back, and she was losing the presence of these calm and peaceful men of God.

The next morning, Tekakwitha said to the priests, "Let me walk with you to the path by the river."

"They can find their way," Moneta said.

"Prepare me some breakfast," Iowerano ordered her.

The priests thanked her for her hospitality and spoke to Iowerano: "You have an intelligent and personable daughter."

"Have a nice journey," he said dismissively, and he turned away, ignoring them. The look that passed between the priests and the young woman was one of fondness and gratitude and, on her part, hope.

CHAPTER SEVEN

KRYN DEFENDS HIS VILLAGE AGAINST A
MOHICAN ATTACK

I.

Two years passed. With peace in the valley, cycles of sun and moon spun in the sky above the winding river. Mohawk women planted the three sisters in mounds, and corn, squash, and beans sprang to life with the spring rain, flourished in the summer sun, ripened, and were harvested in the colorful fall to be stored in underground pits. Hunters ranged over the hills and into the mountains after bear, deer, elk, and moose. Fishermen caught trout, bass, shad, and pike with nets and weirs. When the icy blizzards of winter clamped down, old men sat by the fire smoking tobacco, their lined faces flickering in the light, telling stories of ancient wars and hunting expeditions. Young mothers nursed their infants wrapped in fur against the cold.

As Tekakwitha began her fourteenth year, the subject of a husband arose. Moneta approached her one morning with uncharacteristic familiarity. "You are a child no longer, Tekakwitha. Now that you are ready to take a husband. Your uncle and I have a match for you: Distant Thunder."

"I do not wish to marry, Aunt."

"Nonsense! What idle talk. Your fear of men will pass when you gain experience, and you learn to be a wife and a mother."

"No, Aunt, I will never submit to a man."

Uncharacteristically Moneta sat next to the girl. "There are ways, little one, for you to manipulate men. Their wants are simple, and when you learn how to please them, you can get what you want."

"With tricks and deception?"

"It is the way between men and women." She put her arm around the Tekakwitha's shoulders, and Tekakwitha shuddered. She did not like to be touched, and this new intimacy with her stepmother raised her suspicions.

"I choose not to do that."

"Nonsense! How will you support yourself?"

"I can provide for myself with my embroidery and beads."

"What talk!" Moneta scoffed. "Do you think only of yourself? My husband is too fond of sitting by the fire with his pipe. When you marry, we will have another hunter bringing game to our family. We will once again enjoy a steady supply of venison and bear. And you will be happy in the night when he shares your bed. Perhaps you will enjoy what the white man's disease deprived me, children."

"Why would Distant Thunder court me with my scars when so many beautiful girls dress up and flirt and go to the dances? Let him court Rainbow instead."

"He has been approached. He thinks you are fine. Surely, he is not the fastest runner or the most cunning hunter, or the bravest warrior in the village. He tends to brood and keep his resentments alive."

"And that makes him attractive to me?"

"As you said yourself, yours are not the qualities that young men seek. They want beauty, gaiety, and flirtation, not a woman who's so serious all the time."

"So, I should lower my expectations?"

"In order to marry, yes." Moneta was getting impatient. Her

flattery and wiles were not getting her what she wanted. "Be realistic!"

"I am realistic. I choose not to marry, and that's an end to it."

Moneta stood up, angry. "Think of someone else for a change! We need a hunter for our longhouse, and you are of eligible age now. We have provided for you all these years, and now you must marry to provide for us. Distant Thunder would make a good match for you."

"No, Aunt, I will not do it. Let there be no further talk."

Tekakwitha retreated to her corner where the light was dim, and her handiwork kept her occupied so she might ignore the chill that came over the family toward her.

Five days later, Tekakwitha went to the forest spring with earthenware jugs to bring back water for washing and cooking. When she returned, Iowerano and Moneta and the young man Distant Thunder were seated about to have supper.

"Here, daughter," Moneta handed Tekakwitha a bowl of *sagamite*, "give this bowl to him." She nodded at Distant Thunder.

Tekakwitha immediately saw their trick. When a young woman served a young man food, it was a signal they were married. Tekakwitha shook her head and refused.

"Lose your defiance, daughter," Iowerano ordered. "Give this to the young man or leave our hearth fire and shift for yourself."

Tekakwitha said nothing. She turned and walked to the flap and opened it and went out into the bright sunshine. She adjusted her shawl and walked through the lanes of the village.

"Tekakwitha!" she heard Moneta's voice behind her. "Come back! Have supper with us!"

But she did not stop. She walked out through the eastern gate of the village and down through the plantation where the stalks of corn were high and waving in a gentle breeze. She entered a great stand of pine at the end of the corn brake. This is where she felt happy, here, away from all the gossip and chatter of the women, the braying of the men at their gambling or their bragging or, worse, their drinking. Away from the whining and wailing of the children, here, alone in the forest she could sit and ponder things.

How pathetic was their trickery! Imagine! Setting up this purported marriage proposal and expecting it to result in a new family. How could the ritual ever mean more than simply giving a man his dinner? She did not love Distant Thunder. She did not love anyone except perhaps Kryn, and she loved him from afar. She could support herself with her work if she never assumed responsibilities for a husband and children. What did she need? A bowl of porridge and a bit of meat or fish every day? She made the clothes and the moccasins she wore. And as for a sleeping pallet, there were other families in the village that would take her in if Iowerano did not poison everyone against her.

The place she had found here in the woods was pleasant. The sun slanted through the pine, and a clean wind blew from the west. She rarely ventured outside the longhouse and seldom outside the stockade. Still, this place, with its view of the broad blue river, soothed her, and she vowed to return here early each morning to get away from Moneta's nagging and the thick smells of the longhouse. Here she would watch the sunrise. If she returned to the longhouse with a load of wood, who would be the wiser?

And so, early each morning as everyone slept, Tekakwitha left the longhouse and slipped through the eastern gate and came here. On the sixth or seventh morning, as the darkness receded and mists rose from the river, and the first rays of sunlight pinkened the sky, she lay on the pine needles listening to the jays. When she had thought about many things, she rose and climbed a rock, and she looked eastward, out over the valley. Below her, the river flowed in a broad sweep, and as she looked down, she saw a large band of warriors quietly stealing along the river trail. Curious, she looked at them more closely, struggling to focus her eyes. They were not speaking Mohawk, or any language from any of the nations of the Iroquois League.

"Mohicans!" she said out loud. Fear seized her. She turned and ran back through the forest, over rock outcroppings, down along the stream lined with ferns, out into the open air of the cornfields, and up the hill, breathless, hardly able to cry, "Mohicans!"

The eastern gate was open, and she ran directly to Kryn's longhouse.

"Awaken, Great Chief!"

Karitha sat up and shook him. "What is it?"

"Mohicans!" she cried. "Attacking! Now!"

Instantly Kryn was in battle mode. He pulled on his moccasins, took his musket and his war hatchet from where they hung, and was out the door with an instruction to the young woman, "Rouse your family and help us defend."

A loud war-whoop went up. Just as the Mohicans attacked, Kryn blocked the eastern gate. Other Mohawk warriors ran to repel the attackers. High on the ramparts, Kryn was deploying young men here and there to take positions on the scaffold. He called to the village's fastest runner: "Race to Andagaron and Tionontoguen and summon warriors from the Wolf and Bear Clans!"

The young man leapt from the scaffold to the ground, and he darted through the western gate and flew across the cornfields.

Another shrill war cry sent shivers of fear through the village. Kryn called out in response: "Steady. Let us be steady at our posts."

The cry came again, a wild, forlorn wail, and flaming arrows suddenly rained out of the sky, hundreds of them. They landed on the roofs of the bark longhouses, and they stuck to the logs of the stockade. Treated with pine pitch, the arrows spilled fire on the dry bark and the wood.

Kryn had assembled two dozen archers on the scaffold along the eastern wall, and with the Mohicans within range, he raised his arm and cried, "Now!" Arrows flew from their bows and screams from outside the walls indicated many had found their mark. Kryn's archers pulled new arrows from their quivers while another shower of flaming arrows fell from the sky.

"Help me!" Tekakwitha heard. It was Anastasia with a bark pail of water. She was proceeding from house to house, pulling out the arrows and extinguishing flames. When they got to Iowerano's longhouse, Moneta rushed out.

"Cold Wind is drunk. He cannot load his musket."

"Fool!" Anastasia cursed him. Tekakwitha followed her in. Iowerano was sitting cross-legged on his sleeping pallet with a musket in his lap. He had the ramrod down the barrel with the ball and the charge, but his eyes were heavy, and he lost his grip.

"Give me that!" Anastasia said, and she snatched the musket away. "Every hand and every gun are needed!" She took the powder horn and musket balls and left the longhouse.

"Tekawitha! Tekakwitha!" Moneta called. "Stay here with us."

"I must help," she answered and left to follow Anastasia.

Outside, Kryn was on the ramparts in full view of the enemy, ordering men here and there to fire on the Mohicans and to douse flaming arrows that stuck in the walls. Defying musket fire, he walked along the scaffold to the eastern wall where a battering ram was forcing the gate open. Kryn helped three young men lift a pot of pine pitch up a ladder, and, pulling a flaming arrow from the palisade, he lit the pitch on fire and poured it on the Mohicans below. The men screamed from the burning tar, and the battering ceased.

Anastasia led Tekakwitha to a ladder. They climbed the fifteen steps to the scaffold and looked down on the swarms of Mohicans in chest plates and war paint. Anastasia fired and hit one of the Mohican chiefs. Muskets barked from the ground below, and here and there, warriors fell.

As another volley of flaming arrows flew up and over the wall, Kryn called Tekakwitha to him, gave her a gourd dipper and led her to a mossy tank of water.

"Put out the fires, little one. Save our homes."

She looked up into his eyes and saw, to her surprise, joy. She tilted her head quizzically. He smiled, and she suddenly knew: Kryn was happiest in the heat of battle.

"You, there!" he cried and hastened to order a pair of warriors to the northern wall. The flaming arrows kept flying. Anastasia reloaded and fired and reloaded and fired.

More battle cries rose from outside the walls, the musket fire roared, and now the battering ram began again. Kryn called to young warriors who had another kettle of pine pitch ready. Similarly, they hoisted it up, lit it, and poured it over the wall. The Mohicans below screamed in pain, and again the battering stopped.

Directly opposite, at the western gate, a battering ram began its deadly work. Kryn called to his warriors and climbed down the ladder and raced through the lanes of the village to reinforce the western gate.

As Anastasia fired and reloaded, Tekakwitha moved along the southern wall which faced the river, pulling shafts of burning arrows from the wood, dousing the flames with water. Now she heard a chopping as the Mohicans hacked with their hatchets at the base of the stockade. Looking out over the cornfields, the mob of Mohicans seemed endless, but then a war cry rose in the west.

"Our brothers!" Anastasia cried, and over the ridge from the west appeared an army of warriors from the Bear and Wolf Clans. By now, she and the girl were on the southern wall. Across the shallow ford of the river came a hundred Mohawks screaming and brandishing war clubs and hatchets. Some with muskets stopped, fell to one knee, and fired at the Mohicans. Caught between the palisade and the onslaught from the Bear and Wolf Clans, the Mohicans cried out and ran in retreat.

The ferocious Mohawks from the Wolf and Bear Clans rushed into the fray, hacking, and beating the enemy with axes and warclubs. From the palisade above rained a steady stream of arrows and musket fire, and now, caught in a pincer move, the Mohicans fought to escape. The Mohawks were merciless, though, and cut down the Mohicans as fast as they could move through the crowd.

A cry of retreat went up then. The Mohawk counterattack never eased, but the Mohicans turned north and fled across the corn plantation and then eastward, away from Kanawaka.

Kryn leapt from the scaffold, ran to the gate, threw it open and led his men out. "After them!" he called, waving his muscular arm, and they ran after the Mohicans, pausing here and there to shoot a musket or fire arrows at the stragglers.

Anastasia and Tekakwitha climbed down the ladder to help the wounded who lay groaning in the lanes of the village. Twenty or so warriors had fallen along with three women who, like Anastasia, had seized weapons and fought to defend their homes. A young boy caught an arrow in his left eye. The useless shaman, painted yellow, was dancing around in a frightful mask with rattles, but everyone ignored him.

2.

Kryn returned on the third day. His victorious band led prisoners tied with rawhide cords around their neck like leashes, and nineteen Mohican scalps hung from their belts. Rage at the insult of the attack filled the villagers, and as the sun set in bloody splendor, they formed a gauntlet to welcome the prisoners with rods, clubs, sharp flints, and burning brands.

Iowerano took command of the festivities. He ordered that fires be kindled to torture the prisoners. Tekakwitha kept away from the gauntlet and retreated to her corner to work on a wampum belt so she might avoid the villagers' rage. She averted her eyes and tried to close her ears to the incessant screaming of the captors and their prisoners, to the beating drums and whoops of joy. She thrilled, though, when Kryn entered the longhouse and sat with Iowerano. He was solemn and dignified as he accepted the pipe from the chief.

"You have distinguished yourself, Half-Breed," Iowerano said. "Tell me of your valor."

"Valor needs no boasting," Kryn said, drawing smoke from the pipe, then handing it back.

"Tell me of the massacre then."

As the darkness outside deepened and the screaming grew louder, Tekakwitha moved closer to listen.

"I sent White Hawk to Andagaron and Tionontoguen, and our brothers, Peoples of the Bear and Wolf, ran to our rescue. As we crushed the Mohicans between our forces, many of them fled to their homeland Massachusetts. The English muskets they carried leave little doubt who sent them."

"The English have been our friends," Iowerano protested. He took a long pull of the pipe. Outside, in the night, Mohican prisoners were singing death songs.

"The English resent the treaty we have formed with the French. They fear losing our trade."

"We shall visit them in Albany and display the scalps," Iowerano said. "That will stop the Mohican attacks."

"If only they could witness tonight's ceremony," Kryn said.

"Cowards!" Iowerano spat into the fire. "Tell me how you reduced them."

"I ordered the Wolf and the Bear Clans to trail them, to engage their party from behind as it fled home. Then I led Turtle Clan warriors along a parallel path down the falls at Cohoes and across the broad River That Flows Both Ways to the land they call Hoosick (The Stony Place). We arrived at the narrow pass through which they must travel, and we waited in ambush.

"As they approached and entered the pass, we held our fire until our brothers blocked the rear entrance. Once trapped between our armies," Kryn drove his fist into a dried gourd, smashing it to pieces, "we struck! We left no one standing. The seven we bring back as trophies, three who are singing just now, and the four our brothers took home to Andagaron and Tionontoguen, are the only warriors left. Let the account of this reprisal dissuade all others from attacking us."

"You have fought bravely," Iowerano said. He handed Kryn the pipe. "We shall hold a feast in your honor."

"I care not for feasts, Great Chief. I only want to go to my home and rest with my wife."

"You two shall produce great warriors to protect our people."

"But she cannot bear a child."

"Alas, my wives were also infected with the white man's illness and cannot bear me sons." He spat again in disgust. The prisoners outside were screaming in the throes of their death agony. "Go home to her and rest. I recognize your valor, and from this day forward, all shall refer to you as 'The Great Mohawk.'"

"It is not a name that matters."

"Yes, but a name signifies qualities within," Iowerano touched his fist to his heart.

Kryn rose and dusted himself off. He walked to Tekakwitha. "You still work to produce the beautiful skins."

Her unfocused eyes roamed until Kryn touched her on the cheek and tilted her face up. She shuddered. "I will make whatever the Great Mohawk needs."

"She will," Iowerano promised.

Screams from outside filled her ears as she squinted and marveled at how blue, like the sky, his eyes shone.

"I predict the English will approach us with caution now," Kryn said. "No longer do they consider us weak for our treaty with the French."

"That is why I forbid blackrobes from residing here," Iowerano said with satisfaction. "Let us remain on guard," he struck at a gourd with his fist in imitation of Kryn, but it did not break.

Kryn smiled kindly at the young woman, and she knew then that all the violence, the fire, the blood, and even the screaming outside just now protected her and the village. She understood it was necessary, but she wished it were not.

3.

Flaming arrows from Mohican archers had burned six of the eleven longhouses at Kanawaka. The clan mothers sat in council and voted to move the village upriver to higher ground. The warriors, flushed with victory from their revenge upon the Mohicans, disassembled the village, and a Dutch farmer from Corlaer, which the Mohawks called "Schenectady," lent his team of draught horses to haul stockade timbers, longhouse poles and large sheets of elm bark from the old village to the new.

At this new site, Kryn drove stakes for the four corners of the palisade. He located the eastern and western gates and then staked out a dozen longhouses and lanes within the village. At his direction, the men dug firepits and cut fresh saplings, then set them in the soil, and bent and lashed them into ribwork for new longhouses. They dug larger holes for the palisade timbers and then set the logs in a double row for additional strength and hung a scaffold near the top of the wall. In the center of the village, they raised a platform and pole.

The leaves were crimson and yellow when the farmer led his horses back downriver for the harvest. The clan mothers again sat in council and called for a ten-day Festival of the Dead to close the old village site by exhuming and reburying their dead relatives before moving. When the Hunter's Moon was three-quarters full, the men dug a large pit just beyond the old walls, and the women began disinterring corpses for the reburial ceremony.

The Turtle Clan had built this old village hastily to escape the contagion of smallpox that reduced its population by half. In the nine years since, dozens had died. Night after night, as the disc of moon waxed full, women processed quietly into the cemetery and dug open the graves with wooden hoes. They sang dirges while they worked. As they stripped away the soil, the skeletons of their relatives appeared in the moonlight, flesh and burial clothes decayed and eaten by worms, empty-eyed skulls grinning up from the graves.

On the eighth night of the festival, Tekakwitha walked across the fields and into the forest with her aunt Moneta, her sister Rainbow and eight other women. She lingered behind and at a split in the path, instead of accompanying them to the cemetery, she split away from them and went to Anastasia's hut. She carried three cornhusk dolls. Anastasia was dressing a beaver pelt on a frame in her yard.

"My beautiful Aurora!" Anastasia dropped her scraper, hugged the girl, and rocked her back and forth. "I have missed you. I hear the women singing through the forest. Are you attending the reburial?"

"Yes," she looked down, "but it is of no use to me. My family was buried in the common pit at Ossernenon."

"I remember. Yes. The day I rescued you."

"I have no family to release from the earth tonight, so I made these dolls. See?" One-by-one she handed the dolls to Anastasia. "This is my mother. This is my father. And this is my little brother."

"Aren't they beautiful? Come, sit with me." Anastasia led her to the trunk of a fallen tree and Tekakwitha sat beside her. "You speak of the Canienga belief that this ceremony releases the souls of our loved ones to fly up among the stars." Anastasia gestured at the galaxies spread out above them.

"Yes," the girl said. "If I cannot rebury my family's bones, they may be trapped in the earth forever. I made these dolls to throw into the pit tonight so perhaps the spirits of my parents and my little brother will be released."

"Oh, my precious one! Do not fear." Anastasia put down the dolls and held up the small wooden cross she wore on a thong around her neck. "The blackrobes teach that at the moment of death, all souls travel to a place where they are judged by God.

Then they are sent either to heaven high in the clouds, or to hell, deep in the earth to be burnt by flames. At the end of the world, all our bodies will be raised from the dead and joined again with our souls to live in heaven or in hell. On that last day, Great Beaver, my dearest friend Meadow and your little brother Aronsen will all be raised up and welcomed into heaven."

In the soft moonlight, Tekakwitha did not need to squint as badly, and Anastasia saw her beautiful mother's appearance in Tekakwitha's high cheekbones, strong jaw, and noble forehead. She cradled the girl's chin and kissed her on the cheek.

"The blackrobes tell us we will all be saved if we are baptized."

"Baptized?"

"They bless the water and sprinkle it on your forehead and that allows you to enter heaven."

"I would like this." She touched the cornhusk dolls. "But it is too late for my parents and my brother."

Flames from the bonfires and torches flickered through dark silhouettes of the trees. They could hear the women singing.

"Come," Anastasia said, "let us go and watch the reburial."

Tekakwitha took Anastasia's hand and they walked down a path through the dense woods. They emerged into a clearing where bonfires lit the eerie work. The women—mothers, sisters, wives, daughters, aunts, and cousins—sang a dirge as they opened their deerskin bundles and hurled the bones of their loved ones into the pit.

"Go," Anastasia said, "throw your dolls in with the rest."

Tekakwitha looked at her for reassurance, made up her mind and stepped forward. She approached the ditch and looking over the edge, her blurred vision revealed the piles of skulls, ribs, and leg bones. Murmuring a farewell to her family, she hurled the cornhusk dolls into the pit, and returned to Anastasia.

"Do you feel better now?"

Tekakwitha nodded and they watched and waited.

When the women had finished the reburial ceremony, four

young men came with wooden shovels to fill in the pit. The women filed down a path to the old village, Anastasia walking with Tekakwitha.

When they emerged from the forest, the river sparkled in the moonlight. The palisade was gone, and the longhouses had been dismantled. The stage and sacrificial post stood in the center surrounded by the skeletal framework of a few abandoned longhouses. White Adder, his face smeared with white clay, danced wildly, and shook his tortoiseshell rattles as the women set fire to the discarded bedding and remaining longhouse poles. As the old village blazed up, crackling into the sky, the women walked in a slow procession upriver to the new village, high on its hill.

One by one the women entered the narrow eastern gate. They filed through lanes between the longhouses to the center where a bonfire and twenty torches lit men dancing to a heavy drumbeat. The men wore their red, orange, and yellow tribal masks of distorted expressions: huge noses, accentuated eyes and pronounced lips. Because this was their dance for the dead, the men danced clockwise around the stage and pole, opposite in direction from their dances for the green corn and strawberry celebrations or their war dance.

Iowerano stood on the stage at the large pole with red, white, and yellow paint smeared on his face and chest. He wore his ceremonial *gustoweh* (headdress) with three eagle feathers straight up to denote his office. His stance and stern expression showed an unyielding air of command. He raised his arms to silence the chanting and the drumming, but just as he opened his mouth to speak, a voice in the crowd shouted, "Stop!"

All faces turned. In the lane between two longhouses the crowd parted, and a figure stepped forward dressed in a long black *soutane* and wide-brimmed hat. Iowerano's brow lowered, and he folded his arms. The blackrobe held a wooden cross high, and he turned this way and that to so that everyone could see.

Kateri, who stood close by, recognized Father Pierron, one of the three missionaries who had lodged in her longhouse two summers before.

"You interrupt our festival, Blackrobe?" Iowerano demanded.

"I do, Chief."

"You risk the welcome we reserve for prisoners?"

Shaking his rattles, White Adder danced close to Father Pierron.

"Do what you will. I am not afraid." The Jesuit spoke evenly with no tremor in his voice. "I have come to tell you that you must give up these superstitious rituals. Your Festival of the Dead, your reliance on dreams to guide your actions, and your treatment of captives," he raised the cross still higher, "these are the work of the devil, and must yield to the one true God."

"Silence!" Iowerano commanded.

White Adder stepped between them and pulled a tomahawk from his belt. "Say the word, Great Chief, and I will rid us of the blackrobe."

"Let him speak!" another voice shouted with authority. The crowd turned to see Kryn, tall and unassailable.

"The Great Mohawk takes the side of the blackrobe?" Iowerano derided him.

"This blackrobe does not come alone," Kryn said. "Hot Cinders has honored us with his presence, and he now bears Garacontie, the great Onondaga chief, up from the river."

The priest spoke: "This is true. I will lead them here."

The crowd murmured as Father Pierron turned away. Soon he was back with Hot Cinders, a massive Oneida war chief, who carried the aged Garacontie on his shoulder. He advanced to the stage and set Garacontie on the ground. Hot Cinders then folded his massive, tattooed forearms, and nodded at Kryn, fellow warrior chief of the Canienga. Ten Oneida who followed Hot Cinders arrayed themselves in the torchlight. Hot Cinders spoke to Iowerano:

"Great Chief Iowerano, *hoyoneh* of the Turtle Clan, I bring Garacontie, leader of all *Houdenosaunee* (People of the Longhouse)." Garacontie wore a red blanket around his thin, frail form, and a headdress with two eagle feathers. One feather stood straight up and the other slanted to the left.

"I am honored the chief of our great league sees fit to attend our festival. May I welcome him up here to address our village?" Showing respect for his elder, Iowerano held out his right arm as Hot Cinders lifted the old chief. Garacontie grasped Iowerano's forearm and was pulled onto the stage. The two chiefs bowed to each other.

Garacontie spoke, "It is the decision of the league that you accept a blackrobe at this new village."

"No." Iowerano held up his hands. "I have forbidden the blackrobes to build a prayer house in our village."

"Let the blackrobe join us up here," Garacontie directed.

Kryn and Hot Cinders lifted Father Pierron and Garacontie took his wrist. Now the blackrobe was standing between the two chiefs and he held his cross above the crowd. He turned to the left and then to the right and spoke in their native tongue.

"I come tonight, brave Turtle Clan, to demand that you give up these practices. It is wrong what you have done. The dead must rest in peace until the resurrection at the end of time when their spirits and bodies will be reunited by the one Almighty God. You must no longer put your faith in dreams, dreams do not predict the future. We are all in the hands of God the Father. His divine will alone is what gives life and takes it away. You must also turn from your war god Aireskou. He demands bloody sacrifices and murder, showing that he is not a true god."

"These are our customs!" Iowerano bellowed.

Garacontie held up his right hand for silence and looked around until everyone in the firelight was quiet.

"Noble Canienga! Two summers ago, we traveled the long route north to Onontio and offered him peace and brotherhood. He promised he would never again attack and burn our villages. We promised him in return that we would receive the black-robes. Your blue-eyed war chief represented your nation." Kryn stepped forward. "At the council fire we agreed, all five nations of the *Houdenosaunee*, that we would allow the blackrobes among us. The Onondaga have received a blackrobe. The great warrior Hot Cinders, veteran of many campaigns, has embraced the Prayer among the Oneida."

Garacontie turned to Iowerano. "The other two blackrobes who passed through this village two summers ago are now settled with the Bear and Wolf clans, but still the Turtle Clan defies the will of the League and refuses to allow a blackrobe to build a chapel and teach the Prayer. Your actions violate the promise we pledged to Onontio and risk another attack like the one that sent you into the forests two winters ago."

"Good chief, Garacontie, . . ." Iowerano stepped forward and extended his arms above his people.

Garacontie raised his hand. "It is not courteous to interrupt," he said softly, "but since you consider your thoughts superior to mine, speak and we will judge if this is the case." He stepped back.

Iowerano ignored the rebuke and continued: "These black-robes soften our warriors, Great Chief, and teach that we must look away when the French come among us to steal our lands. Our village, Kanawaka, the eastern entry to our League, has moved farther inland, but the French still knock for admittance. First a blackrobe enters among us and encourages us not to fight, then the French army follows to steal our furs and our land." He slapped his right fist into his left hand. "We must resist them now."

"Brave Chief," Garacontie was controlling his anger at Iower-ano's disrespect, "you defy the treaty, you defy me and the council of chiefs, and you defy the will of your people. I have traveled from our central council fire at the request of Hot Cinders who has embraced the Prayer to command you to follow the will of the league."

"Of what use am I to my people if I cannot lead them?"

"Such insolence will not be tolerated, Cold Wind." Garacontie turned to the crowd and spread his arms. "The decision to admit blackrobes into our villages is not for clan chiefs to decide. I come tonight with the blackrobe, and with these Oneida Christians to direct you to accept the blackrobe Onontio will shortly send you."

Anastasia bent over and whispered to Tekakwitha: "Now you can learn the Prayer."

"Yes?"

"And war in our land will cease."

"I hope this is so!" Tekakwitha whispered.

Now Father Pierron helped Garacontie off the platform into the waiting arms of Kryn and Hot Cinders, then the priest lowered himself into Hot Cinders' embrace. Iowerano stood alone on the platform in the torchlight, his brow clouded with anger as the crowd dispersed.

"Come. Sleep at my hut tonight," Anastasia suggested.

"No," Tekakwitha said, "They will miss me. I must go home."

CHAPTER EIGHT

KRYN ABANDONS HIS NEWBORN SON

I.

Kryn's wife Karitha loved him for his strength and bravery, and for his wisdom in seeing what was beyond Iowerano's reach. She desired to bear him a son. She watched the shaman try to cure the sick. She watched as he shoved a stick the length of his arm down his throat and vomited all over a sick man, dancing and chanting and rattling to get him to stand and walk. She knew that the shaman could not help her, so she turned to the blackrobe at Andagaron.

Every seven days, Karitha walked along the river trail with Anastasia and five or six other converts, returning in the evening filled with a deep peace and contentment. Though Iowerano railed against the blackrobe, Tekakwitha observed the effect on Kryn's wife. When, after two years, she announced she was with child, the blackrobe's magic proved more potent than the shaman's. Iowerano, of course, ignored the miracle. He wanted the village to thrive so they might return to the old ways, and having children furthered his plan. But the blackrobes threatened his authority, he thought, so any offspring attributable to them would surely be tainted.

Kryn, though, found new happiness in Karitha's pregnancy. Unlike many men who hunted and fished, oblivious to their pregnant wives, Kryn was solicitous and kind. As Karitha grew great with his child, he carried her burdens, helped her with her work, and brought her game and fish to augment the corn porridge and squash.

It was a cold, spitting winter morning when she came to term. She was scraping an elk skin when the labor pains grew severe, and Kryn went for the midwife to assist him in the delivery. Normally women squatted in the fields to deliver their children, then chewed the umbilical cord and wrapped the child in skins, and continued with their work, but Karitha's delivery was complicated, a breech birth. Kryn and the midwife needed to reposition the child for it to descend the birth canal safely. Hour after hour Karitha sweat, groaned, and screamed in pain as life in the longhouse went on around her. In the afternoon, the baby appeared.

"All this for nothing," Kryn said when he saw the child. The midwife handed the baby boy to him, but he refused to hold it. She gave it to the mother then. "We must expose the child," he said to Karitha.

"No," she said, holding the baby to her breast. She smiled at her baby boy. The midwife wiped the sweat from her face and lay her back to nurse the infant as she cleaned up the blood and afterbirth.

"His right arm is withered," Kryn observed. "He will never hold a bow or a tomahawk. We must expose him."

Karitha looked up with defiance. In the firelight, her eyes were ferocious. "I will not allow that. A man is more than his limbs. Our son shall be wise and become a great sachem." She stroked the baby's head as his mouth suckled at her breast. "Go! Leave us now."

Kryn scowled at mother and child, and then he pulled on his robe of elk skin and pushed through the flap, out into the weather. As he stalked through the village, no one dared to look at the Great Mohawk for fear of his rage.

A wet, blinding snow pelted the lanes of the village and smoke hung low over the longhouses. The river was frozen, and men and boys had drilled holes in the ice to fish. Kryn did not know what to do or where to go, so he went to Iowerano's longhouse and sat with him smoking.

"... and the child has a withered right arm."

Tekakwitha listened. She had watched the progress of Karitha's pregnancy with great attention. "This is the blackrobes' magic," Iowerano concluded.

"Can you order her to surrender the child so that I may rid us of this disgrace?"

Iowerano considered Kryn's request. "Matters concerning the family are heard by the Women's Council. I cannot help you."

"Perhaps I can," Tekakwitha offered from the corner.

"You would speak to the Great Mohawk?" Iowerano thundered at the temerity of his niece.

"Yes," Tekakwitha said evenly. She was embroidering the hem of a doeskin dress.

"What is it, child?" Kryn said kindly.

"I urge the Great Mohawk to find patience. My blindness forced me to listen, to use my ears for eyes. Your son's withered arm, will force him to develop other skills."

"You are wise, little one," Kryn observed.

"She should learn her place and not eavesdrop on the talk of men."

"The chief, my uncle, forbids me to speak, and I respect him," she said. "But if he allowed me to, I would urge you to raise your son so he may become a great chief like his father."

"I don't see how he will earn respect. He cannot hunt, he cannot fish. He will never leave the company of women."

"Not being able to play lacrosse with the other boys or hunt of fish, he will grow wise."

"Like you, little one, wise beyond your years." His voice was weary.

"She should learn to keep quiet and not jump in at every crossroad," Iowerano said.

"I must leave," Kryn said. "I cannot dwell at that fire pit, or in that house, or in this village so long as she keeps this infant to remind me of its deformity."

"It is winter. Where will you go?"

"What does it matter, Cold Wind? I shall hunt and live alone in the forest until the spring and then I will decide."

Kryn handed the chief back the pipe and stood to go. Tekakwitha turned away. She felt a tear pressing at her eye. There was a gentle touch on her shoulder. She looked up to see the Great Mohawk towering over her.

"You shall marry a great warrior and become a wise matriarch."

"That one?" Iowerano spat into the fire. "Look those scars. She will never marry. I have arranged two matches for her, and each time they are not good enough for her. She will be like the ancient cult of virgins, living apart from men."

"We all reach our destination sooner or later," Kryn said. "I leave, Great Chief, and ask that in my absence, you watch over Karitha."

"She is descended from an ancient line in the Turtle Clan," Iowerano said. "Despite her consorting with the blackrobes, she need not fear hunger."

"As you say." Kryn turned and pushed through the door flap.

Tekakwitha felt Iowerano's eye of rebuke on her, but she did not turn toward him. After a while, she gathered up her work and retired to her sleeping pallet.

2.

The following day, a howling blizzard blew in from the west. Tekakwitha struggled through the village lanes to Kryn's longhouse to visit the new mother. As she entered with a flurry of snow, she heard the joyful sounds of mother and infant. Around Karitha were the three Christian women who traveled with her to the mission in Andagaron.

Tekakwitha approached hesitantly, not wanting to disturb them, but Karitha saw her and summoned her over. "Come, Tekakwitha, look at little Peter."

"Peter?" the girl asked.

"It is the name of a great man of the blackrobes' faith, one who first led the followers of Jesus Christ, our savior."

Tekakwitha threw off her shawl, and slowly her eyes grew accustomed to the dim light. The baby was nestled in fur, his little eyes still closed and his little lips looking for the nipple.

"Do you want to hold him?" Karitha asked.

Tekakwitha took the baby and held him to her shoulder. Blindly the baby searched for the nipple. She laughed pleasantly at the sensation of holding something so small, like a puppy, yet human.

"As I was saying," Karitha lay back and sighed as if from a great exertion, "Kryn's departure has cleared the way to me take little Peter to the blackrobe for baptism."

"We will bring him as soon as you are ready to walk," one of the women said.

"I will be ready this Sunday," Karitha said. "He is so fragile. I fear losing him and, for want of baptism, excluding him from heaven."

"Baptism?" the girl asked.

"The blackrobe drips water on the baby's forehead," said the young woman who now called herself Martha, "and recites a prayer. Only if he does this can a soul enter heaven. If a baby dies before this baptism, he can never enter heaven."

The girl rocked the infant, and he groped in the air. "And what about us?"

"We are baptized," Martha said.

"You should journey with us," Karitha said. "You could be baptized."

"My uncle would never allow it."

"How can he prevent it?" the other young woman, Cecilia, asked.

"He is chief."

"The blackrobe teaches that we are responsible, each of us, for our lives. No one can control another."

"If only that were true," Tekakwitha said. She handed the baby back to Martha, then she reached into her tunic and pulled out a small, embroidered fur blanket. "I made this for Peter." Karitha took the blanket and held it up. Tekakwitha had embroidered a small green turtle in the middle of the bottom edge.

"It is beautiful, little one."

"It is for the newest of our Turtle Clan."

"That was so very kind."

"When will Kryn return?" she asked as she put on her coat.

"Only he knows," Karitha said. She asked Martha for the baby back, wrapped him in the new blanket, and placed him at her breast so he could nurse.

CHAPTER NINE
KRYN MEETS A HOLY WOMAN AND JOINS THE FAITH

I.

Kryn stumbled through the blizzard on snowshoes, his thoughts filled with rage. Had he not survived fierce battles with smoking muskets and bloody tomahawks? Had he not spoken in the councils with the antlered bonnets of fifty-one sachems nodding as smoke from the calumets hung in the sunshine? Had he not hunted for elk and caribou while the crystal stars twinkled, the northern lights pulsed green in the sky, and wolves and coyotes complained to the indifferent peaks? In all these, he had emerged the victor, his courage, wisdom, and cunning rewarded. But now, undone by a woman's whim? What chance had a boy, a man with a withered arm? His right arm, no less! A cripple.

In everything, he—Togoniron, Kryn, the Flemish Bastard, and now the Great Mohawk—had triumphed, but the simple act of fathering a child eluded him. To make matters worse, the woman, his wife, with her sentimental notions, refused to allow him to correct the mistake. Ancient law required children so deformed to be exposed, so the wolves and bobcats carried them off, yet the woman now suckled it, and her Christian friends embraced and welcomed it.

Kryn plunged into the teeth of the blizzard. As darkness descended, he built a lean-to at the base of a great rock. He shaved wood chips with his knife for kindling, and used his bow drill to start a fire to ward off wolves and coyotes. He bundled himself in his skin robe and gazed into the fire as the snow blew outside. In his haste he had packed only dried venison strips and he pulled these from his buckskin wallet and chewed pensively, looking into the flames.

As night deepened, his anger passed. He recalled his joy at learning Karitha was pregnant. He remembered their hope as she grew heavy with child. The future had seemed secure. Now? He fed a pine knot into the fire and settled into his robe with the fragrant smoke. How differently these Christians reacted. Calm, docile, happy, they accepted everything that came their way with little frustration or care, as if the unexpected and unforeseen were meant to be.

Everything these days was flying apart. The order and ritual and certainty that held life together before was now supplanted by upstart individuals making their own decisions, defying tradition, and rebelling against the old ways. This was the work of Christianity. Its followers refused to work one day in seven; its grown men saw no value in war. Droves of people wended along the riverbank to Andagaron so they might kneel in the little bark chapel and chant. What drew them there? The mystery was as dark and thick as this night's snowfall.

He awoke with light filtering through the pine boughs of his lean-to. The snow had stopped. A faint yellow light stole through the tree limbs furred with snow. He was alone and hungry, his rage cooled by uncertainty about where he would go and what he would do. He considered camping here, snaring a rabbit for immediate food and then hunting for larger game, but he needed to keep moving, to put distance and time between himself and the colossal disappointment brought by the birth of his son.

Kryn readied his pack for transport, strapped on his snowshoes, and set off once more, heading north through the forest.

2.

Next day, the vista rolled out in white and blue, with expansive views of hills and valleys and frozen lakes. The long winter nights crept in early, and the landscape was empty and dead, even as hunger gnawed at him. The second day he snared a rabbit and cooked and ate it. He shot a porcupine on the fourth day, carefully removed the quills, cooked, and ate it. He traveled on through the mountains. He even shot a skunk, carefully butchering it, and ate the meat to keep going.

He had been away a fortnight, without food for four days when he spied a dozen columns of smoke rising far off in the valley by a long, wide expanse of snow, a frozen river. He started for the cabins and as he approached, he saw that one had a cross on its roof. Snow began to fall as he drew closer to the small settlement, and he rapped on the wooden door of the first cabin he reached. A woman answered.

"You are lost," she said. Her manner was knowing, and she spoke the word "lost" as though it had a double meaning.

"I am called 'Kryn' from the land of the People of Flint, eastern gatekeeper of the People of the Great Longhouse. May I warm myself at your fire?"

"Of course," she said, and she stood aside.

Kryn entered the small, tidy cabin. It was made of logs and along the northern wall stood a hearth of fieldstone where a kettle hung above glowing coals. On a split log shelf, she had propped a large cross.

"You are Christian?" he asked.

"Yes. I am Gandeacteua, born Oneida and baptized Christian. Catherine is now my name. Let me dip you up a bowl of stew."

She stirred the kettle with a ladle and dished a steaming

portion of stew into a wooden bowl. A savory aroma came from it, and she handed it to Kryn. The stew was hot and meaty, venison with bits of squash and beans and corn. So delicious was the unexpected food that he barely chewed it, and when he had finished the bowl, she gave him another, along with a cup of water. Finishing that, too, she arranged a sleeping mat for him near the fire, and Kryn lay down and was immediately asleep.

Many dreams came to him. In one, the woman, Catherine, appeared as a gatekeeper to a green land of delicious quiet and peace. He dreamed that birds and fish spoke to him. A white stag with a ten-point rack of antlers grazed in a meadow, its muzzle chewing. He dreamed of the mountains reaching as high as the moon. He dreamed of the rivers flowing as warm steaming water from a sweat lodge. When he awoke, Catherine was kneeling before the cross, passing beads on a thong through her fingers, her lips murmuring.

"What do you do with the beads?" Kryn asked.

Catherine continued to pray and did not respond. Kryn arose and pulled on his fur robe and went outside to the privy. The cabins were built of logs, not bark, and the roofs were of thatch and cedar shakes. Along the riverbank, a dozen or so humps showed where canoes had been beached for the winter. A bell in the chapel rang, and Catherine came outside, bundled in her coat and hood. She nodded to him and ambled along to the prayer service at the chapel. Kryn declined to follow but watched her recede down the lane and enter the warm light of the chapel.

In the ensuing days, Kryn observed Catherine closely. So different from any woman he had ever encountered, she was self-sufficient, direct, and free from any coy suggestions. Her husband, Tonsanhoten, was back with the Oneida for the winter, visiting Father Bruyas and enlisting others to migrate to the mission. She and her husband had built this house, the first native residence at this site around which others had recently clustered, initially at the request of Father Pierre Rafeix and after his death, Father Frémin.

A week passed, and then another. Catherine made life comfortable for Kryn, but she also kept her distance. His curiosity about the service in the chapel led him, one morning, to inquire if he might attend.

"Of course," Catherine said, and she led him down the snowy lane to morning mass.

Kryn entered the dim chapel and saw a dozen Iroquois standing in a line, singing a sweet hymn. Father Frémin emerged onto a platform, and they all knelt. Kryn knelt with them. The priest spoke words in a tongue Kryn had never heard before, and the ceremony intensified until the blackrobe held up a round piece of bread, a Huron altar boy rang bells, and all bowed their heads. The choir sang in joy and triumph. Then, many of the People of the Longhouse rose and proceeded to the railing to receive small pieces of the bread.

Kryn was moved by the singing and by the ceremony. He and Catherine walked back in the howling wind, and when they reached her cabin, he had questions.

"What you just saw is called a mass," she answered. "Although he was God, Jesus Christ allowed Himself to become a victim of torture so He could save mankind. The Romans nailed Him to a wooden cross. He died on the cross, and after they buried Him, He rose from the dead."

"He returned from the dead?"

"Yes, that is the primary belief of Christianity, that Christ conquered death. And the mass re-enacts His sacrifice on the cross."

"Christians are so quiet and calm," Kryn observed.

"It is because we forgive."

"Who do you forgive?"

"Everyone. Everyone who wrongs us. Let me teach you something. Repeat after me." Kryn repeated while Catherine recited:

"Our Father, who art in heaven, hallowed be Thy name. Thy

kingdom come, Thy will be done, on earth as it is in heaven. Give us this day, our daily bread, and forgive us our trespasses as we forgive those who trespass against us, and lead us not into temptation, but deliver us from evil, for Thine is the kingdom and the power and the glory, now and forever, Amen."

She nodded with satisfaction. She saw Kryn understood the Prayer.

"When you forgive others, you release yourself from bondage."

"What bondage?"

"Has anyone ever wronged you?"

"Of course."

"Have you forgiven him?"

"Her."

"Have you forgiven her?"

Kryn looked at Catherine and did not speak.

"Why haven't you?"

"She acted contrary to custom and tradition."

"But did her action injure you?"

"It injured my reputation."

"How?"

"As a warrior. As a man."

"What did she do?"

"She refused to expose our son, who was born with a withered arm."

"So, she refused to murder your baby?" Catherine's eyes bored into Kryn's. "A helpless infant."

"She did," he answered. He looked away. For the first time he saw past his pride and his shame.

"And you won't forgive her because she allowed your child to live?" Catherine shook her head. "This is what Christians understand. Forgiveness frees us. It cancels all debts and allows us to live without anger or envy or revenge. Was this woman your wife?"

"She was. She is. Yes."

"Once you forgive her, you will feel love for her again. A withered arm has no effect on your child's ability to live and to love. Your son will love you without reservation, and you must love him and raise him and protect him. That is the natural order of things in God's kingdom."

Kryn was astonished. He trusted her for her generosity, and now she provided the answer for what he sought during many days of hunger, and dark nights of doubt and despair, and she led him to this understanding without magic or spells of any sort.

"This is what Christian faith brings," she said. She saw understanding and relief illuminate his features.

3.

In further talks by the fireside that winter, Catherine helped Kryn examine his motivations in all things. She showed him how to measure the results of his actions against the impulses behind them, instructing him in a process she called "right-thinking," which required discarding the blind following of custom. Kryn soon saw how each decision he made, each act he performed could uphold his values or not, and then how to measure what he accomplished. Once possessed of this tool, he evaluated how well the Iroquois in general and the Mohawks in particular had fared since the whites arrived. He was disgusted by what disease and drunkenness had brought the Great League.

"We have a chief who urges returning to the old ways," he told her. "Being only half Canienga, I have sought to surpass those of full blood by following him. I see now that it is impossible. The old ways are gone. The only path I can follow must lead away from those ways much as villagers must leave a burning village."

"Consider," Catherine observed, "no longer do we look to the forests and the streams for our every need. The whites bring many things that are good, too—knives and cloth, hatchets, and kettles—and we trade for them. This dependency on the whites weakens us unless we can find new strength. The Prayer shows us this new path."

When Kryn was sufficiently prepared, Catherine brought him to meet the blackrobe, Father Frémin. As Kryn held out his hand to clasp the priest's, he recognized him as one of the three who had visited Kanawaka a few years ago. His greeting was warm.

"You wish to receive instruction?" the priest asked.

"I do," Kryn said.

"It is good you have come."

<h2 style="text-align:center">4.</h2>

As the sun rose in the sky and frost steamed out of the frozen ground in the ensuing weeks, Kryn attended the black-robe's instruction at the chapel. By Easter, he was ready for baptism. The spring sun was sparkling on the river when he went to the chapel that day. The choir sang the *Kyrie* and the *Gloria* and the *Sanctus* and the *Agnus Dei* in soft candlelight with wild-flowers around the altar for Easter morning.

Kryn had replaced his buckskin tunic with a robe of white cotton, and his hair had grown in. He walked down the aisle solemnly and knelt while the priest poured holy water over his forehead: "In the name of the Father and of the Son and of the Holy Ghost, Amen."

"Amen."

"Do you renounce Satan?"

"I renounce Satan."

"And all his works."

"And all his works."

"And all his empty promises."

"I do."

When Father Frémin asked the convert's Christian name, Catherine, his sponsor, answered, "Joseph."

"Welcome, Joseph Kryn," the priest said. And they stood in

the candlelight and the harmonious music with the warm spring sun glancing through the door of the chapel.

5.

Kryn was going home. Using a hatchet and a knife, he built himself a canoe of elm bark, lashing the ribwork and the tholes, smearing pine pitch along the seams. He whittled a long paddle out of ash, and one morning in May, after mass and communion, he walked down to the riverbank with Catherine Gandeacteua and Father Frémin.

"May you have safe passage," the priest said, and he embraced the bigger man.

"I go, but I shall soon return, and with me, I will bring those from our village who wish to live here in peace."

Catherine reached out to take his hand. "Bring your wife and your little son," she said. "We will care for them and everyone who accompanies you."

"I will return before the leaves are blazing."

So saying, Kryn pushed the canoe into the water and jumped nimbly aboard as it glided into the broad current. He seized his paddle, waved to the priest and Catherine, and then threw his broad shoulders into the work, paddling down the river toward the Richelieu.

CHAPTER TEN

KRYN RETURNS TO HIS VILLAGE

I.

Joseph Kryn climbed the mud path up from the river. Entering the village through the narrow gate, he heard loud laughter. Suddenly, around the side of a longhouse, a group of young warriors ran heedlessly toward him. When they saw him, they stopped abruptly and waited for him to speak. They had considered him dead.

"You are in a great hurry," said Joseph Kryn.

"We believed you were . . . lost . . . and many thought you'd never return," one said.

"Why are there no women in the fields? Why no guards on the walls?"

"It's the Festival of Dreams," one of the young warriors said with a snide laugh. "Yesterday, we tore through the village to find a sacred wampum belt one old man dreamed about, and we found it. Quorenta, the old hag, dreamed Bobcat the Hunter came to her as a lover, so we roused him and took him to her. Iowerano dreamed the English visited with a cask of rum, and so we sent Gray Squirrel to Corlaer for a cask, and now everyone drinks the dreamed-for rum."

"Yes," another laughed, "our dream feast becomes a celebration. Iowerano and Moneta host a Drink-All in their longhouse tonight."

"And what of the girl Tekakwitha?"

"She is sent on errands to fetch water and wood and even food from neighboring homes."

Kryn turned from the young men and strode through the lane to Iowerano's longhouse. He heard the beating of a drum inside, and when he ripped open the bearskin flap, the wild scene he beheld infuriated him. A young warrior was drumming, and a group of eight sat swaying on the ground, chanting. White Adder, the shaman, danced wildly among them in an ugly yellow face mask. All the people at the gathering were screaming in laughter at White Adder's antics. Kryn looked in the direction of Tekakwitha's usual place and saw she was gone.

Kryn walked straight up to Iowerano, who sat like a king in his antlered bonnet with folded arms. Iowerano turned to him drunkenly, trying to focus his glassy eyes.

"Ah, the Great Mohawk!" he said. "He humbles himself to return to us."

Kryn ignored the jibe. "Where is the girl who sits over there? The one who embroiders?"

"Around here somewhere," Iowerano said. "What's it to you?"

Moneta added: "She goes her own way now. We cannot control her."

"She refuses to marry." The chief shrugged.

White Adder, shaking his rattles, danced up to Joseph Kryn and moved menacingly about him as if he were fending off an evil spirit. Kryn towered over him.

"I sense the blackrobes' evil!" White Adder cried and shook his rattles furiously.

Kryn ignored him and called to Iowerano over White Adder's head, "Is this how you observe the old ways?"

"My magic is stronger!" White Adder cried.

Joseph Kryn reached down and seized the shaman by the

rawhide thong of his amulet to the war god Aireskou. "You are a fraud!" he said. "Your magic is nothing but tricks!"

"So says the half-breed!"

"Let him go, Kryn!" Iowerano was laughing. "The fool entertains me!"

"He dupes you!" Joseph Kryn said. "He is no match for the power of the blackrobes' God."

With the light from the doorway, Kryn saw the girl Tekakwitha then, entering with an armload of firewood.

"You make this little one with the bad eyes fetch your wood and water? While you, able-bodied men and women, sit inside drinking whiskey?"

"Who are you to rebuke us?" Moneta spoke. "You abandoned your wife and child through this long, cold winter without providing for their well-being."

"Come with me, little one," Kryn said to Tekakwitha. "Who knows what might happen as they lose their reason to the whiskey?"

"She stays!" Iowerano said, pounding his fist into his palm.

White Adder shook his rattles in Joseph Kryn's face, and he spun and leaped and shouted imprecations.

"Get your quills and your skins," Kryn said to the girl, and he turned to her uncle. "I have some work for her to do."

"Ah, take her away," Moneta said. "She annoys me with her long-suffering face."

"Yes, go!" Iowerano said with disgust.

Tekakwitha dropped her bundle of wood by the side of the fire pit, collected a few scraps of doeskin and her basket of dyes and porcupine quills, and she left the longhouse. She adjusted her shawl against the bright sunlight and walked along with Kryn toward his home.

"You have work for me?" she asked.

"Do you know the symbol of the blackrobes? The cross?"

"Yes, of course."

"You know my son?"

"Peter grows strong," she said. "He is a happy baby."

"He does not yet know how men will abuse him, but enough of that. I want you to stitch the cross of the blackrobes on a skin for his mother to put around him on the cradleboard."

"Gladly," she said.

Kryn started to enter the longhouse where he had once lived.

"You are seeking Karitha and Peter?" she asked. "They now live outside the village with Anastasia."

"Lead me to them."

She led him through the cornfields to Anastasia's cabin. As they approached, they heard the baby laughing inside.

"Shall we go in, little one, or do you think Karitha will turn me away?"

"I have visited here through the dark winter months. She has often prayed for your return."

Kryn pulled the great curtain aside. The girl followed him into the cabin. "Karitha?" Kryn said. His wife turned, looked at him with surprise and shock, stood, handed the baby to Anastasia, and embraced him. "You have returned!"

"I was a fool," he said, and he took her in his brawny arms.

After they had embraced, she handed him the baby. "Hold your son."

Kryn's face lit up as he opened the soft deerskin and saw his son. The baby's left arm was waving at him in the air. With his big fingers, Kryn tickled the baby's chin, and the baby laughed. The Great Mohawk cradled the infant against his chest and rocked him.

"Here," Anastasia said, "sit down on the mat. How long has it been long since you ate?"

Joseph Kryn shrugged. "I can't remember."

"You too, little one," Anastasia gathered Tekakwitha to her, "please sit." She handed the warrior and the girl wooden spoons and began to fill two bowls with *sagamite* from the kettle.

"You seem changed," Karitha observed.

"I am," Joseph Kryn said. He looked at her with a pene-trating gaze. "I am Christian."

Anastasia dropped a bowl of porridge, and Karitha cried out, put her hands to her face, and they both fell on him, embracing him and crying in thanksgiving. When the emotion subsided, Kryn explained:

"When I left you, I traveled blindly through the snow for days and days. I had little food with me. I hardly cared whether I lived or died. My steps drew me into the mountains along the frozen lakes and then down to the great river of the north. Half-starved, I stumbled toward a cabin, and a Christian woman, Catherine, an Oneida, took me in. She met my arguments with such logic, and it was as if she had been sent to me for that very purpose."

"The blackrobe calls such people 'guardian angels,'" Anastasia said.

Tekakwitha listened, amazed by his change of heart.

"I was proud and unforgiving," he said, clasping the child to his chest. "I learned from Catherine and the priest the prayer they call the 'Our Father' where it says 'forgive us our trespasses . . .'"

The women joined in, "'. . . as we forgive those who trespass against us and lead us not into temptation but deliver us from evil.'"

Joseph Kryn put out his hand and touched Karitha's cheek. "Can you forgive me?"

"I did long ago," she said. "Please, have your supper." And she served porridge to everyone. Anastasia sat next to Tekakwitha and put her arm around the young woman's shoulder, welcoming her into this family.

2.

Joseph Kryn was indeed a changed man. While other warriors and hunters idled away their spring and summer smoking and gambling as their women worked the fields, Kryn doted on his wife and his son, even helping Anastasia in the garden and around her cabin where they all lived together. In the lanes of the village, Kryn could be seen carrying the boy on a cradleboard. It was a decidedly unmasculine, un-Mohawk sight, and in the early afternoon, he began a sort of academy for young people, both boys and girls, to teach them about the faith and the Mission of St. Francis Xavier.

"A dozen cabins surround a chapel," he told the nine or ten children who clustered around him near their swimming hole. "The chapel has a cross on it and a bell to ring for services. We attend mass early in the morning, and in the afternoon, we return for prayer. When workers are in the fields, or building new shelters, or down along the river repairing canoes, we kneel when the bell rings, and we pray Matins or the Angelus. In this way, we stop every few hours to turn our minds and hearts to our Creator."

"Is there a stockade?" one of the young men asked.

"Yes, for defense," Joseph Kryn said. "Unfortunately, war has not been extinguished. But at the mission, there is nothing to fight for. There are no muskets or bundles of furs to trade, no incentive to conquer. And there is no whiskey. We grow what we need and live humbly. We turn the other cheek to an aggressor, and so all aggression disappears."

"Do they marry?" another asked.

"Yes, but only one wife and they pledge to spend a lifetime together in work and in worship."

"I was asking about the blackrobes," the youth said.

"Oh, no. We are allowed to marry, even encouraged to marry to create families, but the blackrobes take no wife. They do not know women, and religious women do not know men. They dedicate their lives, everything, to God."

"Do the blackrobes work?"

"They do not till the field or build the cabins or cook the

food. They do not trade or hunt or fish. They work by praying and by counseling us to lead us into heaven."

"Are all nations welcome?"

"Yes, and it is a miracle. The say the fawn lies down with the bear. Never would I have believed it, yet I have seen it. Men and women from all nations live together in harmony: Hurons, Mohawks, Algonquins, Abenaki, Neutrals, Adirondacks, and Mohicans. All resentments and jealousies are left behind. We devote our time to prayer, and we work in the field free from grudges and revenge. Once you live that way there is no other way to live."

Early each Sunday morning, as the sun was clearing the hills, Joseph Kryn and his extended family met other Christians at the western gate and left the village in high spirits. They walked along the river, talking, and laughing, Kryn carrying little Peter. Still living with her uncle, Tekakwitha heard them assembling each week, then watched them depart, happy and excited about attending mass and receiving communion. Her life was drudgery. Moneta, sensing her desire, ridiculed the Christians openly.

"Look at them! While the rest of us work to clean the skins and till the fields, they go off on a lark, laughing and skipping along the trail without a care."

Iowerano chimed in: "Gone is any respect for the old traditions, for the Dream Feast or the Corn Planting dance or the Harvest Festival. Instead, they worship the torture victim that Ondessonk first told us about, the man who advises warriors not to fight."

These criticisms were meant for her ears, but the ridicule only increased her desire to accompany the others.

As the summer ripened, the talk went around that Joseph Kryn was soon departing from Kanawaka for the northern mission, and he was inviting any Christians who wanted to leave to join him. All the cousins through his mother's line vowed to accompany him, with many others who had been baptized. Hearing of their departure, Iowerano bitterly resented the half-breed's allegiance to the white side of his parentage, and he ordered that true Mohawks seal up their ears, not listen to him and be led astray.

When the nights and the days were equal, and a chill began to tinge the maple leaves, Joseph Kryn assembled his forty emigrants with their packs and hunting gear.

"You must join us someday," Anastasia told Tekakwitha and hugged her tightly.

"My uncle will never let me go."

"Our faith teaches that we are each responsible for our own decisions. Others cannot control us. Become a Christian, little one, and join us at the mission."

She hung her head and did not answer.

After saying their farewells, the Christians left in a happy group. They wended down the hill and into the forest toward the trail that led to the lakes where they would fashion canoes to bear them north to the great river and their new life.

Watching them leave, Tekakwitha was deeply saddened. For a long time, she stood alone at the gate to the village, wishing she could call out and join Kryn and the Christians on their happy sojourn.

CHAPTER ELEVEN
FATHER CLAUDE CHAUCHETIÈRE,
MISSIONARY TO NEW FRANCE

I.

For weeks, it seemed, Claude Chauchetière had gazed out his latticed window at the pelting rain. Clouds billowed in the western sky like smoke above a battlefield. On his brisk walks to the refectory or on those few days where, needing air, he paced slowly and deliberately in the cloister to quell the zeal that burned within him, the wind played with his black *soutane* and his wide-brimmed *chapeau*, winds of change, he believed.

In his small whitewashed cell, his pencils and paint box, quill, and ink bottle lay unused. The output of his letters fell as impatience gnawed at him. *La Belle Yglantine*, a small, square-rigged transport from the Marseille shipyards, was well-suited for Mediterranean trips but not an Atlantic crossing. The ship sat at the quay, waiting for the sky to clear. And then, the sun beamed on the sodden fields, and the wet slates of the turrets and spires of La Rochelle, and Claude's doubts flew away. Bells rang the hours, and he shivered in anticipation.

The ship was bringing sixty *habitans* and their livestock— sheep and swine and milk cows and half a dozen horses for the governor's stables—to New France. Barrels of salt pork and hard tack, and water, kegs of brandy and wine were stacked in the hold. The wind fluttered in the loose sails as Claude climbed the ramp, a large carpetbag over his shoulder. He looked up at the gold and azure pennants flying from the masts, and he felt pure joy. Claude was leaving behind the spiritual morass into which his soul had fallen and was—dare he even breathe a comparison with the great Jogues?—striking out into a native wilderness with only faith and zeal to guide him. He tried to imagine his destiny in the harsh wilderness. Along with apprehension, he also felt certain that a spiritual consummation awaited him in the primordial forests.

The sailors called up and down the quay, casting off the hawsers that bound him to France. He looked up. Gulls wheeled and cried above the twin turrets at the harbor's mouth, beckoning him on. Oarsmen in three pilot boats pulled at their oars to tow *La Belle Yglantine* into open water. Barefoot sailors danced above in the rigging, and as the ship cleared the towers and the breakwater, they unfurled the sails that dropped and filled with wind, flexing the masts with a cheerful groan to be moving at last.

The *habitans* nestled comfortably amid their bleating sheep and lowing cattle. They were simple peasants, small, thick, swarthy men with long filthy hair and knotted beards who wore leather vests, homespun flannel shirts, canvas breeches, and clogs. Their simplicity pleased the priest far more than his two Jesuit companions, who seemed fastidious when sleeping below deck or eating their first meal of salt pork and biscuit or seeking privacy where there was none. He slept close to his fellows. He used his pencils to sketch the captain, the crew, the spars and sails that caught the wind and propelled them into the future. As he sketched, each new blank page brought a daydream about what scenes he soon would be drawing.

The first storm hit four days out. The seas had been strong and steady, large swells that lifted the gliding ship and carried her along and then eased her down into a trough. Toward evening on the fourth day, Father Claude stood with his two fellow priests, watching a thunderstorm sweep toward them across the water like the hand of God.

"Trim the sails!" the first mate called through his speaking trumpet. The crew sprang up the rope ladders and out the yardarms and hauled up the swelling canvas as the sky darkened and rising seas bent the masts leeward. Then a flash of lightning and thunder crashed, and the storm enveloped them. Up, up, up the ship rose, pointed at the sky where it hung, frozen for a moment before plunging, down, down as if the bowsprit would stab through the gates of hell. Sweet rain and salt spray lashed at them as they clung to ropes and belaying pins. Only the leather thong beneath their chins kept their hats from ripping off. Father Claude felt a mortal fear as the once-placid, shimmering ocean suddenly became curling mountains of black water and chasms into which they dropped. His gorge rose with the heaving motion, and although he struggled to lean over the bucking deck rail, the wind blew vomit on his clothes and his shoes.

"Below! Get him below!" someone cried, and Father René and Father Michel put their shoulders beneath his arms and carried him to the companionway.

Below all was mayhem. The floor of the lower deck rose and fell at impossible angles. The beasts bleat and whinnied in fear. The *habitans* cried out in superstitious panic and clasped their hands above their heads with rosaries and crosses, screaming out prayers for deliverance. The smell! Vomit, diarrhea, manure all mingled with the pervasive body odor of stale sweat. Father René seized a bucket for Claude, and he vomited and vomited and vomited until he felt his insides would rise in convulsions and spew through his mouth. Then Father Michel was sick. Then Father René. They shared the bucket, and between episodes of sickness, they fell on the heaving floorboards and tried not to slip backward and forward as the ship rose and fell.

Through an eternity of screams and bellows and the slosh of

fetid water, somehow the night passed. In the gray light of morning, the storm abated, but waves still dashed against the hull and sent enormous clouds of spray high across the deck where Claude, René, and Michel struggled now to breathe fresh air.

"Gives one a new appreciation for the suffering of Jonah," René said. He was a young, irrepressible slip of a boy with a cowlick of red hair and bright blue eyes. His pale eyelids made him always seem sleepy. "At times last night, I would have preferred to be cast into the sea."

Indeed, it seemed to Claude that the storm arose only to admonish him for his vanity. The block-shaped captain was passing at that moment. He had a tired, weary look to him as if he had gazed too long into the abyss. The mortals he transported were cowering landlubbers who could not possibly understand the forces of his world.

"Aye, Fathers," he said in derision, "was your God asleep last night?"

"He listens to our prayers," Michel said, "but he tests us too."

The captain shook his head at the absurdity of these skinny young men with their crosses, rosaries, and breviaries. He swaggered to the bridge to set a new course after being blown off course at the whim of a storm.

"His many sins weigh him down," René whispered to comfort Claude, who, in truth, seemed about to burst into tears. If last night was any indication, what horrors had the captain witnessed? Abused as a cabin boy, cheated by wharf men and merchants, bested in tavern brawls, cast into prison for smuggling, the possibilities fired Claude's imagination and, with his stomach in revolt, all he wanted was to curl up and sleep.

Father Claude never fully recovered during the six weeks at sea. Five more storms hit during that tempestuous spring in the trade latitudes and fear that the precarious craft would not make the climb of the next wave or pull out of its plummet into the following trough frightened him beyond his abilities to cope. He ceased to think of himself as a priest, knowing himself to be nothing more than a cowardly wretch, huddled in his sweat and filth on stinking blankets. He watched the *habitans* and came to envy their simplicity, their stupidity. To be dull seemed a blessing. Not only did lack of imagination reduce fear, but lack of memory reduced its duration and apprehension too of its inevitable return.

Claude tried to believe in his courage, that he would never regret his departure, but his soul was lost at sea. Gone were the gothic limestone arches of the seminary that shielded him from the limitless depth of the stars at night. Gone were rituals marked by priests, sextons, and hooded monks when they rang bells through the city and countryside. Gone were regular meals and digestion and even the clean, simple joy of voluntary fasting. Present only was the agony of a sick stomach, a thirst for fresh water, and the spiritual doubt that his ambition or devotion or faith was nothing more than adolescent vanity. In seeking to transcend the narrowness of a French clerical life, he found now, in a swinging hammock, that his rampant willpower had nothing to feed, warm, or comfort it.

Claude's crisis of faith, which he hid as a shameful secret from his fellows, persisted long after the seasickness. On the forty-fifth day of the voyage, they spied land, Anticosti Island, and soon they made landfall at Havre-St. Pierre. They stopped briefly to take on fresh water, then sailed up the Gulf of St. Lawrence into the embrace of the estuary and on to Ile d'Orleans. They floated upriver on the tide into the evening shadow of the massive rock of Quebec. Michel and René were excited by the arrival, but Claude was pensive. The rock rose suddenly from the narrow channel, a natural fortification. Indeed, a century and a half of hardy French explorers and soldiers had settled on its brow, their wooden stockade like a sort of beret. But the sheer size of the gray stone cliff made him shiver with a deep awareness of the elemental, primordial nature of the place. Like the fabled Pillars of Hercules, this rock served as a gateway, not to the civilized sea at the middle of the earth, but to all the horrors and privations he had read about in the *Relations*.

Never robust, Claude Chauchetière was now emaciated, his eyes staring out from dark sockets above caved-in cheeks, his bony chest and his spine hunched over. His brown eyes were dulled by illness, and he faltered walking down the ramp with his carpetbag, now almost empty since he had long ago thrown his stinking blankets and clothing overboard.

While the captain supervised the unloading of cargo and the *habitans* breathed and stretched in the clean new air of the lower town, Claude Chauchetière climbed with his two fellows to the Jesuit provincial house on top of the rock. They were welcomed warmly and given mutton stew with potatoes and carrots that Claude strove to keep down along with a goblet of wine that made his head swim. The middle-aged *donne* who managed the house gave Claude a new cassock and showed him a cot with a straw tick in a cell up under the eaves. Claude slept the remainder of that day and the next, awakening on the third day at the matins bell, surprised that the earth was not rocking beneath him.

He rose, knelt, and recited the *Lectio divina* in his cell; then, he crept down the stairs and out into the yard. The air was crisp and clean. The green leaves of trees and, in the garden, the fragrant herbs and blooming roses and lilies flooded his eyes with color after six weeks of gray ocean. For the first time since he left Poitiers, he wanted to paint.

After a silent breakfast, Father Gabriel Bernier, superior of the house, met the new missionaries in his office.

"We welcome you." The ascetic old priest tried so hard to smile that his face seemed to crack. "We need you just now. We recently founded a mission for poor Hurons displaced by the Iroquois who settled three leagues upriver. Do you know the fate of the Huron nation?"

"Father Jogues first mission?" René asked.

"Indeed," the priest nodded. "Nearly forty years ago, Father

Jogues went there. He spent six years ministering to the Hurons, who grew in faith under his care. He was returning to them a second time when he was captured by Mohawks who abducted him to their land." The priest shook his head sadly. "I arrived in Quebec five years after Father Jogues was martyred." He bowed his head and made the sign of the cross. "Shortly afterward, the Iroquois massacred the Hurons, burned their villages, and sent all survivors fleeing like swallows from a cannon shot.

"At first, our surviving missionaries gathered a band of fugitive Hurons on the shores of St. Joseph Island in Nottawasaga Bay. Starved and fearful of more attacks from the Iroquois, about three hundred Hurons and sixty of our priests and assistants came downriver to Quebec, where we quartered them on a property we hold by royal grant. Still, the Mohawks do not cease their attacks."

"Why do the Mohawks perform such demonic acts?" asked René.

"The Iroquois are unique among all the native peoples," Father Bernier explained. "They are the most ferocious warriors by far, and they are very prideful. They never forget a slight and, once roused, they fight to the death without any concern for survival. On the other side of the coin, I have heard from Fathers Bruyas and de Lamberville that once converted, their piety also knows no equal either in France or in New France. Their singleness of purpose, the depth of their character, and their natural loyalty permit no backsliding. While not as ferocious, the other Iroquois nations are equally as fervent and true in their faith.

"As to the Hurons, after de Tracy's raid and the treaty, they again ventured outside these walls of Quebec. Seven years ago, Father Chaumonot established a new mission, Notre-Dame de Foye, about two leagues west. With the influx of some Christian Iroquois, the mission found itself cramped for both land and timber, so three years ago, they moved to a new site three leagues upriver. It is there that Father Chaumonot built a chapel modeled after the Holy House of Loretto. We call the village 'Notre-Dame de Vielle Lorette' or simply 'Lorette.' This is where Father Claude will be assigned."

Claude bowed in obedience.

"We have need of Father René in our chapel at Trois-Rivières, and you, Father Michel, we have assigned you to a mission farther upriver, near Montreal, which is relocating this year."

Fathers René and Michel bowed their heads.

"Your mission, Father Michel, St. Francis Xavier, illustrates what I have said about Mohawk converts. One who is known among his people as the Great Mohawk exemplifies what I say. Our order possessed a seigneury, La Prairie, on the south bank of the St. Lawrence, opposite Ville Marie on the island of Montreal. Given that the land is flat and not well fortified and open to attack along the river, it was worthless so long as the Iroquois were raiding. But after de Tracy burned the Mohawk villages, Father Rafeix built a house there. His initial plan was to surround himself with *habitans* who would farm and raise live-stock and increase the value of the land. But soon another use, by the grace of God, announced itself.

"Knowing only a smattering of the Huron language, Father Bruyas had journeyed among the Oneida, the second nation of the Iroquois. This language bears a resemblance to the Iroquois tongue about as close as Portuguese does to French, so he could make himself understood only with laborious effort. But an Oneida woman called Gandeacteua tutored Father Bruyas in the Iroquoian tongue until she and her husband Tonsanhoten left Oneida to accompany a fur trader to Montreal. It was winter when Gandeacteua, Tonsanhoten, and the fur trader arrived in Montreal, and spent the winter of 1668-1669 there. They visited our church for the Christmas service. Because Gandeacteua had absorbed much about Christianity from helping Father Bruyas learn the language, she and her husband asked to be baptized.

"The missionaries urged them to live at Notre-Dame de

Foye, but they declined and started home. Yet when they stopped at Father Rafeix's house at LaPrairie, they saw how close it was to their homeland and stayed. That year Catherine Gandeacteua tilled the ground as she had at home. Catherine's husband built a wooden house that served as an inn to wayfarers up and down the river. A new community of converts took root there and was called Kentake. Until this spring, it thrived at its original location, but I have just received word it is moving upriver to the place where travelers must leave the river and portage their canoes beside the rapids. This new place, where you will be assigned, Father Michel, is called 'Kanawaka,' which means 'At the Rapids.'

"Four years ago, the Great Mohawk, perhaps the fiercest warrior of his nation, left his village alone in the dead of winter and happened into the Kentake settlement. Catherine Gandeacteua, whose husband was away, invited him to lodge with her, and she instructed him in the rudiments of our faith. He was baptized 'Joseph.' He returned to his village, also called 'Kanawaka' for it is also built at a set of rapids, and he enlisted many of his community to come to Kentake.

"Unfortunately, the good Gandeacteua died last summer, but the mission she helped found continues to thrive. Each summer Joseph Kryn returns to his native village to escort more converts to the mission. By now he has escorted two hundred souls from Iroquois villages to this mission. His devotion knows no bounds. He has the highest degree of personal honor and is possessed of great skill in all things, building houses, making canoes, and negotiating peace.

"You, Father Michel," Father Bernier said, "will be assigned to help my old friend Father Frémin at Kanawaka."

"It will be my great honor to be of service." Father Michel bowed humbly.

"Now, Fathers, let us pray for the success of all the missions." Father Bernier stood and reached for the hands of the young priests, and they knelt on the floor.

"Let us pray as our Savior taught. 'Our Father, who art in heaven, hallowed be Thy name. Thy kingdom come, Thy will and not mine be done on earth as it is in heaven. Give us this day our daily bread and forgive us our trespasses as we forgive those who trespass against us and lead us not into temptation but deliver us from evil, for Thine is the kingdom and the power and the glory now and forever, Amen."

2.

The Jesuit house hosted a dinner to fete the three new priests. The next morning, they departed, Michel and René up the St. Lawrence to Trois-Rivières and Kanawaka, and Claude Chauchetière, kneeling uncomfortably in a canoe, up the St. Charles to Lorette. Father Bernier's stirring accounts and the natives' heroism in resisting Mohawk raids encouraged Claude during the short journey in a flimsy, tipping birch bark canoe. Landing on a mudflat and climbing a small rise, he came on a dismal, smoky, stinking collection of hovels where filthy humans sat in idleness and skinny dogs prowled for scraps. The squalor far exceeded any filth and poverty he ever saw in France.

Four hundred refugees, mostly Hurons, lived in thirty long-houses at Lorette. Lazy smoke curled from the chimney holes, emanations of the squalor inside. Mangy dogs growled at him as he walked up the mudflat where a naked child of two welcomed him by squatting and defecating in his path.

Brother Paul, a leathery-faced Huron who sang baritone in the choir, led him to the rectory, a low log cabin with a thatched roof beside another small cabin that had a cross on top—the chapel. Father Claude met Father Pierre Chaumonot, founder of Lorette. They would now share the hut they called a rectory.

"Welcome to our mission," Father Chaumonot said with an ironic smile. "How do you find it?"

"In need of some improvement."

"Quite so."

After a tour of the grim little hut, Claude and Father Chaumonot went together into the chapel, little more than a shack. The altar was a slab of wood, and the tabernacle a small wooden box. Six benches on each side could seat perhaps forty worshippers. The priests walked through the village where naked children ran, and dogs looked at Claude suspiciously, and barechested native women pounded corn in tree stump mortars. Claude sensed that his every move was watched by these small, swarthy people with accusations in their eyes. The sordid reality of the mission did not begin to measure the grandiose, romantic image he had invented.

"Unimaginable barbarity!" he wrote to his younger brother Jacques. He described the primitive hunting, planting, cooking, and eating, but he did not write about the lack of privacy, which suddenly confronted him with surprising scenes of men and women urinating in his sight, and now and then a coupling pair grunting in passion.

"Are there no taboos?" he asked Father Chaumonot.

"Yes. Young people of one clan must look outside their clan to marry."

"I meant about copulating where others can see."

"The Hurons consider copulation a normal function, like eating. We have done our best to ask converts to engage in that privately."

"It cannot be good for the children," Claude observed, though in truth, it was his sensibilities, not theirs, that were affronted.

As the weeks passed, he tried to be tolerant, but the squalor, ignorance, and filth shocked and dismayed him. A familiar depression and lassitude fell like a shadow over him. Each morning he said mass in Latin, and the communicants seemed to know what transpired—at least they knew when to stand, when to sit and when to kneel, and when to come up the aisle for the host—but the language barrier made him dependent on Father Chaumonot whom he regarded as a happy fool. Unkindly, Claude tried to fathom whether the priest was that way before he arrived or if this place removed whatever spark of intelligence he ever possessed. After mass, Claude visited his parishioners in their longhouses. The poorest of the poor in the slums of Paris lived like royalty compared to the filth and privation of these Hurons, he thought, and he poured out his heart to his older brother Jean:

> "They live communally in long bark huts through which the wind and rain, and in the winter, snow, readily penetrate. Each bark hut belongs to an extended family ruled over by a matriarch and forms part of a larger clan. Five, six and seven open fire pits run down the middle of the houses.
>
> "In clusters loosely aligned with couples and their children they cook, eat, and copulate. In summer, the men walk about with breechclouts to cover their genitals. Since the advent of the whites, they make these of cotton or wool, fastened with a leather strap about their waists. Prior to the white man's appearance, these were no doubt made of buckskin. The women wear fabric skirts, and many of them work and pound the corn with a wooden mortar or plant in the fields wearing no garment on top, their dugs readily observable. In summer, the children all run about naked and get into all manner of mischief."

His observations soured in subsequent letters to both his brothers:

> "I considered at first that I would grow used to this, or that I at least would cease being shocked, but the smell of these people is such that I find myself standing upwind when there is a wind, and when there isn't, I must gulp to hold down my gorge. They never bathe and at the latrine they do not wash, but simply wipe with handfuls of leaves. Mothers cleanse their infants with sawdust from rotten stumps. They eat corn porridge, *sagamite*,

with their fingers and they bite into huge sections of meat and then saw off the piece they are chewing with their knives so that it looks as if they might amputate their noses. Everywhere is the stench of burnt meat and excrement. I do not see how I might lead them closer to God when the proximity of Europeans for more than a generation has had no effect on their sanitation.

"Oh, my brother, I despair of the graces I sought by this assignment. I have been banished from my home, my books, my studies, my fellows, from my chores instructing the youngsters in mathematics which I so hated. On this foreign shore I have been cast among heathens who cannot read, will not learn, and though they are fervent in their worship, I suspect they have merely supplanted their sun god with some vague notion of ours. The mystical presence of the Eucharist interests them, but I doubt whether they can understand its meaning in any way. I keep asking myself, 'What have I done? Why has God deserted me?'"

In his letter to Jacques, the younger brother, he observed:

"From the time I first read of Father Jogues's suffering and death at the hands of these natives, I admired how he forgave them, loved them and tried to save them. My admiration for his Christ-like patience and tolerance has increased tenfold since I have been here. Not only do I not suffer at their hands, but these simple natives do me honor and give me great respect as the minister of the rites of our faith when I cannot summon one-hundredth of the love Father Jogues felt for them. I cannot see them as children of God, but only creatures bowed by ignorance and superstition, chained to rites and sorceries and dream rituals that seem to the western mind haphazard and inexplicable."

The responses from his brothers, also Jesuits, were diametrically opposed. His older brother, Jean, worried about his well-being and wrote back that Claude should examine his conscience to discover what the Lord expected of him, that this assignment had been his choice and certainly now was not the time to reconsider every step of the process. Jacques wrote him to cease his unedifying correspondence. In the usual manner of sharing letters from New France with the provincial house, his peers had insisted on reading what Claude wrote, and Claude's failings had caused Jacques untold embarrassment.

Winter howled down the river. Wrapped in infinite darkness, pelted by relentless snows, frozen by the bitter cold, Claude utterly despaired. His most ardent desire, to find in these people the worthy vessels of faith and divine love, had been dashed. Just as a spiritual ecstasy had lifted him into a heavenly realm one Christmas Eve only to abandon him soon after, leaving him dazed and confused, his zeal failed him. He now believed that anyone who imagined these people could rise and embrace the holy faith was delusional. The simple ignorance of the Hurons allowed them to survive. They ignored the insult of frostbitten toes and fingertips. They laughed and sang as they chopped wood for the fire. With generous hearts, they invited the priests to their communal feasts of venison and bear stew, and Claude now saw the children in their leggings and hoods of fur as small and joyful embodiments of a survival urge that he, with all his theology, lacked. He no longer poured his out despair in letters to his brothers, but he strove in prayer, both his private prayers and those in the chapel attended by the furred and feathered Hurons, to find peace in his heart.

Nor was Father Chaumonot much help. While he possessed a kind heart, the ancient priest was weakened and desiccated by three celibate decades in the wild, and seemed disengaged from the denizens of Lorette.

One day near the equinox, as the ice on the river was groaning and breaking into floes as big as Parisian city blocks, the senior priest announced, "Father Superior has asked whether I can spare you, Father Claude, and I replied I could."

This news stung Claude. Try as he might to conceal his unhappiness and vent it only in letters home, somehow it had leaked out. He feared that his despair and weakness were universally known.

"Why would he make such a request?" Claude could not disguise the reedy pitch to his voice.

"He seeks to deploy you upriver at Kanawaka."

"But Michel Cocteau was sent there, was he not?"

"Michel has petitioned to be reassigned."

"Has he given any reason?"

Father Chaumonot shrugged. "Living with Jacques Frémin? Isn't that reason enough?"

"I don't follow you."

The sense of great unseen forces moving behind the veils unsettled Claude.

"Father Frémin is a headstrong man, nearly fifty, I'd wager. He is a most effective manager, and Kanawaka grows each year. Do you need to know more than that?"

"Is there more to know?"

"There is always more to know, my son. Nothing immediately reveals its deeper secrets."

"What is it, then?"

"Father Michel, it seems, caused some concern to Father Frémin with how well he might be keeping his vow of chastity."

"That can't be true!" Claude said. "I knew Michel in the novitiate, and though I haven't known him well since I went as an instructor to Tulle, I cannot believe such a temptation would ever lure him from the path."

"Well," Father Chaumonot smiled cynically, "Frémin's eye might be keen enough to see what is not even there."

"And he will be my superior?"

Father Chaumonot's eyes twinkled. "Although you have not settled your heart in this place, you will grow to miss me."

Claude sighed. "Where can one ever find peace in this world?"

"Not in the missions," Father Chaumonot curtly answered the rhetorical question.

Claude realized that he despised the smug superiority that Chaumonot thought age and experience conferred on him. Father Jogues had also left the Hurons for the Mohawks, he consoled himself, though under far different circumstances.

A month later, when ice floes no longer threatened the delicate bark canoes, Claude knelt in the bow of a canoe while in the stern knelt the brawny Marcel, a scarred Huron warrior with an enviable collection of scalps. In the center sat Gasçon, a youth of twelve summers. They were one of nine canoes making the journey in a flotilla, paddling through the blistering sun and the chilling rain fourteen and sixteen hours a day, camping at night along the river where the ferocious Mohawks were still known to prowl.

The journey upriver worked an odd change in Father Claude. Behind him lay his despair in embracing this raw country, seeking a benign Eden but finding instead a brutal wasteland. He saw how, in his failed first effort to acclimate himself, the readings of the *Relations* merged into the physical world and he, a humble denizen of Poitiers and son of a jurist, was now fully immersed in this primitive land where titles and lineage and rank held no meaning. Survival was all that mattered here. Beyond the elitism of his priestly status allowing him to administer the sacraments, he was nothing more than a man, a set of arms and shoulders, a spine bending into the paddle to haul himself to his next assignment or else into an ambush, whichever lay ahead.

Day by day, they paddled against the current. They stopped at Trois-Rivières, then passed the palisade of Fort Richelieu where water flowed down from Mohawk country and where Jogues had been dragged to a Mohawk fort. They pressed on to Ville-Marie (Montreal) and paddled around the island to the rapids of La Chine. The journey took seven days, including a stop at a parish in Trois-Rivières to visit Jesuits there. When they approached the mission of St. Francis Xavier at the Sault, Marcel called excitedly, "Kanawaka! Kanawaka!" and slapped his paddle on the side of the canoe between strokes to announce their arrival.

As if in welcome, the sun broke free of the clouds and radiated down on the flimsy stockade and the cluster of small cabins and longhouses, one peaked building in the center with a cross. Two dozen canoes were inverted on the bank, and a grass swale rose from the river to the flat land. A large man on the shore raised his arms in greeting. He was lashing a bark panel to the bent ash framework of a new canoe. Chauchetière reached behind himself and located the wide-brimmed hat that identified him as a priest, and as they drew closer, he observed the large man leave his work and walk easily along the bank to welcome them.

"Kwe! Kwe!" the man called with his right hand upraised. He was over six feet tall, light-skinned, and broad of frame. He wore no paint or tattoos. His hair rose above his scalp about three inches in the distinctive Mohawk rooster comb. Down his back was a long braid tied up with a red eel skin ribbon. He was working bare-chested, and he wore fringed buckskin trousers and moccasins. Around his right wrist was a rawhide bracelet. "Welcome, Marcel! And our new Father! And who is this young man you have doing all the work?"

"He is Gasçon," Marcel grinned. "My sister's son. A most skilled navigator."

"Who is that man?" the boy asked his uncle.

"It is Joseph Kryn, the greatest of all the Mohawks."

Claude looked at the man with admiration. Whether from his presence now or the legends he had heard, Claude immediately felt Joseph Kryn's charm and air of command.

Marcel leaped into the water from the rear of the canoe to push it ashore. Kryn waded into the water, took the canoe's bow in his left hand, and stretched his right arm out in salutation to

Father Claude. Claude could not help but notice Kryn's size and bulging muscles, but looking directly into his eyes, he sensed Kryn's powerful masculinity was held in check by a strong will and an even stronger intelligence. Joseph Kryn beached the canoe and helped him out. Marcel approached the canoe, his leggings and moccasins sloshing, to pick up his wiry nephew and toss him toward the war chief.

"I'll wager you're a skilled hunter!" Kryn said, holding the boy high in the air. He flipped the young man so that he landed on his feet but, looking around, the boy could not understand exactly how. Marcel then ran at Kryn and nearly knocked him over. Kryn lifted him in a great bear hug, and the two were as foolish and playful as boys.

"Come, Marcel, you'll share my longhouse. Things are growing a bit crowded here, but that is good!"

"They say in Lorette that you built a house of timbers and planks with a pitched roof."

Joseph Kryn laughed. He motioned toward the building with the cross on top. "I built a house for myself and my family, but the Lord had other plans. The fathers needed a larger chapel, so I donated it to the mission. I now work to build another. We will feed you and make you comfortable, and you," he threw a brawny arm over the slender priest, "we'll stash your bag in the rectory, and I will introduce you around."

Father Claude paused a minute to turn and look out over the river. Upriver to his left, the rapids boiled and thrashed over rocks, and a well-worn path showed where the portage trail ran. Across the river to the west rose a cluster of thatched huts, the village of La Chine. Far to the north, just visible in front of the pale blue of distant mountains, was another village, Ville Marie, behind a low stockade. To his right was a large headland, the three-peaked Royal Mountain, where it was rumored, but he could not see, Governor Maisonneuve had planted a cross twenty-five years before when prayers to the Blessed Virgin saved the settlement from a rising river.

"Come along, Father!" Joseph Kryn urged. "It's time to eat and rest."

"Thank you," Father Claude said, and then he noticed something shocking. He was speaking in the Iroquois tongue without effort! Father Chaumonot's instruction had finally taken hold.

With Kryn carrying Gasçon on his back, the three men walked together through the swale, past the broad fields and along the plain where women were planting, away from the blue river that flowed so purely and boiled white over the broken rocks.

Nautæ suis infensum vitijs in deser-
tam Insulam expofituri, subito vento re-
pelluntur, ac inuiti licet ad Cyprum vehunt.

25

**Missionaries braving the North Atlantic to spread the word of
God**

CHAPTER TWELVE

TEKAKWITHA IS BAPTIZED

I.

Three winters froze the land with blizzards and ice since Kryn departed; three springs bloomed with wildflowers and strawberries; three summers of corn ripened in the drone of lazy bees. Tekakwitha still lived with her uncle and aunt, an empty life of duty and drudgery in subservience to Iowerano's power and his apparent desire to keep the old ways. But he had made one concession. Obeying Garacontie's order, he agreed to let a blackrobe settle at Kanawaka shortly after Kryn's departure. Elderly Father Boniface set up a chapel in a small hut and named it St. Peter's, and in 1674, Father James de Lamberville, came to the mission at Kanawaka to replace him. Tekakwitha saw the young blackrobe in the lanes of the village and wished to speak with him but passed him because her uncle forbade it.

As she walked through the cornfield with her hoe one morning, the shawl shielding her eyes from the bright sun, Tekakwitha stepped into a gopher hole and sprained her ankle. Not wanting to draw attention to herself, she stood up and worked all day. By evening the ankle had swollen so badly, she needed to be carried from the field on a stretcher. She lay by the fire that night, in such pain that she broke a sweat, and after a fitful rest, Karitha looked at her ankle, swollen to twice its usual size, and told her she must rest for a couple of days.

The following morning Father de Lamberville was making his rounds from longhouse to longhouse, seeking out the old and feeble to counsel and bless, as well as infants to baptize. Iowerano had paddled down to Albany, and Rainbow and Spotted Fawn were preparing to go into the fields. As Father de Lamberville entered the longhouse, he spoke:

"Hail, sisters. What have we here?" He waved his hand at Tekakwitha.

"She's hurt her ankle," Rainbow said.

"Let's see," the priest drew closer.

"We have to be off," the other girl said, and they excused themselves and left for the fields.

"Is it painful?" The priest knelt beside her pallet.

"No, Father. The swelling just needs to go down, and I'll be fine."

She looked into the priest's kind face. He had eyes of pale blue and a warm smile from years of meditation and prayer.

"I hope you feel better," he said, and he touched her hand.

"Father?" she asked. "Do you think . . . would it be possible for me to learn the Prayer?"

He smiled and looked intently into her eyes. Her eyes, so impaired from smallpox, were unfocused. He looked from one eye to the other to guess through which one she saw better.

"Everyone can learn the Prayer."

"I've wanted to for so long."

"Did you ever meet with Father Boniface?"

"No," she looked away. "My uncle hates the blackrobes. My aunt heaps ridicule on the ceremonies, yet I long to become Christian."

"Well, then," de Lamberville said, "shall we begin?"

"Yes, oh, yes!" she said, and a sob welled up within her.

"Can you come with me?"

"Of course."

"Let me carry you."

He lifted her and carried her out of the dim longhouse. Tekakwitha was quite small and light, and she put her arm around his neck and rested her head on his shoulder. As they emerged into the light, she adjusted her shawl. He carried her out of the village to a hill in the middle of the vast fields of corn. They looked down on the flowing river and the clouds that swept over the low hills. He sat her on a large rock.

"In the beginning," he began, "God created the heaven and the earth."

"Our elders teach that a woman created the world on the back of a large turtle."

"It will help you learn the Prayer if you put these legends aside. There was nothing before God spoke the word, no heaven, no earth, no water, and certainly no turtle. The universe was formless and void, and when God said, 'Let there be light,' there was light, and God saw it was good."

Tekakwitha groaned as he said this, so he asked: "Does the light hurt your eyes?"

"Sometimes it is too bright."

"Such is the majesty of God in heaven, my daughter. How are you called?"

"Tekakwitha. She Who Gropes Her Way."

"And yet, sometimes you see what is hidden from others. We are created not only to see the physical world, what is of the world, or in the world. We are also created to see the light that shines within."

"Yes," she breathed audibly. She knew this but never knew that anyone else did too.

"It is a light God has placed within each of us, and it is good."

"I have seen it," she whispered.

"God created the firmament and called it 'Heaven,' and he collected the water below heaven in one place, and dry land

135

appeared. He created the two great lights and put them in the sky, one to light the day, which he called 'Sun,' and the other to light the night, which he called 'Moon.' These lights were to rule the darkness, and He saw that it was good. God called the gathered the waters 'sea,' and the dry land 'earth,' and He saw that they were good. Then God spoke, 'Let the earth bring forth grass, and the corn-yielding seed and the sweet berry bushes and all manner of plants,' and the earth did as He commanded, and it was good."

Tekakwitha leaned back, closed her eyes, and lifted her veil so the sun might kiss her face.

"And God brought forth life from the seas, fish of every sort, the great whales, and to fill the air He brought forth winged fowl, and God blessed them and said, 'Be fruitful and multiply,' and fish filled the water and birds filled the air. And then God created the beasts of the earth, the deer, elk, bear, moose, wolf, bobcat, and every animal that moves on the land, and He saw that it was good. Then God saw His creation was lacking, so He created man in His image and likeness, walking upright, speaking, thinking. He formed man from the dust of the earth and breathed into his nostrils the breath of life, infusing man with a living soul. He named the first man 'Adam' and gave him dominion over all the earth, the fish of the seas, the birds of the sky and the beasts and every creeping thing."

Tekakwitha smiled. This account of creation explained so much.

"Then God planted a garden to the east, in Eden, and from the ground, He caused to grow every tree that is pleasant to the sight, and in the middle of the garden He planted the Tree of the Knowledge of Good and Evil. And a river flowed into Eden to water the garden, and God put the man into the garden to keep it, and He told the man, 'You may eat freely of the fruit borne by every tree in the garden, except the fruit of the Tree of the Knowledge of Good and Evil. You may not eat fruit from that tree, for if you do, you will die.' Then God said, 'It is not good that man should be alone. I shall make a helpmate for him.'"

"Was Adam white or Haudenosaunee?"

"Adam was the first man, father to all of us, to people of all races, white and red and black and yellow."

"There are black and yellow men?"

"In the far corners of the earth, there are people who are black and people who are yellow, and even now, my brothers, the followers of St. Ignatius, teach them about God."

"But it is the white man's God, is it not?"

"God is the God of all. He is everywhere. He is all-powerful, all-knowing, and He loves us without limit. Once we learn of God, we turn to Him with all our love, gratitude, and trust. After the man Adam named all the creatures, God caused a deep sleep to come over him. Then God removed one of his ribs, and from the rib, He made a helpmate. He brought her to Adam, and Adam awoke and said, 'Bone of my bones, flesh of my flesh. She will be called "Woman" for she was taken out of a man,' and he named her Eve. And in the order of things, a man leaves his father and mother and cleaves unto his wife, and they become one flesh. Adam and Eve were both naked, but they were not ashamed."

Tekakwitha pulled her shawl tightly about her.

"But then evil entered the world," Father de Lamberville said. "The serpent was more devious than any of the other animals. He slithered into the garden and spoke to the woman."

"Snakes could talk?"

"Back in that magical time before original sin, all the animals and birds spoke, and the man and the woman understood them. So, the snake asked the woman, 'Can you not eat of every tree in the garden?' and the woman answered, 'We may eat the fruit of every tree but one, for God said if we eat of that fruit, we will die.' And the crafty serpent said, 'You certainly will not die, but you will be gods when you know good and evil.' So, the woman picked the fruit of the beautiful tree for she thought that she would be wise and that wisdom would be good. Then she ate the fruit and gave it to her husband. He ate, too, and their eyes were opened, and for the first time, they understood that they were naked."

Tekakwitha pulled down the shawl against the bright sunlight and opened her eyes to look at the priest. She looked steadily, unflinchingly at him. She felt as if he were the first person in her life who knew what she knew and imparted true wisdom. Gazing into her eyes, the priest saw her struggle between belief and fear. He also saw a fleeting glimpse of hope until her eyes squinted with their customary doubt, and she looked away.

"What did they do, knowing they were naked?"

The priest heard in her voice how vulnerable she was, and his voice was soothing and gentle. "They picked fig leaves," he said softly, "and sewed them together, and they made aprons to cover themselves, and when they heard the voice of God who came walking in the garden, they hid from Him. The Lord God called, and Adam answered, 'I am here, Lord.' And God asked him why he was hiding. 'I am afraid,' the man said, 'for I know I am naked.'

"'Who told you that you were naked?' God asked.

"'No one,' said Adam.

"Then God asked, 'Have you eaten of the fruit of the tree that I forbade you to eat?'

"And the man answered, 'The woman you gave to me told me to eat of the fruit, and I did.'

"So, the Lord said to the woman, 'What have you done?' and the woman answered, 'The serpent tricked me.' And the Lord said to the serpent: 'Because you have done this, you are cursed to live below the cattle and the beasts of the fields. On your belly you will crawl, and you shall eat dust all the days of your life. I will make the woman your enemy, and she shall crush your head with her heel.'

"Then God turned to the woman and said, 'In pain shall you

bring forth children, and your husband shall rule over you.' Then to the man, He said, 'Because you listened to the woman and disobeyed me, thorns and thistles will spring up in the garden, and you will make your living by the sweat of your brow until you return to the earth for out of it were you taken. Dust you are, and unto dust you shall return.'

"And then the Lord made coats of animal skins for the man and the woman to clothe themselves, and He expelled them from the garden to till the earth by the sweat of their brow. So they could not return He placed an angel with a flaming sword at the gate of Eden to guard the Tree of Life forever."

They sat together on the stone, the slender ascetic priest in his black *soutane*, with a weathered face and long bony fingers, and the small, scarred, half-blind Mohawk girl, shrouded from the sunlight by her shawl.

"Were they ever allowed to go back?"

"No. They lost Eden forever. These were the parents of the whole human race, yours and mine and everyone's, condemned to work and bear children and suffer from disease and pestilence because of their sin."

"And God punished them and us, too, and never relented?"

"You are wise, little one, far beyond your years. Yes, He did relent. He did forgive. That is the message I bring to you. God sent His only son down into the earth. God gave His son human form, Jesus Christ, our Savior, who was born to lead us to the eternal kingdom of heaven."

Tekakwitha was nodding. Anastasia had spoken of this.

"You know of Jesus?" he asked.

"I have seen Father Boniface place the wooden baby Jesus in the manger in the chapel in the winter." She turned to look at him and her eyes, again, were unfocused. She spoke softly. "I have longed to learn of Jesus, Father, but my uncle threatens to banish me from the longhouse if I learn the Prayer." She looked up and tried to focus her eyes against the bright sun.

The priest plucked a long stem of the grass and snapped off

seeds at the top. "Do you go to the fields to plant the corn and squash and beans in mounds?"

"Yes. I have a planting stick, and we do that after the snow melts and the earth softens."

"Are the seeds you plant alive like these?"

"No, the corn is dried from hanging in the rafters all winter, the beans, and squash from being stored in bark bins."

"You already understand, then. Before it can be reborn in the soil, the seed must die. In such a way, we must die to be reborn and to grow."

"But I do not wish to die."

"This is the heart of my message, Tekakwitha. God saw how men and women were killing each other and suffering from their lies and betrayals, and so He took pity on us. He sent Jesus to walk the earth as a man, but a man without any fault or sin. Jesus performed many miracles and taught us that we are all on earth to help each other. We are to forgive, and above all, to love each other. Jesus loved mankind so much that He was willing to die like a slave so we could be pardoned for our sins. The Romans nailed Him to a cross, like the cross we place above the chapel."

"When you pray at the altar, do you pray to God or to Jesus?"

"To both. Before Jesus went to His death, He blessed bread and wine and told his followers that the bread and the wine were His body and blood and to eat and drink them in His memory. Christians celebrate Christ's sacrifice at mass and God sends His power through the Priest's hands to transform bread and wine on the altar into the body and blood of Jesus Christ. When we take communion, His spirit works in us. In this way, our life of sorrow and pain has a purpose, Tekakwitha. Our destination is heaven."

"Joseph Kryn led Anastasia and many others to La Prairie. And each summer he returns to lead others there. I want to go with him."

"The Great Mohawk is a good man and an able leader."

"He believes that the northern mission is a place of salvation."

"It is. If you go you will progress very rapidly."

"I have longed to know this Prayer my whole life. My mother was Christian, a friend of Anastasia, and I see now what they shared."

"Yes?" the priest encouraged her.

"My mother was filled with love. I remember how she held me. Unlike my aunt now, my mother never showed envy or anger, or frustration. If only I could be like that."

"You are, Tekakwitha, and you will learn the Prayer." He stood and helped her to her feet. "I will show you the path."

After this initial talk, Father de Lamberville inquired about Tekakwitha among the villagers. Reports of her virtue were universal. Although she embroidered designs on the skins and made the wampum belts for the councils and treaty ceremonies, she was plain in her dress and simple in her habits, retiring, shy, and docile. He heard no whisper of criticism whatsoever. Villagers told him how she often went alone into the forest, and the priest believed she had mystical insights. He saw this in her embroidery with its brilliant colors and vivid shapes. From her blindness, she was showing others the beauty she saw within, and he would guide her in the faith until she could leave for the mission.

2.

In the ensuing months, Father de Lamberville observed how Tekakwitha's compliant behavior disguised a firm willpower and strong opinions on marriage. She never wavered on the subject of chastity, but she hardly needed to. Her scars and diminished eyesight caused lusty hunters and young, untested warriors to pass her by when they attended the Green Corn Moon festival and the Harvest Home for flirtatious girls who braided beads and put feathers in their hair. Tekakwitha who had lived apart

141

for all her nineteen years, asked only a subsistence while she served her longhouse by fetching water and firewood, pounding corn into meal, weaving wampum and embroidering garments and robes with imaginative pictographs. Now she opened her heart to him, and her intuitive grasp of abstract concepts surprised him.

All through the winter, Father de Lamberville counseled Tekakwitha. He gave Tekakwitha a rosary, and he taught her the *Pater Noster*, the *Gloria*, and the *Ave Maria*, showing her how to tick off the beads as she prayed. She carried the rosary secretly to avoid her uncle's scorn, clutching onto it as a symbol of her new faith. The priest instructed her in doctrines of the church: the holy trinity, the virgin birth, transubstantiation. He showed her in his picture book the golden bliss of heaven, the fiery tortures of hell. He read to her from his hagiography of saints, and she hungered to hear how so many suffered torture and death to keep their faith. Witnessing her swift progress, Father de Lamberville soon offered to baptize her. She accepted immediately but sensing that his well-being and that of his mission might be in jeopardy for converting the "daughter" of the chief, he conditioned her baptism on obtaining her uncle's permission.

Never duplicitous, Tekakwitha approached her uncle directly. She waited until he was content after a good meal of trout and venison and was sitting back smoking his pipe.

"Have you had enough to eat, Uncle?"

"Our hunters and fishermen please me," he said, "and you are skilled in preparing meat and fish on the fire. Peace brings many benefits."

"I am happy to please you," she said. "Can I ask for your blessing on something I wish to do?"

"You have chosen a husband?"

"No, Uncle." She bowed her head, astonished again by his insensitivity. "I have spoken with the blackrobe."

"Oh?" His eyes turned sharp with anger. "The one who

encourages women to be upstarts and our villagers to leave for the north? That same blackrobe?"

"He is not like that, Uncle. He is a good man."

"He brings the double-tongued words of the whites to un-man us in battle, telling us to turn the other cheek as they steal our lands. Is that a good man?"

As he grew excited, she spoke calmly. "The blackrobe reveals a world beyond ours, a place of peace and beauty and sunshine where there is no hunger or sickness or suffering, and he shows us how to get there."

"Daydreams!" Iowerano spat into the fire pit. "He tells fables, and the gullible believe him. One day we will be cleared from our lands, and the whites will plant our fields and dig their metals from our hills and sweep along our rivers in their sailed vessels. Their lies about a better place are only meant to lull us into passivity."

"I do not seek to persuade you of this, Uncle. I am of age. I want to be baptized."

"You are honorable, at least not to go behind my back." He smoked his pipe and considered. "Perhaps it is not as foolish as some of the girls who chase after young men, and then must wear the cradleboard, a child with no hunter to bring in meat."

"I will be going to the chapel each morning," she said, "and on Sundays, one day in seven, I will not work. Yet I will make up for it by working harder during the other six days."

"Impossible."

"I promise."

"You will if you wish to eat," was his curt response.

She left him smoking his pipe. She pulled up her shawl into a hood and went out into the bright afternoon and hastened along the lanes to the chapel. The chapel had a door of split logs, fashioned in the manner of the French with leather hinges. She opened the door and drew in the smell of sanctity—pine from the boughs decorating the altar and beeswax candles. She knelt and blessed herself as the priest had instructed her and gave herself over to a joyful prayer of thanksgiving that a great obstacle had been removed.

On Ash Wednesday, Father de Lamberville told Tekakwitha he would baptize her on Easter Sunday.

"Oh, yes, Father!" She wept for joy. "Oh, thank you!"

She chose the baptismal name 'Catherine,' pronounced 'Kateri' in the Mohawk tongue. Catherine of Siena had been a mystical virgin from whom Catherine Gandeacteua, the woman who converted Kryn, likewise took her name.

It was too early for wildflowers, but the pious congregation decorated the rustic chapel with pine boughs, feathers, and furs. Father de Lamberville rehearsed the choir—all shapes and sizes and ages—to sing the mass of Christ's triumph over death.

The morning of April 16, 1676 was sunny and cloudless in the valley of the Mohawks. New and old converts sat on log benches in St. Peter's chapel as Tekakwitha glided up the aisle in a simple tunic of white doeskin, her hair braided and tied with a red eel skin ribbon, her leggings tied with leather thongs. Her eyes were humbly downcast, but her heart was soaring with joy. She knelt, and Father de Lamberville asked:

"Do you renounce Satan?"

"I do."

"And all his works?"

"I do."

"And all his empty promises?

"I do."

The priest sprinkled holy water on her forehead, and as the choir sang about the risen Lord, he traced the sign of the cross with aromatic chrism:

"I baptize thee 'Kateri' in the name of the Father, and of the Son, and of the Holy Spirit."

"Amen." Joyful tears fell from her eyes as Father de Lamberville handed her a simple wooden cross. She kissed it and bowed her head and folded it in her arms.

CHAPTER THIRTEEN
KATERI'S LIFE AS A CHRISTIAN

Kateri's joy at being baptized a Christian knew no limit. It was not the label or the association with others of like mind; it was that her natural yearning for transcendence had found its path at last. All confusion vanished before the two great commandments of Jesus—love the Lord your God and love your neighbor as Jesus loves you. The crucified Savior above the altar where the priest consecrated bread and wine reminded her constantly of Christ's blood sacrifice, freely given to end all blood sacrifices, and she knew happiness at last.

Tekakwitha attended mass each morning at four and remained in the chapel afterward praying. At sunrise, she took breakfast and then went into the fields to help with the planting and sowing. Once or twice during the day, she broke away from the workers and hurried to the chapel to kneel in the dim quiet and pray a rosary. Always retiring and shy, she retreated even further from the life of her longhouse and village, hardly speaking to others. She never fussed over her appearance, nor did she gossip or malign others. As much as she retreated from village life, she joined more enthusiastically in the life of the small congregation and Father de Lamberville guided her spiritual impulse with wisdom and care. He was repeatedly astonished at her progress in the knowledge and love of Jesus Christ, and all in the Christian community felt touched by her grace, humility, kindness, and inner peace.

At first, Moneta and Iowerano gave her complete license to practice her faith. Viewing it as a silly indulgence, they ignored her comings and goings. She had always been such a phantom among them they rarely noticed her absence. But as reports of her good works reached them, about how sweet and kind she was to a child, how she came to pray at the difficult delivery of a baby, or how she brought food to the elderly, envy filled them. She thought more about others than the family who had raised her. They began to torment her.

Moneta found chores in the fields surrounding the village to keep Tekakwitha from returning to the chapel during work hours. If she were planting, Moneta assigned her the farthest section of the fields, gave her the largest bag of seed corn, and then ridiculed her for not properly weeding the mounds where she planted beans, squash, and corn.

One day, Kateri did not appear for the noon meal. All the other women and girls assembled under a spreading oak and reclined to eat dried fish, venison strips, and corn porridge, but Kateri never came. As the women went back to the fields, Moneta went searching. She was not in the field where Moneta had assigned her. Rather than call out and alert her, Moneta decided to surprise her. She found Kateri's planting stick and doeskin bag at the forest's edge near a path into the trees. Moneta entered the shady grove stealthily, her bare feet on the cool earth of the path. Fifty, a hundred steps, two hundred she went until she found the thicket where Kateri knelt, her arms spread, her head back and her mouth moving in prayer. On the great pine tree before her, Kateri had placed her small cross.

"So, this is how you waste your time when the rest of us are working?"

Kateri turned, an otherworldly smile on her face. "I am sorry, Aunt, I did not realize so much time had passed." She stood.

"You missed your meal, and all the food has been eaten."

"I am not hungry for food," Kateri said. Seeing such happiness and joy in her face, Moneta exploded in rage. She seized Kateri's ear and twisted it.

"Give up this madness! Get back to work!"

"I will work, Aunt. Do not be concerned about that."

Moneta tilted the young woman's face up as if to slap her. "The disease has pitted and scarred your face. What sort of man would have you?"

"We resolved that long ago, and need discuss it no more. I will work. You need not fear." Kateri nodded to her respectfully, walked out of the wood, and submissively picked up her planting stick and her bag of seed and returned to work. Moneta watched her suspiciously, wondering how she could be so content. From that day forward, Moneta's resentments lay closer to the surface. Hadn't her mother, the beautiful Kahontake (Meadow), lured the handsome chief Tsaniton-gowa (Great Beaver) away from her? Moneta who had hated Kateri's happy mother now took Kateri's happiness as an insult. The girl needed to be punished, to lose that composure, and so Moneta actively persecuted her.

When Kateri remained home from the fields each Sunday, Moneta deprived her of food: "If you don't work as a Canienga, you can't eat as a Canienga."

Kateri quietly retreated to her corner and fasted, offering up her hunger to Jesus. After four or five Sundays of this, she told Father de Lamberville, and he responded.

"The persecution shows they hold you in high regard."

"A high regard by depriving me of food?"

"They want to break you. They are testing the strength of your faith. The punishment is a measure of their admiration. If they were indifferent, they would do nothing. Can you bear it?"

"I am Canienga. I have been hungry on the hunt. This is not so difficult for the body. It is difficult only because it seems so needless and cruel. I wish I could heal my aunt."

"Go about your life with cheer and hope, Kateri. They will soon see their punishment has no effect and will stop."

And yet, rather than abate, the criticism and ostracism grew more severe. Moneta spread rumors about her so others would scorn her. Young children threw stones at her as she returned from mass and mockingly called her "Christian." Kateri was not angered or even saddened, though. Other young women, never close to her or sympathetic, looked at her with disdain as they decorated themselves with dyed eel skin and necklaces of wolf teeth and quartz. Her uncle hardly noticed her anymore, and when he did, he merely grunted as if she were a dog.

One rainy morning, as she embroidered in the longhouse, a young warrior rushed in and waved a war hatchet high above his head: "Christian! Renounce your faith!"

Kateri showed no sign of fear. She kept to her embroidery and never looked at him. He screamed and waved his hatchet and danced about, but it had no effect. Finally, seeing he could not penetrate her equanimity, he left. But by this incident, she saw how she must keep her soul in a state of grace, always ready to die.

The worst test of her faith again came from Moneta. As the trees mellowed with fall, Kateri accompanied her uncle on a trading party to Albany. They were gone ten days. Soon after their return to Kanawaka, Moneta heard Kateri call her uncle by his name, and in a sour mood, she visited Father de Lamberville.

"I have news about your precious little Christian. She traveled with my husband, her uncle by blood, and on the journey, she seduced him."

"You don't believe this."

Moneta grew aggressive at his skepticism. "All along, I have suspected a secret relationship with my husband, and now I have it confirmed. She was serving food to him, and she called him 'Iowerano.'" Moneta nodded. "And he looked at her as he has never looked at her before."

Father de Lamberville smiled. "Well, that is surely proof of mortal sin."

"You have said it, not I." Moneta folded her arms. "What do you think of your precious little Christian now?"

"I will speak with her." As he escorted the woman out of the dim chapel into the sunshine, he mused at how Kateri's rare purity gave birth to such envy. "Send her to me."

Later that afternoon, Kateri appeared at the chapel. "Father, my aunt said you wished to speak with me."

He observed her expression and her posture—not a hint of guilt or defensiveness.

"She told me you addressed your uncle by his name when you served him food."

"I did."

"Why did you do that?"

"He has put our relationship on a different footing."

"How do you mean?"

"Since baptism, my name is 'Kateri,' and as 'Kateri' I wish to be known. As I served him the other day, my uncle called me 'Tekakwitha,' my former name, which means 'she who gropes her way.' I am no longer groping, Father. In the light of faith, I see more clearly now. His name, 'Iowerano,' means 'Cold Wind.' When he called me by former name, I called him by his for he gives off a cold wind. Was this a sin?"

"Your aunt says it signifies you have been intimate with him."

The young woman looked at him directly. Her eyes, usually bedimmed and clouded, were now clear, deep, and direct. "She knows that is not so," Kateri said quietly. "Why does she try to discredit me?"

"The world hates purity and will do everything to destroy it." The priest waved toward the crucifix. "Look at how our savior was treated."

"I am no threat to her or anyone else," Kateri said. "They are behaving the same as when I refused to marry. I will live as I wish. It should be nothing to them. Why should I respond to their criticism and gossip?"

"Does it make you angry?"

"No," she bowed her head. "A little sad, but not angry. What business is my conduct to anyone? Their lies are harsh and waste so much time. I will not respond."

"Come with me," the priest said, and he led her to the chapel. Kneeling together at the split-log communion rail and gazing upward to where the crucifix hung above the altar, they prayed. Later, emerging into the sunshine, the priest said:

"I think you should leave this village. You should not suffer from their gossip and back-biting."

She inclined her head toward the priest. "Tell me."

"You should live where people love and respect each other as Jesus taught. Your faith must grow, but they try to pull you back into the old ways even as you move forward into the new. You will not prosper with these villagers always ridiculing you."

"Where would I go?"

"To the mission in the north."

"With Joseph Kryn and Karitha and little Peter? And Anastasia?"

"Yes."

"Even my sister Rainbow is there!" Kateri began to cry. "Is it possible, Father?" He nodded. "How often have I wished for that! Prayed for it!" She wiped her tears away. "Rainbow's mother divorced my uncle and moved to the mission. He still controls me, though, and Moneta is opposed to my leaving. My uncle will never consent."

"Perhaps," the priest said gently, "you don't require his consent anymore."

"I don't?"

"No, you don't."

The following day Father de Lamberville visited Moneta as she was pounding corn.

"I have spoken to Kateri," he said. "I am satisfied she committed no sin."

"I knew you would ignore it. Such are her wiles that she can deceive even you."

"Your hatred and suspicion will never end, and they seek to ruin her peace of mind," he said. "That is why you are losing her."

"Humph!" Moneta grunted. "Where would a blind cripple go?"

"The mission."

"Oh, let her go! Let her go! Rainbow deserted us! Kryn and his family. What does it matter anymore? Tekakwitha will not embrace our ways. It took bribery for me to get a young man even to consider marrying her. Who will have her? Let someone else take her in."

"Be careful," the priest said. "Sometimes we get what we wish for."

"The blackrobe speaks in riddles. Let her leave our family if she wishes. It will be no loss."

"As you say," he nodded, tipped his wide-brimmed hat, and walked away.

CHAPTER FOURTEEN

KATERI ESCAPES

I.

Joseph Kryn came to the village each spring to encourage his Kanawaka friends and relatives to join him. This year, however, another great warrior arrived before he did. Hot Cinders, the powerful Oneida chief, came to Kanawaka just after the big melt.

Like Joseph Kryn, Hot Cinders was respected for his valor in war. His name reflected his smoldering temperament, which easily burst into flame at the slightest provocation. Years before, when Hot Cinders heard that his brother was killed in the north, he concluded the murderer must be French and left in a rage toward Ville Marie, vowing to kill the first Frenchman he found. While he camped for the night at the mission of St. Francis Xavier, he learned that an Algonquin, not a Frenchman, had killed his brother. Instead of returning to Oneida to rouse the fury of his nation against the Algonquins, Hot Cinders stayed at the mission to receive instruction in the Christian faith. After a few weeks, he summoned his wife, and she brought their children north. In due time they were all baptized together, and Hot Cinders built a house. Hot Cinders and Joseph Kryn, who had constructed another large house at the mission, became dear friends.

When the Oneida realized that they had lost their great chief, they sent an emissary to the mission to inform him they would welcome him home and allow him to live among them as a Christian. He sent back the message, "I care for nothing but my faith, so I will remain here." Then, considering how they valued his leadership, he saw his opportunity to convert many, so he went to Oneida to recruit new converts. To accompany him, he chose a young Huron and a young Algonquin from Trois-Rivières. The Algonquin, Jean-Baptiste, had just married Kateri's adopted sister Rainbow, who had been baptized Camille. Hot Cinders and his two companions paddled down the St. Lawrence in a long elm bark canoe, continuing up the Richelieu with its steep portages and then across the long lakes, Champlain and Blessed Sacrament. After beaching and concealing the canoe, they continued overland to Kanawaka.

When news of Hot Cinders' arrival reached them, the villagers came out to meet him. He paraded among them like a conquering hero, and just outside the palisade, he called for the villagers to assemble.

"My people!" he cried with raised arms raised, "I have come from the mission where good Joseph Kryn now makes his home. He wishes you well and encourages all of you to join us at our village there. It is also called 'Kanawaka.' At the mission, we have built a chapel, and the bell in the chapel regulates our days, calling us to prayer or sending us into the field. There is no idleness. There is no drunkenness. We live in peace and tranquility, working and praying together."

The crowd who heard him numbered three hundred, and in the front stood Kateri.

"Here, in this land, you have constant war," he continued. "The English and the Dutch flood your villages with brandy and gin to addle your brains so they can cheat you of a fair price for your furs and serve the interest of their kings across the sea. We can no longer ignore the whites in our land. Even if we were to wage war for a generation, they will keep arriving in their great ships. If we cannot rid this land of whites, we must give our loyalty to those who best serve our interests. The French treat us with respect. Father Frémin has rid us of the whiskey traders, and black-robes teach us how to live in peace and harmony. If you wish to live in peace, leave this place and journey to the mission."

Hot Cinders spoke for three hours, and the crowd listened in rapt attention. When he finished, Kateri approached him.

"I wish to accompany you to the mission."

"How are you called?"

"Kateri Tekakwitha."

A huge smile spread across Hot Cinders' face. "Joseph Kryn told me to seek you out and guide you to the mission if you are ready."

"I long for nothing else."

Hot Cinders called the Algonquin lad over. "This is Jean-Baptiste. He is married to your sister, who is now called Camille."

Jean-Baptiste bowed respectfully. "Camille asked me to locate you and bring you back."

Kateri nodded, closed her eyes. She knew God was opening this path for her escape.

"I am not returning to the mission immediately," Hot Cinders said. "I am traveling among the Oneida to speak with my countrymen. I hope to lead many of them back to the mission. But these two young men will be returning tomorrow, and you are welcome to take my place in the canoe."

Kateri nodded and looked toward Jean-Baptiste. "Thank you."

"I left Camille at Fort St. Louis," Jean-Baptiste told her. "Once we reach the St. Lawrence, we will are proceeding east to Trois-Rivières, not west to the mission. I will take you to Fort St.

Louis, and we will send word to the mission for someone to come for you."

"I will be ready," Kateri said.

Iowerano and Moneta happened to be in Albany negotiating new terms of trade with the English. Kateri went to see Father de Lamberville.

"Hot Cinders' speech has stirred me to action."

"Will you go now to the mission?"

"Yes, never to return."

"I know Father Frémin well. I will write a letter of introduction. He will welcome you."

"Anastasia is there," she said, "and Joseph Kryn and Karitha and Rainbow who is now called Camille, and many others of our village. I am certain to find a home there!"

She returned to her longhouse and put her few belongings in a pack. After a fitful night, she met Jean-Baptiste and the other Huron youth at the eastern gate. The autumn sun was rising over the mist on the river. With her pack on her back and her cross in hand, she set out with them on foot toward the Dutch settlement of Corlaer, where they would buy bread for their journey.

Although Kateri only told the priest of her plan, White Adder, the shaman, observed her departure, and he sent a boy to summon Iowerano. Iowerano had just portaged the Cohoes Falls on his way home when the boy reached him and breathlessly related that Kateri was fleeing.

Iowerano exploded. "This is what comes of the blackrobes' meddling!" He put his back into the paddling, leaving Moneta with the messenger. When he reached Corlaer, he disembarked, loaded his musket, and set off across the pine barrens to intercept them on the trail.

At this time, Kateri and her guides were just west of Corlaer. Jean-Baptiste told Kateri and the Huron to hide in a clump of pine while he went into the village. At Corlaer, Jean-Baptiste saw Iowerano lumbering across the shallows toward the stockade with his musket held high.

"Hiro!" the chief called in greeting, and Jean-Baptiste answered him. "Have you seen a girl on the trail?" Iowerano asked. "She is small, only this high. She wears a shawl to cover her eyes and carries a cross. Her face is marked with scars, and she walks slowly because her eyes are poor. I am her uncle. She is running away, and she must come home."

"I have seen no one like this."

The chief expressed his frustration. "She is in the company of two young men!"

"I have not seen them."

"If you do, tell her to return to the village at once. If I catch them fleeing, they will pay with their lives."

"Why would she ever think to flee such a household?"

Iowerano paused, narrowed his eyes suspiciously to consider the sarcasm as Jean-Baptiste bowed and moved past him. After buying bread with a string of wampum, Jean-Baptiste returned to Kateri and the Huron lad, and they set out through the pine barrens.

When they reached the bank of the great lake three days later, Jean-Baptiste and the Huron brought Hot Cinders' canoe out from the brush where they had hidden it. They helped Kateri step into the middle and then began paddling the ten leagues up the lake.

2.

At the point of land where the Richelieu pours into the St. Lawrence, beneath the rickety wooden stockade of Fort St. Louis, a cluster of huts had been thrown up to house traders who paddled up and down the river with pelts, wampum and, occasionally, tin or iron goods. Camille was on the shore to meet Jean-Baptiste's canoe at the docking place and she cried out in joy when she saw Kateri. After first embracing her husband, Camille hugged Kateri and held her tightly.

"It is good you have come," she said. "You will be so happy at the mission."

Kateri continued to hold Camille tightly. "How I have prayed for this day."

"We live now with Anastasia. She will welcome you, and we will all live together."

"Anastasia!"

Joy soared in Kateri's heart, and tears streamed down her face. Together the four of them went to a low hut and shared a meal of *sagamite*. A canoe was leaving the following day for the mission, but it was filled and had no place for Kateri. They agreed to carry a message to the mission that Kateri was at the fort downriver. The following morning, Camille, Jean-Baptiste, and the Huron left for Trois-Rivières. Kateri stood alone on the riverbank, looking out over the broadest river she had ever seen.

CHAPTER FIFTEEN
KATERI ARRIVES AT THE MISSION

I.

Father Claude knocked gently on the rectory door and entered. After living with Father Chaumonot, he was apprehensive about sharing close quarters with two other men who had so much more experience as missionaries. Also, Father Frémin and Father Cholenec had just ejected Michel Cocteau on suspicion of impurity.

"Is that our new father?"

"Father Frémin?"

A white face loomed out of the shadows. It had small brown eyes and thin, abstemious lips above a lean jaw and a pointed chin.

"Welcome, my son." Frémin was in his fifties, but his months in the winter had aged him prematurely. "You may put your bag on that bunk. You will share a room with Father Cholenec. He is across the river in Ville Marie at present but will return in a few days."

"I have met Joseph Kryn, and he has invited me to supper. Would you care to join us?"

The priest tightened his thin, bloodless lips and worked his neck up out of the Roman collar. "I don't believe fraternizing helps us with the natives," he said coldly. "They hold us in reverence and we must keep them from witnessing our more human natures."

"Are you saying I should not attend the supper?"

The priest's eyes bored into his. "Do not put words in my mouth. I said nothing of the sort, nor was I hinting at it. I merely suggested that fraternizing with these natives has its perils."

"I was impressed with Joseph Kryn," Chauchetière said.

"Kryn is one of our hardiest warrior chiefs."

"There are others?"

"Yes," Father Frémin said proudly. "We have an Oneida chief named Hot Cinders who is mercurial, exploding anytime he senses someone opposing him. He and Joseph Kryn protect us now and have become good friends. Hot Cinders returned to the land of the Mohawks and Oneidas recruiting more converts. Our mission grows and grows." Father Frémin's tone and smile indicated that he took personal credit for the expansion.

"Soon, you will have the entire Iroquois League here."

"This mission is God's special place," Father Frémin said firmly to address the irony he heard in Claude's words. "Here, Iroquois from all five nations assemble to free themselves of violence and drunkenness and superstition. Together we plow the earth, grow corn and live simple lives. They cut timber and build houses. They go into the forests for game, and they dress the skins for clothing."

Claude looked around with appreciation. This place surely had a more beneficent feel than Lorette. "St. Francis does seem to be a very holy place."

"Consider, Father. We do not enslave the native people as do the Spaniards in Mexico, nor do we corrupt them as the English do with their liquor and warfare. In return for the respect we show, our mission grows so rapidly that we require a new chapel which is now under construction by French carpenters."

"Ah yes, Joseph Kryn took me there," the younger priest said.

"The spiritual gifts of these people are exemplary. They have proven that God is universal to all races, not dependent on language or place. Opening their hearts to the message of Christ is our gift to them, and their gift to us is the affirmation of our highest ideals."

"I was a year at Lorette, and the ignorance and squalor overwhelmed me. Here the ground seems fertile indeed."

"One caveat, Father."

"Yes?"

"The devil lurks everywhere. The temptations of liquor appear each time a trader beaches his canoe. The temptations of the flesh follow these native peoples from their homes and spring up when they get lax or fall away from our regimen. The temptation to backslide into dream ceremonies or shaman cures occurs during times of personal stress. We must be ever vigilant against the wiles of Satan."

"I understand."

Father Frémin raised his index finger. "Caution and vigilance, Father. We have a duty to them, yes, but our first duty is to ourselves, our order, and above all, to God."

"I told Joseph Kryn I would sup with him," Father Claude said, anxious to get away.

"Then go along. That generous fellow gave us the house he built for his family to use as our chapel until the new one is completed. He lives in the next row of longhouses directly behind here. Stow your bag in your room and I will show you."

Father Claude entered and looked at his new quarters. The room was small, five-by-six and seven feet high, with two narrow bunks. A window, its vertical shutter propped open with a stick, looked down to the river. In the corner was a pile of skins and three makeshift shelves that served as storage. An ornate crucifix, carved from walnut in France, hung on the wall. Gazing at the crucifix and feeling the clean wind off the river, he was comforted. He had paddled and portaged fifty leagues to reach this outpost. He took his paint box and his chalks from his bag and placed them on one of the shelves. Father Frémin's reservations aside, he already felt at home.

"Shall we go, Father?" Frémin adjusted his wide-brimmed hat and led Father Claude out into the evening.

The sky was resplendent, long reaches of pink cloud deepening in hue with the sunset. As they walked, the sun lanced from behind the clouds and cast a bright ruby light on the river, the fields, and the houses of the mission. It lit the cross atop the chapel so the wood gleamed like red gold. Gulls were flying in wide circles overhead.

"It is peaceful here," Father Claude observed.

"It is a place God has blessed," Father Frémin agreed.

Children playing in the lanes stopped their games to greet the pastor, who introduced the new priest. Father Claude held open the bearskin curtain when they arrived at the longhouse, and they entered the long, dim, smoky room. At the center, a large group of Iroquois was sitting and squatting on the ground. The house was bigger than those at Lorette, and the vaulted ceiling seemed like the nave of a church. Corn with braided husks hung from the ceiling as they picked their way along the sleeping shelves. Antlers hung as trophies and animal skins here and there were rigged as modesty shields for the sleeping shelves.

"Hello, Father!" Joseph Kryn called, and all eyes turned. "Our new priest," he said to the others.

"May the Lord be with you," Father Frémin said to the assembled. "Let me introduce Father Claude to you. He will be helping me and Father Cholenec, and I know you will extend every kindness to him."

Father Claude bowed, and all those who had gathered for the meal bowed in respect.

"I will leave you now," Frémin said. "Feed him well. He looks as though he could use a good meal."

"Please sit down, Father," Kryn said. "This is my wife

Karitha, this is my son Peter, and this is our kinswoman, Anastasia."

Father Claude nodded and greeted each of them. Anastasia stood to make room for him. She was a large, commanding woman with penetrating eyes. He sat on the mat they cleared for him and accepted a bowl of *sagamite* sweetened with maple sugar and strawberries. He ate with his fingers, as they did, and listened to the men planning a fishing expedition.

He understood much of what they said, and he observed them closely. These were the fierce Mohawks he had read about in the *Relations*. They were larger than the Hurons of Lorette, and their skin color was not as dark. The Mohawks were vigorous and quick, gifted speakers and natural storytellers with a sense of humor that often caused them to burst into laughter. Father Claude observed that they often spoke about the faith. They must surely approach learning and practicing the tenets of Christianity with fervor, he thought, so different from Lorette and even from the Jesuit cloisters of France.

After dinner, Father Claude walked alone on the mudflats. He gazed up at the moon and murmured a prayer of thanksgiving for his assignment here and for the great virtue and magnetism of Joseph Kryn that, despite the caution of Father Frémin, seemed to be innocent and good. After so much doubt and so much searching, Father Claude had arrived at last where he could do good work.

When he returned to the rectory, Father Frémin was asleep. Claude quietly unpacked in the moonlight. He counted the sheets of paper he had brought and found there to be seventy-three. He had a used set of chalks and six pen and ink drawings along with four paint brushes and a case of pigments. He would employ these to sketch and paint the people and objects around him. With his back against the log wall of the hut in the moonlight, he began to sketch the tale of the late Catherine Gandeacteua as she and her husband trudged on snowshoes over the river from Montreal to found this mission nine years before.

2.

In the coming weeks, Father Claude began to believe the very air around the mission was charmed. He said daily mass in the chapel. On Sundays, the men's and the women's choirs sang the high mass—*Kyrie, Sanctus,* and *Agnus Dei.* They sang the entrance, communion, and recessional hymns. Joy pervaded the square where the children played, the fields where the women planted, and the new chapel that Iroquois men helped French carpenters build. Claude's spirit was lifted with hope as he saw the bonds of these people from twenty-two nations being knit into a community devoted to Christ.

By now Father Pierre Cholenec had returned from Ville-Marie. He was a few years older than Claude and seemed agreeable if a bit distant. He volunteered to answer whatever questions Father Claude might have. Naturally shy, Father Claude kept mostly to himself, and as the youngest of the three priests, he drew the most menial of duties. All the fathers celebrated mass and administered the sacraments. Father Frémin, the superior, set policy, approved or disapproved building projects, resolved whatever complaints the villagers had with each other and policed the riverbank to keep traders from landing with their liquor. Father Cholonec, next in seniority, attended to most of the spiritual needs: confessions, counseling, instruction in the faith, and visiting the sick and dying. Father Frémin assigned Father Claude to instruct the children and fill in as necessary with the other duties.

As Father Claude was beginning his second month, a messenger arrived to announce that Hot Cinders, on his way back to the Oneida nation, was sending a young convert north to the mission. Since her traveling companions were headed for Trois-Rivières, they had deposited her at Fort St. Louis. Father Claude heard Kryn and Anastasia discussing the arrival of this young woman.

"She has received the Prayer then," Anastasia said, overjoyed. "I doubt Iowerano approved."

"No," Kryn said. "He feels the bite of an insult when anyone acts contrary to his wishes. He does not understand we all have free will."

"True, true," Anastasia said. "And from her infancy, Tekakwitha has displayed a strong will."

"Yes, and she shows exceptional talent, patience, and diligence in her beadwork and embroidery," Karitha added.

"Who is this woman you speak about?" Father Claude asked.

"As close to me as a kinswoman," Anastasia said. "Her mother was a Christian Algonquin from Trois-Rivières. We were captured by the Mohawks and transported to their village. When the girl was still a babe, the family was stricken with the pox. Her parents died, but the girl lived, though she is badly scarred, and the pox has diminished her sight. She refuses to take a husband and is therefore considered poor and destitute. She is the adopted sister of Camille who lives here with me, so I will lodge her at my fire."

"She is a favorite of Karitha and little Peter," Kryn said. "I would be happy to house her when the chapel is completed and I return to my home."

"Let us see what she will say of the matter when the time comes," Anastasia said.

"I will go and bring her back," Kryn said, and he set out alone in his canoe, beneath a bright moon.

3.

Days later, Father Claude was saying his office, walking along the bank of the river. Sunset colored the water with deep red and violet. He walked slowly; his head bent to his book, a lone, slender figure in a black *soutane* and wide-brimmed black hat. Gulls cried and circled in the flaming sky.

"Father?"

It was the voice of Joseph Kryn, and it seemed quite close. Father Claude stopped and looked up, only then noticing the hushed, fiery evening. He closed his prayer book.

"Out here, Father. Look who I bring!"

Father Claude turned. The voice had floated across the water from a canoe gliding toward him. He saw the bulging arms and shoulders of Joseph Kryn in the stern, his skillful paddling scarcely breaking the surface.

In the bow of the canoe knelt a small figure, stiff and bolt upright, a blue shawl covering her head. Joseph Kryn's face beamed in the rosy light. With two strong strokes, the canoe scraped on the pebbles. Joseph Kryn vaulted easily from the rear of the canoe, his moccasins and leggings splashing in the water. He pulled the canoe high up the shore and gently helped the small woman stand and step over the gunwale.

The priest approached curiously. Joseph Kryn was beaming with joy. He had his big arm around her narrow shoulders, her face still covered. "This is Kateri, Father. From my village. Kateri Tekakwitha."

Father Claude leaned forward to see her face. She was quite small and slender and appeared painfully shy. She wore a white tunic and leggings and moccasins, and carried a small wooden cross. She kept her head down, not looking at him. He waited to see her face, but she continued to stand there, head bent under the shawl.

"Kateri has a letter." At Kryn's urging, the small woman produced and hesitantly held out a folded paper. Father Claude took it from her and read. Father de Lamberville's ornate hand greeted him from the creased paper. "To Father Frémin: I entrust to you the treasure of my mission. Care for her as I have."

Curious, the priest bent to look into the shadow of the woman's veil.

"It's Father Claude," Kryn explained to her. Slowly, she lifted her shawl. Expecting to see the comely features of a young

Iroquois woman, Father Claude gasped when he saw instead a squinting face disfigured by pox scars. Her hair was oiled, braided, and tied up with a red eel skin band. Despite her scars and half-closed eyes, she held herself with dignity. When she opened her eyes sufficiently to take in light, they were filmy.

"Welcome to La Prairie," Father Claude said, trying to hide his shock.

"I have long dreamed of joining you," she said simply. She sensed his revulsion. She pulled her shawl back to hide her face.

"Greet our father in the manner of the French!" Joseph Kryn said and took her hand and offered it to the priest. When Father Claude touched her hand, he felt a surge of energy that made him shudder involuntarily. Sensing this, Kateri looked up at him imploringly from the shadow of her shawl in the gathering darkness. Pity for her flooded his heart. Her hand was small but strong and calloused from hard work. She quickly put the hand back beneath her shawl.

"Anastasia and her mother were friends," Joseph explained.

"Is your mother back in the land of the Mohawks?" Father Claude asked.

"My mother lives now in heaven," Kateri said.

"I am sorry," the priest said.

"No. She is happy, as you teach," the young woman said. "She died long ago, and she is with my father and my little brother."

The sun had set. Its fading purple light reflected on the dark flowing water.

"Let us make you comfortable," the priest said. The touch of her hand, interrupting his prayer, had awakened him.

"Come, Father, we will bring her to Anastasia's house."

Joseph Kryn placed one arm around the young woman and her pack, gestured to the priest with his other and they moved off together.

4.

Anastasia was sitting outside, pounding corn in a wooden mortar, when she saw the three walking up the lane. Recognizing the small woman between the men, she dropped the pestle, brushed her hands on her apron, and rushed to greet them.

"Can it be? Aurora! My little bird!"

Kateri, still under the shawl, curled into the older woman's embrace.

"I've known this child since her birth," Anastasia gushed to the priest. "My precious, precious one! Her mother was my dear friend, who died, and now Tekakwitha joins us!" Radiant with joy, Anastasia pulled back the blue shawl and held the young woman's head in her hands, kissing her scarred face all over. "My beautiful, beautiful child!" she said. Kateri opened her eyes as wide as she could and spoke. Her voice was a soft whisper:

"I am baptized, Mother." She showed Anastasia her cross. "I am Kateri now."

"Kateri! Yes. We recently lost our Catherine here, and now the Lord sends you to replace her. Come inside! You must be tired and hungry." Anastasia nodded in thanks at Joseph Kryn and Father Chauchetière and led the young women into her cabin.

CHAPTER SIXTEEN
KATERI MAKES HER FIRST COMMUNION

I.

In the morning, Kateri stood on the riverbank near the large cross that marked this northern Kanawaka. Her weak eyesight drank in light from the shimmering waters of Lac St. Paul, and the foaming rapids of Sault St. Louis and, far to the north, the slumbering mass of Mount Royal. Thin tendrils of smoke from the chimneys of Ville-Marie cheered her. She stood on a rise at the foot of the elevated cross, awestruck at the magnificent sweep of this vista, the green of St. Paul Island, and at the base of the rapids, Heron Island where thousands of birds fluttered and chattered. She was thrilled with a certainty that she had been delivered. She now inhabited the place Father Cholonec read that Sunday from the Book of Isaiah—

"The wolf also shall dwell with the lamb, and the leopard shall lie down with the kid; and the calf and the young lion and the fatling together, and a little child shall lead them. He will judge between the nations and will settle disputes for many peoples. They will beat their swords into plowshares and their spears into pruning hooks. Nation will not take up sword against nation, nor will they train for war anymore."

Father Frémin assigned Father Cholonec to be her confessor, and Father Cholonec, immediately observing her spiritual gifts, wrote to Father de Lamberville:

"On arriving here, the child could scarcely find words to express her happiness. She possesses a true and noble heart; a strong spirit and a courageous character and, as far as myself and Father Chauchetière were able to discover, an insatiable thirst for spiritual knowledge with a great zeal to put into practice all that she understands.

"Her soul was well disposed toward perfection; and throwing herself into her new life with singular devotion, she adopted all the practices which she saw were good in the older converts. In a matter of a few weeks, she stood out among all the other women and girls of the village. Here we see Kateri Tekakwitha, having preserved her innocence and holiness through twenty years among evildoers and unbelievers, become at our mission in such a short time, a saint among the just and the faithful."

Kateri immediately adapted to the rigors of her new life. At four each morning, she hastened through the lanes between the longhouses to the chapel. She knelt and prayed until Father Cholonec or Father Chauchetière celebrated the first mass of the day at dawn. She returned to Anastasia's cabin for breakfast, and then she assembled with the entire village to attend the Matins mass. She remained behind in the village while the others went to work, the women to the fields and the men to building the chapel and other houses for new emigrants. Kateri worked at her embroidery and beadwork by the cabin fire. Whenever the flood of her feelings for Jesus and Mary overflowed, she quietly left her work, pulled her shawl over her face, and hurried to the chapel to kneel and pray. In the evening, when the villagers returned—always singing from their work—she accompanied them into the chapel for vespers.

If fair weather beckoned her outside, she would sometimes accompany Anastasia into the forest to gather wood or draw water from the spring. Because she hated gossip and small talk, she avoided the society of others and preferred to remain private about her past and her devotions. But she opened herself to Anastasia.

"I loved your mother," Anastasia said. "It is no accident you are given to the Prayer. After her baptism in the chapel at Trois-Rivières, the beautiful Meadow dedicated her life to Holy Mother Mary and had nothing to do with men. We were smoking fish along the river one day when the Mohawks fell on us. They killed the men and hauled us off to Ossernenon, where they enslaved us. Because of her beauty, Meadow escaped torture and death. They spared me as well, though I was far less comely, because I protested so vigorously. The chief of the Turtle Clan was so impressed by her modesty, constancy, and lack of vanity that he took her as his wife. While she wished to remain chaste and apart from men, she acted as a dutiful wife, bearing to him yourself and your little brother."

"Tell me again, Mother, about my family."

"Your mama's joy at your birth was limitless. She confided in me that her capture and forced marriage, as horrible as they were, became happy events when you and your brother blessed her life. For four years she was completely devoted to your father and you, but then the white man's pox swept through our village. How can I speak of those horrors? Nearly everyone in the village was infected, red sores erupting from the skin, and it was so sudden! In a few days, everyone lay groaning on pallets. I was away on a fishing trip, but when I returned, I rescued you."

"Twice the Lord has saved me," Kateri murmured. "Once when my body was threatened by disease, and then when the corruption of our homeland threatened my soul. If the wonders of this mission are mere worldly deliverance, Mother, imagine what heaven will be!"

2.

Sundays and feast days were special to Kateri, and she spent those days in the chapel on her knees. Father Cholonec described the devotion of the mission, how men on one side of the chapel, and women on the other, sang in Iroquois the *Kyrie*, the *Gloria*, the *Credo*, the *Sanctus,* and the *Agnus Dei.* Both priests so respected the natural eloquence and the spiritual progress of the Iroquois that they often allowed one of the chiefs to deliver the sermon in his native tongue.

Father Frémin, an accomplished linguist and musician, adapted Iroquois prayers to the eight psalm tones from medieval Christian services. He trained both the men's and the women's choirs to sing morning prayers, the liturgy of the mass, the Ten Commandments, Iroquois hymns, the *Ave Maria*, the *Pater Noster,* and the benediction of the Blessed Sacrament. Father Cholonec observed that Kateri soon learned these chants and joyfully participated in them. He wrote to Bishop Laval in Quebec:

"Her devout love for the church services is wholeheartedly sincere. In attaching herself to God, she pursues all avenues to remain in communion with Him, and to preserve throughout her entire day the good sentiments she experiences early in the morning at the foot of the altar."

"Her piety exceeds all others," Cholonec observed to Father Chauchetière as they watched Kateri hurrying to the chapel one morning. They were sitting on a bench outside the rectory.

"I felt her holiness the moment I met her," Chauchetière replied. "God chooses special vessels to carry His grace among us, and as I bear witness, Father, I have never met anyone with her spiritual gifts."

Father Cholonec agreed but advised caution. "We must not

question His choice, Father. We must bow to God's will, which makes us not only witnesses but ministers to this young woman."

"Beauty and purity shine around her," Chauchetière said. "She is the fairest of flowers. I worry about the fate of such purity and virtue in this world."

"You don't worry she will be corrupted?"

"I pray her faith will be sustained." Chauchetière thought for a moment. "Her holiness is different in quality, not just degree. She is a daughter of these people, yet even from beneath the hood of her shawl, she cannot hide the light of her spirit from view."

Father Cholonec considered something, and then he spoke: "When Kateri appears for the service, could you bring her to me?"

"Of course."

As the mission bell rang for vespers and the workers in their humble clothing filled the lanes of the village, Father Chauchetière waited for her.

"Kateri?"

"Yes, Father?" She had been in deep meditation, preparing herself for the service, but she smiled, and her dimmed eyes strove to focus on his face.

"Father Cholonec asks that I bring you to him in the sacristy."

"I have not displeased him, have I?"

"No, of course not."

As he touched her elbow to guide her toward the chapel door, he felt again her extraordinary energy.

Dressed in his alb, stole, and cincture, Father Cholonec welcomed them.

"Shall I leave you?" Father Claude asked.

"No, please sit." Father Cholonec motioned them to two chairs and prayed silently as he donned the green chasuble. Then he spoke, "Father Claude and I have observed you, Kateri, and your progress is exemplary."

"Oh, Father!" she sighed. "It is heaven on earth for me to be here with nothing in the way of my devotion."

"Yes." He went to her, reached down, and took her chin in his hand. "We have seen backsliders among those we baptized, and so we have become cautious . . ."

"I am not one of them, Father."

"No, you are not." Father Claude wondered what this portended. "I have decided that you are ready," Cholonec said, "or rather you will be ready after receiving instruction from Father Claude from now until Christmas, to receive the Eucharist Christmas morning."

"Oh, Father!" Kateri fell to her knees, folded her hands, and sobbed: "I want the Eucharist so much, but I am so unworthy!"

"No, Kateri, you are a ready tabernacle."

"Oh, Father!" she sobbed. "To welcome Our Savior into my body which I so detest! To think that He will live within me! It is more than I ever hoped."

CHAPTER SEVENTEEN
KATERI LEAVES THE MISSION FOR THE WINTER HUNT

I.

Two weeks before Christmas, Camille and Jean-Baptiste asked Kateri if she would join their party on the winter hunt. Kateri took the matter to Anastasia.

"Camille wants me to join her family on the hunt, Mother. I declined."

"Why?"

"I have found my heart's delight here. I never want to be away from the chapel and the sacraments."

"But the mission will be deserted. Our food stores are running low. There will be fresh meat and much idle time on the hunt, which you can use for praying and encouraging others by your prayer."

Kateri mulled over the idea. She visited Father Cholonec and asked his guidance.

"It is true that the hunt is a time away from mass and the sacraments," he said, "but Anastasia is correct; food will soon be scarce here."

He rose and went into the next room to summon Father Chauchetière, who brought a folded paper with him.

"I asked Father Chauchetière to draw calendars for each hunting party. We give them to an advisor in each party to keep track of Sundays and holy days and to calculate when Easter will fall so that you may return the week before to celebrate Palm Sunday." He handed her the folded paper. She looked at Father Chauchetière. He was the quietest of the three priests and surely the most sensitive. She felt he understood more than the others. Father Cholonec continued: "Take this calendar with you, observe it, and all will be well."

"You're going off with a hunting party?" Chauchetière asked.

"I wish to remain at the mission, Father, to pray and receive the sacraments."

Father Claude turned to Father Cholonec and spoke in French words that she did not understand, "Why don't we employ Kateri to help us in some way?"

"No," Father Cholonec said, "the hunt is a time of renewal. It removes our villagers from the discipline of mission life, and they return renewed and rededicated."

"But she is so fervent."

"Kateri should not be singled out for special favors. It would not serve her progress." Father Cholonec turned to her and spoke in her language. "Your sister desires to be near you on the hunt, Kateri. Keep your hunting party to the schedule and return for Easter."

"As you wish," she said quietly and then bowed and left them. She returned in obedience to Anastasia's cabin to ready herself for the journey to the hunting grounds.

2.

For Christmas this year, Father Claude and Father Cholonec coached the choir to sing the four-part harmonies of the Shepherd's Mass. The villagers took great pains to decorate the chapel with evergreens, soft furs, and embroidered coverings for the altar and the communion rail. Late Christmas Eve, they lit the interior with candles and rush lamps, so the chapel's light shone out on the snow.

Anastasia had stitched a fringed tunic from a white doeskin for Kateri's first communion. She braided white beads and feathers into Kateri's hair, and together they labored through the deep snow to the chapel where the choir was singing carols.

As Kateri entered, the congregation rose and sang *Adeste Fidelis*. She bowed and walked to the front bench. Fathers Frémin, Cholonec, and Chauchetière emerged from the sacristy in vestments of white and gold, and they began the mass: *"Introibo ad altare Dei."*

The mass proceeded with great joy, a festival of lights near the longest, darkest night of the year. During the procession at the offertory, Father Frémin lay a wooden carving of the infant Jesus in the *creche* they had fashioned from pine boughs. At communion, before any of the other communicants received, Father Frémin turned from the crucifix and held a host above the ciborium, waiting for Kateri to approach.

Bowing her head as the choir sang *The First Nöel*, Kateri walked slowly up to the communion rail and knelt. Father Frémin approached with the ciborium, and Father Chauchetière with the patten. Kateri gently pulled back her veil. Making the sign of the cross with the host, Father Frémin held it up.

"Corpus Christi."

"Amen." Kateri opened her mouth, and the priest placed the host on her tongue. She shuddered, closed her mouth and bowed her head, then made the sign of the cross. As the choir lifted the melody in the flickering candlelight, she stood and found the way back to her pew and knelt and bowed her head in deepest communion with her savior, not noticing all who watched her.

Gandeacteua (who converted Kryn) and her two companions
arrive at Montreal on snow shoes from the winter hunt.
Drawing by Father Claude Chauchetière

3.

When Kateri awoke the morning after Christmas, Camille was packing the kettle and bowls while Jean-Baptiste packed his musket, spear, bow and arrows, hatchet, hunting knife, and fire bow-drill. Kateri arose and folded her doeskin blanket on a large square of canvas. She added her woolen tunic, her bone and metal needles of various sizes, her array of dyed porcupine quills, a two-pronged iron fork, a knife, a bowl, and a bark plate. She placed her rosary and a small wooden cross in the pocket of her coat.

Before they left on the hunt, the families gathered in front of the chapel. They went in together, knelt and prayed for good hunting. Then they emerged to the overcast day, fastened on their snowshoes with leather thongs, and set off south into the hills.

The wide, bright vistas hurt her eyes, so Kateri kept her shawl pulled down. She walked in the path behind Jean-Baptiste and Camille. Her heavy pack hung down her back from an eel skin band looped around her forehead. The snowshoes made walking slow and laborious. She was so accustomed to sitting by the fire that she found the exercise tiring and painful, but she did not complain. She bowed her head and leaned into the path and kept up while three dogs fanned out as their scouts.

For five days, they walked, a party of twelve—four men, five women, a youth, and two little girls. They slept two nights in the shelter of pine bushes on the plain. Reaching the hills on the third night, they slept in a thicket of pine. In the darkness of the cold morning, Kateri awoke in her sleeping robe beneath a dusting of snow. She arose and knelt on the snow with the others, praying to the gray, silent sky. She missed the small chapel with its railing and altar and tabernacle and crucifix. After a quick breakfast of cornmeal, she fastened the band across her forehead and started once more.

As the hills rose into low mountains, Jean-Baptiste looked for a suitable camp. Water was essential, so when he came upon a level tableland sheltered in a pine forest beside a frozen brook, he signaled they would stop there. In a few hours, they had erected the hut they would inhabit until spring, and while the women set about fetching firewood and water, the men went off to hunt.

"Bring water from upstream," Camille gave Kateri a kettle to use as a bucket and a hatchet to cut through the ice. The evening was dark and still, and the stars glittered like ice crystals. Kateri fastened on her snowshoes and walked upstream where she could hear water gurgling beneath the ice. She chopped a hole in the ice, cleared away the snow, and dipped the kettle into the cold running water. As she pulled the kettle up from the water, she recalled the story of Jesus and the woman by the well, and her heart ached again to be in the mission chapel. There she could kneel and listen to the priest recite in broken Iroquois those stories of Jesus and His apostles from the New Testament, and from the Old Testament, stories of nations and kings of Israel and the long exiles into Babylon and Egypt.

A stone's throw upstream, Kateri saw a thicket of pine. She left the kettle in the snow and walked a few steps to duck under the low branches and enter the thicket. It was as sheltered as a chapel, boughs above her forming an arch and boughs on all sides enclosing her in a snug little praying cell. She knelt in the snow and wept bitterly. It would be three long dark months before she returned to the chapel and Holy Communion. Until then, she would be minding the children and listening to the gossip and petty complaints of the women, and the stories of their lives before the mission.

"Help me, O Lord, to be patient," she prayed. "Help me show love for my sister and her family, who have welcomed me among them. Help them not to return to the old ways. I will ask them to recite the lives of the saints and sing the hymns as we work, and I will come here as often as possible to pray."

She picked up the kettle of water and carried it down the hill where no one noticed how long she had been gone.

The following day, fetching water for camp, Kateri brought a hunting knife, and in the thicket, she carved a cross in the bark of the largest tree to sanctify her grotto. She cut boughs, too, and spread them as a carpet on the snow where she could kneel. She prayed in thanksgiving for this place of solitude and for her knowledge of the prayers and the stories of the lives of the saints and the hymns that gave her such comfort.

On the fourth day in camp, young Eugene killed a caribou. The men came back, Jean-Baptiste proudly carrying a forequarter. Eugene and his brother Daniel each carried a hindquarter, and Jean-Baptiste's brother Pierre carried the head on one shoulder and a forequarter on the other. The youth, Lucien, who had remained behind with the woman to chop wood, pestered Jean-Baptiste to take him along hunting now that they had found game.

The women stoked up the fire. Jean-Baptiste skillfully butchered the meat, and they hung it by ropes in four deerskin bags from the branches so their dogs, coyotes, bobcats and racoons could not reach it. Kateri took charge of the hide that she would scrape and sew into a robe with her long needles. In the evening Jean-Baptiste spoke as he sat cross-legged in front of the fire. Rib-eye slabs of the caribou were cooking.

"Before we eat of this gift, let us thank the Lord for sending the caribou to us. Let us also thank Eugene for being vigilant in tracking him and courageous in running him down and killing him." He looked about the small gathering. "I am mindful that in our former lives, we'd be praying to Aireskou and then eating until we grew sick or until all the meat was gone. Let moderation always regulate our lives. Let us now recite the Our Father." In the ruddy glow of the hut, the small group recited the prayer, their voices rising at "Give us this day our daily bread."

Jean-Baptiste served meat to them on bark plates, and hungrily they ate until they were full.

4.

Late in January, the deep cold set in, and the skies were cloudy all day. Snow fell for twenty or thirty hours, piling up at the entrance of the hut, requiring the hunting party to dig out. Life in the camp had settled into a routine. Kateri kept the calendar, marking off the days, reminding Jean-Baptiste to observe Sundays with an hour of prayer before they set off to hunt, and the women performed their chores. Her strategy to initiate discussions about the saints or sing hymns worked. The prayers and songs crowded out the usual tittering about romance and courtship and any backbiting or gossip.

Two or three times a day, Kateri left the hut for water, and she went to her chapel in the pines to pray. Here in the deep, white heart of the forest, she emptied herself of memory and fear and dreams about the future and opened her heart to let it fill with the grace of God. There were no candles, no decorations, no vestments, no golden props—chalice and ciborium and monstrance—of the mission chapel. Here there was no priest to deliver parables and sermons. Here there was no choir to help her in her quest to feel God's presence. Yet it was here, alone in the forest, that she allowed her heart and soul to open, and she meditated —

— *on wisdom* of the Holy Spirt, a white dove! If she closed her eyes, she heard the fluttering of snow-white wings, and she opened herself to the wisdom brought by solitude and the reward of her chastity.

— *on sacrifice* in the offering of Christ crucified looking down from His cross. His face streaming red with blood from the crown of thorns, His hands, and feet pierced with sharp iron nails, hanging on the cross as torture victims hung on the pole on the platforms when she was a child, "Father, Father, why have you forsaken me?" She felt His despair, tortured, and slowly murdered in humiliation, alone, betrayed, cursed, and reviled until the moment of death. What agony! "And You did this for me!" she sobbed, beating her breast. "You suffered, and you died for my sins!"

— *on order and reason and the peace of God the Father*, a white-bearded old man, older than Deganawida and Hiawatha. He was the all-powerful God, possessor of winds and thunder and light-ning bolts, the looser of frosts and blizzards. He held the sun like a fiery ball, sending it up from the East each morning and guiding it through the sky, even behind the darkest clouds, in and out of the occasional eclipse. He cast the moon in its phases, like the shaman juggler tossing bones after a feast, brightening, then darkening the land and then brightening it again, and finally her favorite:

— *on purity* of the blessed virgin Mary. How Kateri wept when she considered the perfection of the mother of Jesus, able to keep her virginity and to bear the savior of the world. Mary responded instantly, without hesitation, to the call of Gabriel, and in the secret recesses of her womb, the Holy Spirit placed Jesus. Mary gave birth to the infant Jesus in a stable and placed him in a manger while the shepherds came, and magi from the East following the star. Mary nursed the savior at her breast, soothing and comforting him, teaching him to walk and speak. And then she was rewarded for all this with the seven sorrows, *Mater Dolorosa*, which she bore until God and her son Jesus sent for her, opening the clouds to assume her bodily into heaven.

When she finished her meditations each day, Kateri felt complete. The Holy Trinity, together with the Blessed Virgin Mary, formed a perfect union. All lay within a divine circle while chaos, darkness, and violence raged outside. This circle was as timeless as the sun and solid as the earth. The seasons would blow in and blow out, and days would lengthen and shorten, and the weather would grow cold and then hot, the crops would give them an ample harvest and then die, all in the order of things. But the Holy Trinity and the Blessed Virgin Mary would always remain above and beyond this physical world, eternal.

5.

Weeks passed. The days were lengthening, and one day from the shelter of her praying chapel, she heard the song of birds. The Lord had blessed their camp with much success. The hunters had brought back deer, elk, and caribou as well as hares, possum, and raccoon, all of which she and Camille butchered and skinned. They hung strips of meat above the fire to dry and smoke and stacked it near a great pile of hides in the corner facing the door. The hides would purchase hatchets and scissors and knives and bolts of cloth when the traders came upriver from Quebec.

They still hunted during the mornings, and Jean-Baptiste and Daniel and Eugene and Pierre used the afternoons to build four canoes so when the streams melted, they could paddle downstream to the lowlands and the river. It would be far easier returning to the mission than it had been trudging through the deep snow to get here.

One evening, the young men, Daniel, Eugene, and little Lucien, returned to camp, but Pierre and Jean-Baptiste had continued on the trail of a moose. The boys concluded that they had enough meat and skins, but the men—brothers who hunted together when they were young—wanted to demonstrate their prowess and bring back the moose. The others ate their evening meal and settled down to sleep.

Deep in the night, the hide curtain opened. Kateri awakened briefly and saw stars through the opening, and then she fell back to sleep. The men jostled the sleepers as they found themselves places on the ground where they could wrap up in their robes. In the morning, Camille was up first. Kateri awoke to see her looking down, arms fold, scowling above her. She did not understand Camille's expression, but needing to use the latrine and fetch water, she rose and went out with her kettle and escaped to her shrine and her morning prayers.

According to the calendar Kateri kept, Palm Sunday was two

weeks away. The sun was spiraling upward in the sky each day, and clumps of snow fell through the branches of pine. Birds brightened the wood with singing.

"Help me," Jean-Baptiste asked her one morning. She and Camille were sweeping the hut. Kateri put her broom aside. "The boys are gone, and I need help sliding our last canoe to the riverbank." Kateri followed him out the door, leaving Camille to finish cleaning.

Days later, the hunting party loaded in their canoes and shoved off. The creek was high with meltwater, and they descended in two days to a tributary river. The river was thrashing between smooth icy banks, treacherous and slippery, impossible to climb out if the canoe swamped. They rushed past standing waves of whitewater, around protruding rocks and across pools that swirled with strong currents. What had taken seven days to hike took only two to travel by water, and soon they emerged onto the broad St. Lawrence, filled with giant ice floes from the uplands. They paddled carefully through the blocks of ice, slept on the riverbank, and watched with delight the following day as the palisade and bastions of the mission appeared on the south shore. The chapel bell was ringing. Small birds skittered across the snow. With relief and joy, Kateri climbed out of the canoe and waded onto dry land.

Many other villagers were on the riverbank unpacking, and they shouted greetings. Joseph Kryn, Karitha, and Peter called to her, and Kateri went over and embraced them. Later in the afternoon, when the mission bell rang, the villagers assembled in the old chapel—men on the left and women on the right—to intone hymns and listen to the gospel of the Prodigal Son returning home, then Father Cholonec's homily welcoming them back. At the consecration, when the host was held high, *Hoc est enim corpus meum,* as Father Chauchetière rang the bells, Kateri wept in adoration of the blessed sacrament, and joy at being home.

6.

Father Cholonec was surprised two days later when Camille came to see him. Her manner was subdued, a gravity he sensed did not portend anything good.

"One of our most revered members, Father, may not be what she pretends."

The priest scowled. He often preached against gossip. "Who?"

"My sister. Kateri."

The priest hid any surprise he felt. "Yes? I have heard nothing but testaments to her faith, her purity, and her virtue. Are you saying these are *false?*"

Camille nodded. "We all know what men are like, Father, you more than I for you hear their confessions."

"You mean their behavior toward women?"

"Yes." Camille folded her arms and set her jaw and nodded. "I caught Jean-Baptiste in a tryst with an Abenaki woman four years ago."

"But that occurred before you arrived at the Sault. Before you were married."

"Exactly," she nodded. "So now we are married, and he and my adopted sister have been carrying on."

"Oh, no, you must be mistaken."

"I am sure of it."

"Tell me what you saw."

"As we were preparing to leave the hut where we had wintered, Jean-Baptiste came in late one night. In the morning, he was sleeping, not next to me, but next to her."

"Were they under the same sleeping robe?"

"No," she scoffed. "That would have given away their game! But they were close enough to show me what happened."

"Hunting camps are usually cramped, are they not?"

"He knew where I was. He always found me in the night before. No," she shook her head sadly, "but that's not all."

"What else?"

"When we were about to leave, he asked her to accompany him into the woods to get a canoe he had built."

"And she went with him?"

"Yes."

"And was there a canoe?"

"There was. They slid it out on the snow. And they were laughing together like children!"

The priest scowled. "What causes your suspicion?"

"It was the way they carried on, laughing and joking, and she referred to him by his name, with familiarity."

"What do you think I should do?"

"Confront her with her behavior and see how she responds."

"But the confessional is secret. I can't reveal what others confess."

She tossed her head with haughty disdain. "I care only about her soul, not about my husband. I already know I cannot trust him with young women."

"I will speak with her."

That evening, Cholonec related this to Father Chauchetière.

"Impossible!" Father Claude said. "Camille has the problem, not Kateri. Camille envies her sister's purity. I have never known Kateri to stray from the path of chastity in the least. She is incapable of such a thing."

"I told you when you arrived, Father, that one must be vigilant to the snares of the devil. We know morals can often become lax on the hunt."

"I would stake my life on it, Father. Forget what you heard. To confront her with this calumny would be to credit it and demean yourself as a carrier of rumor."

"No one is above temptation. I shall get to the bottom of this."

The following day, after he had slept on the issue, Father Cholonec summoned Kateri to the rectory.

"Yes, Father?"

"Do you know why I asked to see you?"

"No."

"You were on the winter hunt with Jean-Baptiste and Camille?"

"Yes." Her eyes were unfocused and cloudy.

"How well did you know them before the winter hunt?"

"Camille and I were sisters in the land of the Mohawks, and Jean-Baptiste was the one who carried me away from the land of the Canienga."

"And are you grateful to him for that?"

"More than I can ever show."

"How well do you know Jean-Baptiste now?"

"Much, much better than before. He is a good man."

"There has been an allegation that you have engaged in improper conduct with him."

She looked at the priest, and her eyes cleared and focused on him. Her brown eyes penetrated his. She was not defensive in any way. She looked evenly at him and slowly shook her head. "Whoever has spoken this, it is not true."

"Camille said she saw you sleeping near him early one morning."

"I remember. He came in late when we were all asleep. He lay down near me and went immediately to sleep. Her suspicion is unfounded." A look of sorrow passed across her face, pity for Camille and her pettiness. "This same charge was made by my stepmother before I arrived here. Why do people suspect evil in each other, Father? Don't they know they are only seeing the evil they carry within?"

"Camille also said," the priest tried to demonstrate to her the reasonableness of his doubt, "that you helped him slide his canoe out of the forest."

"Yes, I did. He asked for my help, and I helped him." She looked at the priest with perfect frankness. "You are my confessor, Father. You don't believe her suspicions, do you?"

Father Cholonec bowed his head. He had harbored a suspicion which, in her presence, now seemed baseless and mean-spirited.

"No, of course not, Kateri, but it is my duty to inquire into your spiritual well-being."

"I am grateful for your concern," she said evenly, and she rose from the chair and started for the door.

"Kateri," he said, his voice catching in his throat.

She paused on the threshold and turned around. "Yes, Father?"

"I should have said nothing."

"It is, as you say, your duty." She looked at him with beneficence and love. "I will pray for Camille that she may trust her husband again. I have already made a vow, Father, which you now confirm."

"Yes?"

"I will never go on the hunt again. Next winter, I will remain at the mission no matter the scarcity of food. The hunt is a custom from former times, and I will not honor it. This allegation will not be repeated. I will keep company with women only. I will stay away from men." She pulled the shawl down over her eyes, tucked her cross beneath the tunic, and went out into the spring sunshine.

Father Cholonec sat in his room in front of the hearth filled with wet, gray ashes. He was depleted of energy. Now he had the unenviable task of telling Camille.

Before he could, though, Father Claude returned:

"Have you spoken with Kateri?"

"I have. She was not defensive or upset in the least."

"She is God's chosen one, Father. I feel it whenever I'm near her."

"I wish I had your faith in her," Father Cholonec said.

"I wish you did, too."

CHAPTER EIGHTEEN
KATERI'S BAND

I.

Kateri was watching the men work on the new church. A framework of hewn timbers rose thirty feet with a peaked roof like the massive church across the river in Ville-Marie. Wearing a leather apron, the architect stood at a table made of planks on sawhorses while men, half of them *Haudenosaunee*, were on scaffolds of lashed saplings, sawing, and hammering the thick timbers of the superstructure. Sensing someone near, Kateri turned and saw a woman gazing as intently at the work as she had.

"Which side will the men occupy, and which side will the women?" Kateri asked.

The woman was older. The lines on her face and her manner revealed that she had lived through considerable hardship.

"Surely it will be as it is now. Women on the right, men on the left."

They entered the roofless structure.

"This chapel of wood is not all that God asks us to build," Kateri said in a low whisper. "Our souls, too, must be temples for Him to live in." She looked around, then bowed her head. "I do not deserve to enter here when so often I have driven God from my heart. I should be ordered to remain outside with the dogs."

"I too," the woman said, also bowing her head and making the sign of the cross, "am a great sinner."

"I have not met you."

"I have been at the mission for three summers. I arrived when it was downriver at Kentake."

"I arrived last summer."

"Yes, Hot Cinders sent you. I know of you," the woman said. "You are Kateri."

"I am."

"I am called Tegaigenta and was baptized Marie-Thérèse. I am Oneida like Hot Cinders. He has asked me about you and how well you have acclimated to life here at the mission."

Kateri kept her eyes cast down. "I can't control what others say."

"No, but Hot Cinders asks about you from concern. He is a good man, if a bit explosive. My husband grew up with him in the same *ohwahchira*."

"You are married?"

"I was," she said with sorrow. "My husband died on the hunt."

The noise of the hammers was distracting. Kateri spoke: "Each morning, I walk down to the tall cross that stands on the knoll above the river. Let us go there now."

The two women walked together.

"I went on the hunt this winter," Kateri said. "I shall never go again. Being away from mass and the sacraments grieves me deeply. Our people revert to the old ways when they are away from the priests."

"Truer words I have not heard." They reached the cross on a low mound overlooking the broad sweep of the river and sat together on a large stone. "Since you know this about the hunt, I will tell you my story," Marie-Thérèse said. She took a deep breath and expelled it. "Three winters ago, we went into the woods, eleven of us, my husband, myself, my sister's son, three other men, three other women, and two children. We journeyed north to the river of the Ottawa to hunt, but the snows came so heavily that the deer, caribou, and moose could not migrate. After some days, we had snared only one rabbit, and it was quickly eaten. Famine threatened us. We boiled and drank hot water to cease the agony in our stomachs. We boiled and ate leather we had packed for moccasins. We dug for roots and boiled the bark of trees to eat. At last, we gave up the hunting camp and fled downriver to reach the valley and find meat.

"One of our number, a Mohawk, indicated he wanted to split off from the group and go hunting alone. He took the other man, a Seneca. In three days, the Mohawk returned, and no longer did his eyes burn with the glow of hunger. It was clear he had killed and eaten the Seneca.

"At this time, my husband became sick, delirious. I knew the others wanted to kill and butcher him, but along with my sister's son, I guarded him day and night. Seeing that we would not agree to sacrifice him, they moved on without us, and soon after, when the three of us were alone, my husband died. After my nephew and I buried him, we hastened to catch the others. Now there were nine of us. The Mohawk eyed the woman who slept alone with her boys, thinking to kill and eat her since she was the most vulnerable. He asked me, as the Christian of the group, whether Jesus Christ excused murder because of necessity."

"He needed to ask?" Kateri whispered.

"Yes! Perhaps he needed my approval, or maybe he was only joking!" Marie-Thérèse clasped Kateri's arm. She was sobbing. "But I did not reply! The Mohawk asked me a question about the teachings I had studied. I was struck dumb with fear as to what he would do to me and my nephew if my answer displeased him. So, he went ahead and killed her and her two boys. And we," she was sobbing inconsolably, gripping Kateri's arm, "we . . . ate . . . them!"

The bright spring sun shone on the river where great white

sculptures of ice floated breezily along. Kateri put her arm around Marie-Thérèse and held her. "The winter hunt puts our souls in peril."

"I feared that if I tried to stop them, they would kill my nephew and me and butcher us too. At that moment, I promised the Lord, our God, and Savior," Marie-Thérèse spoke in earnest, "that if He delivered me from that ordeal, I would confess my sins and change my life."

Kateri hugged her. "Let us vow that when the winter comes, we will remain at the mission, two women without men. Our bodies might suffer but our souls will not be in peril."

"It shall be so." Marie-Thérèse took Kateri's hand in hers, and they sat together on the mound above the river, Kateri's arm still around her new friend, who tried to stop weeping.

2.

In the ensuing weeks, the two women established a deep friendship and their conversations focused on spiritual matters. They examined their past lives for sins and shortcomings, and they vowed to avoid the gossip and quarrels of other villagers. One cloudy afternoon, Marie-Thérèse initiated Kateri into the practice of mortification. She led her into the forest and cut a handful of willow shoots. In a secluded place, she exposed her back and instructed Kateri to whip her. She did this for penance, she said, to chastise her flesh for its weakness.

Confused by this, Kateri paused with the switches in her hand.

"Please, please," Marie-Thérèse asked, and so Kateri whipped her, first gently and then more vigorously. Biting her lip to remain silent, Marie-Thérèse closed her eyes and accepted the pain. Soon, her shoulders were a deep red. When blood showed through the skin of the abrasions, Kateri stopped. Marie-Thérèse pulled her tunic down to cover the marks, and she answered Kateri's quizzical expression: "The pain takes away my sorrow and replaces it with joy. Now the Lord knows I am truly sorry, that I accept this penance for my sins."

"May I try?"

"Yes, of course."

Kateri loosened the tie of her tunic and pulled it down, exposing her back to Marie-Thérèse. The elder, more experienced woman stood to the side and, holding the willow shoots firmly, whistled them through the air to whip Kateri's pockmarked skin. Kateri cried out at the pain, but at the second blow, she closed her eyes and pressed her lips together to internalize it. Marie-Thérèse administered a dozen blows, then stopped, tossed the shoots aside, and went to Kateri. She gently pulled up her tunic and held her as the younger woman trembled and wept.

"Are you in pain?" Marie-Thérèse asked.

"It soothed my heart," Kateri said. "I meditated on Jesus as the Romans scourged Him at the pillar."

"Let us return to the chapel and pray," Marie-Thérèse said, embracing her. "May this help us both to receive the Lord with deeper reverence."

They met daily and walked to the small rise above the river where the large log cross stood to mark the mission to wayfarers. One day, looking upriver, across the rapids of La Chine, the rising sun caught the buildings of Ville-Marie and made them shine.

"I have long wanted to journey to Ville-Marie," Kateri said. "Anastasia, whom I call 'Mother,' grows old and set in her ways and will not make the journey."

"I will go with you," Marie-Thérèse said. "Let us borrow a canoe and go tomorrow."

"Yes," Kateri said. "I will ask Father Claude for a letter to take so we may visit the convent chapel."

Marie-Thérèse agreed to borrow the canoe, and Kateri

approached Father Claude after evening benediction for a letter of introduction.

"What is it you wish to see?"

"We wish to see how the French live in their community."

"Yes, I think that would help you understand many things." The priest went to the rectory and composed a letter of introduction to the Sisters of the Hôtel-Dieu and the Sisters of the Congregation.

The next morning, the two friends glided downstream to see the new French settlement on the Isle of Montreal. They paddled around the island and along the riverbank where it faced East, past wooden docks and warehouses built on piles driven into the mud. Eventually, they landed and climbed up the hill into a wondrously busy village of French soldiers and clerics, log cabins, natives, and women in religious habits.

With her smattering of French, Marie-Thérèse asked directions, and soon the two were received at the convent of the Sisters of the Congregation. They were shown into the small room Mother Bourgeoys used as her office. When the nun entered in her long habit with a rosary at her waist, they stood to greet her. Kateri and Marie-Thérèse were pleased to find that the mother superior knew their language and welcomed them warmly. They had many questions.

Mother Bourgeoys introduced them to a sister who took them on a tour of the school. The two young women marveled at the white habits, the cleanliness of the place, and the order in the classrooms where the young Canadian girls were taught. At midday, they were brought to the mess hall, where they ate with the nuns. The nuns prayed before and after their meal, and one of them read from a holy book while the others ate. They watched in awe as the nuns wielded slender iron knives and forks to cut and spear their meat, boiled squash, and fluffy white potatoes.

Later in the afternoon, they visited the Hôtel-Dieu, a hospital operated by the Hospitallers of St. Joseph, where the ill and wounded were brought to be nursed and cured, and the dying kept comfortable until the end. Again, the two Iroquois women were in awe of the order and cleanliness of the halls and the wards, the spotless white habits of the nuns, and the calm way they ministered to the sick. There were crucifixes throughout the hospital.

It was close to evening when they walked back to the river-bank, pushed off, and paddled home.

When they met the next morning by the great cross, Kateri shared an idea:

"I wish to live and serve others as those women do. Do you know how one joins that house?"

"I have a friend who lived for many years in Quebec," said Marie-Thérèse. "She also spent a long time at the Huron mission of Lorette. Let us ask her."

They walked together through the village to a longhouse at the eastern end. An Iroquois woman in her fifties greeted Marie-Thérèse warmly, and upon meeting Kateri, embraced her. Her name was also Marie. Marie-Thérèse put the question to her:

"We visited the nuns in Ville-Marie yesterday and toured the hospital and the girls' school. How does one become a nun to serve in that way?"

The older Marie shook her head and smiled sadly. "The black-robes share with us the mysteries of their faith, and they counsel us to receive the sacraments and lead lives of virtue and prayer and tell us we are equal in the eyes of the Lord. But they do not allow us to join their nuns. The whites keep such secret knowl-edge to themselves. I doubt that any People of the Longhouse will ever become nuns or priests, but I was told once how it is done."

"Well, tell us what is required, and we will ask Father Frémin. We are strong workers and would do anything to join the nuns in their holy way of life."

"Come, let us walk," Marie said. Kateri and Marie-Thérèse led her down to the cross overlooking the river. At the foot of the boiling rapids, there was a small island named for the blue and white herons who frequently landed on great flapping wings to fish in the shallow water.

"The biggest rule they enforce is that women and men, when they enter the order, renounce sleeping with each other. They do not marry, and they do not have relations or bear children. They must promise to be obedient and humble and not care about possessions."

"That poses no difficulty," Kateri said.

"The priests retreat from the world and study for ten or twelve years. Only after they have read many, many books and proved themselves to be dedicated are they allowed to submit to the bishop and be accepted as priests. And only men can become priests."

"Why?" Kateri asked. "Among our people, the women have always ruled the *ohwahchiras,* appointing and removing chiefs. Why is it that among the French, only men can be priests?"

"They view women as unclean," Marie said. "That is why they worship the virgin."

Kateri looked at them both in wonderment. "Unclean?"

"Yes," Marie said.

"Unclean and weak and changeable," Marie-Thérèse added. "Don't you know?"

"No," Kateri said. "That is nonsense. Men are unclean until they receive the Prayer. Men are crude and insensitive. They take more than one wife, and change their wives at will. Women are life-givers. They till the field and bear the children while men kill. Men hunt and wage war. I have kept myself away from men not because I was unclean but because they were. Not until I met the blackrobes did I understand that men could be gentle and kind."

"The religious take vows, both the men and the women," Marie explained. "They vow three things, poverty, chastity, and obedience."

"We have not done it formally," Kateri said once more, "but those vows apply to us."

"Yes," Marie-Thérèse agreed.

"Why don't we ask the priest if we can take the vows and become nuns?"

"Who will ask him?" Marie did not want to do it.

"I will," Kateri said.

"And where shall we remove ourselves if he allows us to do this? Surely we cannot remain in the village!"

Kateri looked across the boiling water. "Heron Island."

"Yes," Marie-Thérèse said.

3.

Kateri vacillated on whom to ask for permission. Father Claude was agreeable and pleasant and never declined any favor, but Father Cholonec, though more austere, was her confessor, so he would be preferable. Father Frémin was superior of the mission, though, so whether she asked either of the other two, they would need to ask Father Frémin anyway. She went to the rectory that afternoon to see him.

"Yes, my daughter," Father Frémin said cordially, escorting her into the sitting area, "what can I do for you?"

Kateri took the chair that was offered and pulled back her shawl. She looked at the priest with blank, unfocused eyes.

"I need guidance, Father." She placed her cross on his desk.

The priest rubbed his chin and thought to himself that it was no wonder she never married. The smallpox scars marred the skin of her face and, no doubt, the skin of her body. Additionally, as it had with others who contracted the disease, it may have rendered her barren.

"I am happy you came to me."

"Marie-Thérèse and I visited the convents attached to the hospital and the school in Ville-Marie."

"It is good you have seen that. They are holy women who

198

dedicate their lives to others. They live according to the highest aspirations of our faith."

"Yes," Kateri said, "and we wish to live as they do."

The priest put up his hands and shook his head. "That is quite impossible. The rules forbid any religious orders accepting natives as members."

"We understand that. We have also spoken with Marie, a woman of much experience who lived for a time in Quebec and then at Lorette. We have a proposal, and we hope you will agree."

Father Frémin's eyes were lit with mirth. He admired how composed and undaunted she was. The childish thinking of the natives amused him. Their response to the pictures Father Claude drew of heaven and hell, and a whole line of saints and sinners proved to him that their spiritual gifts, even after much instruction, remained primitive and superstitious.

"Tell me."

"We want you or the great Onontio or else your king across the salt sea to grant us Heron Island so we can build a convent of sisters there."

"You want to begin your own order of sisters?" The thought tickled him. She nodded in earnest, which only made him laugh harder.

Kateri leaned back in her chair and watched this grown man, this holy man, clap his hands and laugh. "Oh, that is good!" he said. "Wonderful! You three want to start a convent!" And he laughed and laughed as she stoically observed him.

"Do you think we are joking? Why should we not?"

"Why you're . . . you're too . . . too young in the faith! Where would you live?"

"Heron Isle."

"Young people go there to . . . to frolic . . . and hunters camp on that island. You would not have a day's privacy. You would not be safe. Your idea is foolish and completely out of the question."

"Are we less holy than French women?"

"Of course not," he laughed silently and shook his head, "but you need to read and study and go through years of training. It is impossible."

Kateri's fierce sense of justice was offended. "I'm sorry I wasted your time, Father." And she stood and left the rectory.

Building the new church at St. Francis Xavier mission. The
figures praying beneath the cross are thought to be Kateri,
Marie and Marie- Thérèse. Drawing by Father
Claude Chauchetière.

CHAPTER NINETEEN
KATERI AND MARIE-THÉRÈSE MAKE A VOW

I.

K ateri told the others how the priest disapproved of their idea to establish an order of sisters. She did not tell them he laughed at the notion. His laughter made her feel foolish and shamed, quite the opposite of how ennobled and connected she felt when praying in church.

Kateri and Marie-Thérèse went to a cabin in the mission graveyard where they could be alone. They whipped each other's backs in punishment for their vanity in thinking they might aspire to the spiritual height of French women. The priest had made it clear they were inferior. Still, they knew that what he believed did not nullify the message of Jesus Christ.

Concerned that he had offended Kateri, Father Frémin visited Anastasia and told her of Kateri's yearning to do more in her faith. He asked Anastasia to nominate her—but not either of her companions—as a member of the Holy Family Society. This exclusive praying society, like the medicine societies of their homeland, accepted Kateri into its rites and ceremonies, and she attended with devotion.

Anastasia welcomed the opportunity to pray with her young protégé twice each week, and Kateri showed her the utmost respect and affection. But Anastasia noticed a change in her, and she went to Father Cholonec with her concern.

"The girl went to Father Frémin," he explained, "with the idea that she and two others could start a convent on Heron Island."

"Marie-Thérèse has taken Kateri's affections from me, her mother's best friend and her adopted mother. Me, the one who saved her from certain death and serves now as her sponsor and guide."

"I'm sure she loves you as she always has, but she is young," the priest observed.

"She is twenty-two."

"Young people often become distracted by new people and ideas. Kateri might still marry," the priest observed. "That would make her more settled. There are many young men here who could benefit from a union with one so blessed. She need not have children. Many of our married couples have taken a vow to live as brother and sister."

"She will never marry," Anastasia said.

"It hurts nothing to ask."

"I know her heart, so I will put her sister Camille up to this." Anastasia did not know of their estrangement since the episode on the winter hunt.

The following day, Camille caught up with Kateri on her way home from the chapel.

"We have not spent time together in a very long time, sister," Camille said. "I miss the discussions we used to have."

"I have been praying with Marie-Thérèse and, occasionally, her friend Marie. We keep to ourselves."

"Yes, but you still live, thanks be to God, with Anastasia and Jean-Baptiste and me, and we miss your company. I have a request of you that will help all the people you love. Most of all it will help you. If you would do this favor for us and for yourself, we all could be completely happy."

"What is it, sister?"

"Find a good Christian man, someone perhaps like Joseph Kryn, and marry him."

Kateri pulled down her shawl. "There is no other like Joseph Kryn."

"It's not that Jean-Baptiste and I begrudge you the food you eat, but if you brought a hunter into our cabin, we would all benefit."

Kateri stopped, turned to her, and pulled up her shawl to reveal her scarred face so that Camille might see how absurd the idea was. "I know you suggest this because you care for me."

"That is true. Above all, we want you to be happy."

"This is a big step, so I pray you give me some time."

"Oh, of course! Take as long as you need. It is not my intention to pry into your affairs. I know you will see the wisdom of what I ask when you think about it."

"Until I give you my answer, please don't speak of this again. To anyone."

"As you wish." Camille bowed and left her side.

The first thing the following morning, Kateri sought out Father Cholonec and told him what Camille had suggested.

"Please consider it," he said.

"It is out of the question, Father."

"Your conduct is very unusual."

"Not at all. In Ville-Marie, I saw two large houses filled with women who live without men. I suggested to Father Frémin that Marie-Thérèse and I form such a society, and he laughed at me."

"But those were French nuns. Your conduct is highly unusual among your people."

"You teach that there is one God, and we are all the same in His eyes. Why then are there different rules that depend on our races?"

"For one thing, you neither read nor write."

"Does God care about such things?"

"Without study, you can't possibly learn all you need to know to take vows."

"I know that my heart belongs to Jesus Christ. What else is there to know?"

"There are many doctrines . . .'

"Does Jesus care about doctrines?"

"He does."

"Well then, can I make my own decisions?"

"Absolutely," Father Cholonec said.

"Then I have decided I will not marry.

"Think it over carefully because Camille's idea has merit."

"Father, I have thought about it in every possible way. Marriage is impossible."

"Are you not concerned about providing for yourself when you are old?"

"I do not fear poverty. My work will furnish me with the necessities. I can always find furs, rabbit skins if need be, to stitch together as a covering for winter. Didn't Christ say that His father cares for even the birds of the air?"

The priest did not laugh. He felt her resolve. "Do not close your mind, Kateri. Believe that Camille has your best interest at heart."

"How can you say that? Doesn't the virtue of chastity open our hearts to receive grace?"

"But there are other concerns, worldly concerns."

"Not for me."

"Give the matter more consideration. You will see its wisdom."

She bowed humbly and left the rectory.

Learning that Kateri had seen Father Cholonec, Camille sought her out that afternoon.

"Have you reached a decision?"

"We were not to speak of this."

"What did Father say?"

"He told me to consider it further, but I have decided. I will not marry."

"But the way you carry on with your new friends! Don't you see you open yourself to the ridicule of men?"

"I care not what others say."

"But you expose yourself to temptation."

"The flattery of men or their gifts mean nothing to me. Men never give without expectation, and they cannot give me anything I need that I cannot get myself. I will never submit to a man, any man. Nor will I speak of this marrying business again."

She walked away, and Camille let her go.

The days shortened, and relentless pounding rain stripped the trees of their leaves and churned the village pathways into mud. Going on the winter hunt became the topic of discussion in the mission. Anastasia importuned Joseph Kryn to ask Kateri to accompany his family, and he did so the next day.

"Great Chief, I am honored that you invite into your hunting camp, but I vowed last spring I would never leave the mission to live in the wild."

"Such vows are not binding," Joseph Kryn said. "Karitha and Peter and my nephews Matthew and Luke were excited when I told them you might be with us this winter. Please reconsider."

"The use of a vow is that it settles things once and for all," she said. "My mind is made up. Thank you for inviting me, Great Chief, but I will remain behind in the mission this winter."

Marie-Thérèse and Kateri continued to meet in the cabin in the middle of the cemetery to chastise each other before confessing their sins. After one particularly severe session, where Marie-

Thérèse begged Kateri to whip her until she bled, she revealed her reason for wanting such severe punishment.

"I must break my word to you, Kateri," she announced. "I have been asked to join a hunting party, and I have no other means of supporting myself. I cannot remain at the mission this winter. I hope you will forgive me." Marie-Thérèse brightened with a thought. "Perhaps you could come with us?"

"No," Kateri said. "I will remain here at the mission."

"What will you do for food?"

"I am more concerned about food for the soul than food for the body."

Kateri encouraged her friend to whip her soundly for the resentment she felt at Marie-Thérèse's backsliding.

At the next meeting of the Holy Family Society, Kateri walked home with Anastasia.

"What have you decided about marrying?" the older woman asked.

"My decision has not changed."

"It would solve many problems."

"If marriage is such a boon, Mother, why don't you try it again?"

"Ahhh. I see."

"Let there be no further talk about it then."

"There won't be."

2.

When the villagers left for the winter hunt, Kateri remained behind with Anastasia in her cabin. Through the long winter nights, they huddled by the fire as winds howled down the frozen river, whipping the snow up into high drifts against the thin bark walls. In the dark and cold, the idea of another vow took hold of Kateri, and in late February, without discussing it with anyone, Kateri sought out Father Cholonec.

"Father, I have survived the winter without a man in my life.

I have proved to myself, and to you, that it is possible. I want to vow to remain a virgin for the rest of my life. As the French sisters do."

"That would be unprecedented," he said. "Take a few days to weigh this matter, and after that time, if you still want to, I will consider it."

"There is no question of deliberation," Kateri said. "I made this resolution when I was a girl, and I have been living according to it ever since. I will have no other spouse than Jesus Christ, and I wish to proclaim my vow publicly to honor and glorify Him and to settle the matter once and for all."

Father Cholonec thought a moment. "This matter has often been discussed by you and those who care about you. I see that you are sincere, and you wish to do this not simply to emulate the good sisters, but from your own desire to follow Christ."

"Yes, Father!" She closed her eyes, and a look of peace passed across her face.

"Very well, I will allow you to take this a vow before our congregation."

"Oh," she said, releasing a pent-up breath, "thank you! Thank you, Father."

She opened her eyes and looked at the priest. With this deep personal struggle resolved, her appearance changed. An inner quiet suffused her scarred face. She looked serene and deeply happy.

So it was that on the March 25, the feast of Archangel Gabriel's announcement to the Blessed Virgin, in the chapel decorated with pine boughs, as the men's and women's choirs sang the offertory hymn, Kateri walked up the aisle of the chapel in a white tunic she borrowed from Marie-Thérèse. Anastasia had braided white ribbons in her hair. She knelt at the altar rail, and she renounced marriage and vowed perpetual chastity.

"I pray you, Blessed Lady, to present my soul to your Divine Son, for I shall be espoused only to Him until the day of my death. I also pray that you will allow me to consecrate myself to you, my only mother."

She rose from her prayer, weeping for joy, as the chorus swelled:

> *"Immaculate Mary, your praises we sing.*
> *You reign now in Heaven with Jesus our King.*
> *Ave, ave, ave, Maria, Ave, ave, Maria!"*

CHAPTER TWENTY
HEALING THE SICK

I.

F ather Claude had watched Kateri from afar since she
arrived. On occasion, he discussed her progress with the
other two priests. Father Cholonec, as her confessor, and Father
Frémin, as superior of the mission, answered to most of her
needs. She was reserved by nature, so Father Claude had little
opportunity to speak with her. He observed her praying in the
chapel and had often placed the Eucharist on her tongue. They
had nodded to each other in the village lanes. He frequently saw
Kateri and Marie-Thérèse together at the great cross by the
river, but except for half a dozen short conversations, he hardly
knew her.

Shortly after Kateri's vow of celibacy, when the river was free
of ice, Father Frémin went down to Quebec and sailed to France.
He left Father Cholonec in charge of the mission, and Cholonec
put Father Claude in charge of visiting the sick.

Kateri's austerities continued. Confirmed in her vow of
celibacy, the young woman fasted two days a week, often sprin-
kling ashes in her food to make it less appealing. With Marie-
Thérèse, she found new ways to mortify her flesh: they walked

barefoot on the snow; they immersed themselves in the freezing currents of the river. One night in the throes of her devotion, Kateri branded her legs with live coals, as her people had branded their slaves, to prove she was the slave of Christ. Another night she put a live coal between her toes and burned a hole in her foot. She wore a belt with iron studs around her waist when she went into the forest to cut wood. She fell one day and lay on the ground gasping for breath but refused to let Marie-Thérèse remove the studded belt. On learning from the priest that a saint in the Old World had slept on thorns, she cut thorn branches and put them in her bed to remind herself of her suffering Lord.

These mortifications did not come to the attention of the priests for a long time, but when at last Marie-Thérèse confessed about the severity of the whippings, Father Cholonec ordered the women to stop. They continued other practices still, and the fasting, exposure to the elements, and constant prayer wore down Kateri's constitution. When spring arrived once more, Kateri Tekakwitha was weak and thin.

The first time Father Claude ministered to her, she was confined to her sleeping shelf from an injury when a branch fell on her leg as she was chopping wood. Anastasia was stirring the kettle, and she nodded and pointed her ladle to where the young woman lay. Father Claude went to her and sat beside her.

"Kateri?" he whispered quietly.

She lay on her back, eyes closed and palms upward. Only after he spoke did he understand she was praying, not sleeping. Kateri opened her eyes slowly as if waking from a dream. She looked up at him, and his heart stopped.

"Father," she said softly. The light from her eyes bathed him in otherworldly radiance. In her gaze he was enveloped in pure beauty and love. Her aura of grace momentarily encircled him too. The sounds of the longhouse faded, and he felt as if he were floating. His breath caught in his throat, and he dared not stir. He understood and he was overwhelmed to see that Kateri had found a pathway into the presence of God. She was in the divine presence, in that mystical state he had first achieved on Christmas Eve eleven years before.

Kateri lifted her cross toward him, inviting him to hold it with her. When he touched her hand, a force of energy flooded into him and filled him completely. He looked into her eyes and saw that they were struggling to focus. She was in another place, and it was from the depths of a mystery beyond all understanding that she gazed at him. Her look conveyed both welcome and encouragement as if to say, "Approach! Approach!" Overwhelmed, he knelt, humbled and quivering, and hung his head.

"Oh, Father," she murmured, "I love Jesus so!" Her eyes rolled back, and she closed them and swallowed. "Jesus loves us all," she whispered, "and in Him and only in Him can we love each other." She slowly opened her eyes and reached up and touched the priest on the back of the hand. "Release all your doubts, Father," she said as if she knew his thoughts, and she smiled so beautifully that he began to sob. "Surrender," she whispered, "surrender."

Tears flowed down his face, and his heart was bursting. He saw that all the weakness, all the illness, all the wounds were in him, not in her. She was healing *him!* She was opening his doubts and his flaws and shining a brilliant, cleansing light into all the dark corners of his soul.

"You should rest," he murmured, and the noise and the presence of others in the longhouse returned.

"Thank you, Father," she whispered, and as she fell asleep, he traced the sign of the cross on her forehead.

2.

The rest of that day, while he went about his work, Father Claude wondered if he had not created this epiphany. But each time he revisited those moments with Kateri, he felt again the flood of light and love that came from her. She held the healing power that his sick heart sought. Before sleeping that night, he knelt in his small cell and prayed in thanksgiving for her holy presence in the mission and in his life. As he prayed, Father Claude found himself praying to the powerful light he had seen radiating from her, and then he realized he might be praying *to* her! His customary self-doubt whispered "idolatry," but then he silenced his interior critic and lay back and surrendered completely to the heavenly rapture.

The next morning and the next, he returned to her cabin. Rather than be depleted by familiarity, the holy energy increased in strength and brilliance even as her body was wasting away.

3.

The first morning Kateri missed mass, Father Chauchetière waited until sunrise and then hastened to Anastasia's home. He murmured a prayer as he lifted the bearskin curtain and entered the dim, smoky cabin. A shaft of daylight penetrated the murk, then died as the flap fell closed. He coughed at the smoke from the low fire.

"Why, Father!" Anastasia rose from her seat, surprised. She was grinding corn for the day's meals. "What an honor!" There was a stirring on a pallet to the other side of the fire.

"Kateri was not at mass this morning."

"She is weak today," Anastasia said, "and I keep her company."

The priest stepped around the fire pit to squat down at the side of Kateri's bed. She lay on her back, her long black hair unbraided and fanned out on the fur she used as a pillow. She turned her head slowly and opened her eyes. The dim light of the cabin allowed her to open her eyes fully.

"Hello, Father," she whispered in a hoarse voice. Her lips were dry. Anastasia came over, gently lifted her head, and held a

gourd dipper of water for her to sip. Kateri smiled weakly.
"Thank you for visiting. I am not dressed to welcome you."

"You must get back your strength." Gently he touched her
cheek. "We need you here."

"If it is God's will." She sighed and lay back on the deerskin.

"We missed you in chapel this morning."

"I miss mass, too, Father, and communion. Communion most
of all."

He took her hand and squeezed it. "We shall nurse you back
to strength."

"She hardly eats," Anastasia said.

"You must eat," the priest said.

"I try, Father, yet I have no hunger for bodily food."

The priest bowed his head and said nothing. He made the
sign of the cross on her forehead. "I will return at midday."

"Thank you, Father."

Father Chauchetière conferred briefly with Anastasia, and
then he pulled aside the bearskin curtain, and again daylight
briefly illuminated the two women in the smoky room.

"He was weeping," Anastasia said. "He is afraid of losing
you."

"I am so tired," she whispered.

"Sleep, little one." Anastasia went back to grinding her corn.

4.

As he left the longhouse, Father Claude felt again the despair
he had not felt since his crossing from France. The thought of
losing this young woman stirred up a wild gale in his soul. He
vividly remembered the massive rolling waves as they churned
and broke, lifting him up and plunging him down, the wind
howling annihilation in every blast. He felt the same stark terror.
Not since attending at his father's deathbed had he felt the
weight of such a loss. Worst of all, he knew there was no hope.

Soon she would leave the world behind. The divine light she carried within would shine no more on him.

As a boy, when his father died, he threw himself into the arms of God, and his entire life and all its seeming wrong turns had brought him to this moment. Tekakwitha was the opposite of his father. Lacking ambition or vanity or worldly aims, her passivity, docility, and her unyielding Mohawk will had shown him a new path. He had vacillated for decades between certainty and doubt. Now he must throw himself into God's arms again, and Kateri would show him the way.

Father Claude's duties included teaching the children. When he went to class that morning, and they greeted him with such innocence and joy, he knew what to do. They cheered when he asked if they would visit Kateri with him. The children loved Kateri, and they were excited and happy. After class, he led the dozen children along the lane, and when they entered the long-house, the quiet, smoky place was instantly filled with their laughter and happy chatter. Anastasia propped Kateri up on her bed, and Father Claude arranged the children six on each side. He showed them his drawings of the nativity scene, of Jesus as a lad among the elders, of John the Baptist baptizing Jesus in the River Jordan with the Holy Spirit, a white dove hovering in the rays of the sun, of Jesus healing the blind, raising Lazarus from the dead, entering Jerusalem, offering bread at the Last Supper, suffering in the garden, on the cross and then rising from the dead.

As he showed the pictures, the little boys and girls happily recited what each represented. Father Claude called them "my little magpies," and they all tried to win Kateri's approval. When they finished, they all touched her hands and her arms and recited at Father Claude's direction: "Get well, Kateri. Soon it will be spring, and we will play outside with you."

"Thank you for coming to see me," she said softly and smiled at them. "Listen to Father and learn your lessons well."

"We will!" they promised, and soon they were skipping from the cabin out into the clear, chilly sunlight.

"Thank you, Father," Kateri said. "You are so very kind to me." In the dim light, her eyes were fully opened, though unfocused, as if she were looking through him.

"Get well," he said, and his voice broke. Tears pressed at his eyes, and he struggled to keep from sobbing.

"She's so tired," Anastasia said. She helped the priest up. He was slow to stand.

One of the little girls stuck her face through the crack of light in the doorway.

"Are you coming, Father?"

"I am." He was weeping now, peering down at Kateri's small, wasted form recumbent on the skins in the smoky cabin. "Do not leave us, Kateri," he said, sobbing softly. "These . . . these little ones have so much to learn . . . from you."

"We must do what is willed," she whispered. Her eyes fluttered, and she nodded her head, folded her hands, and closed her eyes.

"Come, Father," Anastasia put her hand under the priest's elbow. "She sleeps." He hid his face in a handkerchief. The woman led him from her firepit to the door and then out into the sunlight. The sun on the brown mud of the fields and the sparkling blue water startled him after the smoky confines of the sick chamber.

"Get her to eat and bring her back to us," Father Chauchetière said, pressing her hand strongly between both of his. "Please, Anastasia, bring her back."

"I am praying, Father."

**Iroquois traveling in bark canoes. Drawing by Father
Claude Chauchetière.**

CHAPTER TWENTY-ONE
KATERI'S DEATH

I.

Walking on snowshoes, Joseph Kryn carried the bloody haunches of a caribou, one on each shoulder. Behind him, his twin nephews, Matthew and Paul, each carried a forequarter, and his son Peter proudly held the head by the antlers in his good hand.

Kryn had taken his family far into the northern woods. The hunting was favorable this year, deer and elk were plentiful, and now the caribou were migrating south for the sweet grass. Kryn had waited in a blind while the boys chased a large male caribou into a defile, then he killed it with his spear. He field-dressed the carcass with his hatchet and knife. In former days, he would have cut the heart, warm and pulsing, and held it to the sun god before cutting it into strips and feeding it raw to his fellow hunters. Today he offered the heart to his Lord, who watched over him and sent plentiful game so he could provide for his family.

The small procession emerged from the forest at the hunting camp by the river. The camp faced south and east and so had sun all day. It was sheltered from the stiff west wind and the bliz-

KATERI – A BEACON IN THE WILDERNESS

zards that pounded the mountain's western side. A long, blue panorama of the lowlands and rivers opened before them.

"Again, you return with meat!" Karitha said. She was outside, scraping an elk hide stretched on a frame. "God be praised!"

Joseph Kryn deposited the haunches on the snow and went to his wife. His shoulders and arms bulged from the physical work of the hunting season. He embraced her and brushed his nose against her cheek with affection.

"Good wife," he said. "The time of the sun now exceeds the time of darkness. Easter will soon be here. Let us break camp and return to the mission."

"Why? The hunting is good, and we can rest for a week or so. The skins we have cured will bring us cloth and the knives-that-meet (scissors) and hatchets and saws for cutting wood to work on Father's new church. The earth will not be ready for digging and planting until the moon grows full. There is no hurry."

"There is, though," Joseph nodded solemnly.

"Tell me, husband."

"I have held brave warriors as they died on battlefields. I have sat beside the sick as the death rattle sounds. I have returned from the hunt and from warfare to find loved ones gone, and in sorrow, I have lamented not being with them at the last moment."

"What has this to do with returning?"

"Kateri."

Karitha narrowed her eyes. "You believe Kateri has died?"

"She was so weak when we left. She was in my thoughts today."

Karitha scowled. "But you always think of her."

"I sensed she was with me at the moment I killed the caribou. It was as if I heard her whisper that she is being called but wanted to give us a final benediction before she leaves."

"What was she wearing?" Karitha asked with a smirk.

"You trifle with me. What does that matter?"

"I wish to judge if it was truly Kateri."

"She wore moccasins and leggings and a white tunic. She wore her blue shawl like a veil pulled down over her face and she carried her small cross."

"Did you see her eyes?"

"What is the meaning of these questions, wife? Do you doubt me?"

"It is comfortable and easy here," Karitha said. "Look how the sun shines all day and how we have been blessed with good hunting. We have gone so much farther north than usual. The journey will be difficult now with ice in the river and the rocks so slippery on the portages. If we capsize in the rapids, we will perish. Let the Sugar Moon die, and the Fishing Moon rise before we leave, and our journey will be far less perilous."

"Kateri has called me, and we must go," Joseph Kryn said.

"We gave up the dream feast when we embraced the Prayer," Karitha pointed to the cross near the entrance to the hut. "A dream is only a dream."

"We leave in two days," Kryn said. "This caribou will provide meat for our journey. Tomorrow you may dress the skin and ready the packs for departure."

"As you say." Karitha turned away, but Kryn went to her and turned her toward him.

"Please understand, wife. Many of the others are coming home from the hunt. Kateri wishes to bless us all before she leaves. This was her message to me. Let us go down to the valley and receive her graces."

"And what if she is gone by the time we arrive?"

"Have faith, wife. Faith brought you our son, and faith brought us back together. Faith will bring you peace and understanding. I wish to see Kateri one last time."

"As you say."

The following day, Karitha dressed the caribou hide, scraping off the fat, and then she collected their bundles of fur from the winter's kill and stowed them in the canoes. They packed their cooking utensils, knives, spoons, and the kettle. On the morning of the second day, a dark, lowering day that threatened snow, they struck camp and set off.

Joseph Kryn manned the lead canoe, his huge shoulders and arms skilled in whitewater navigation. His nephew Matthew steered the second canoe, following him closely. The current was high and strong with meltwater. Ice floes rattled along with them through the churning water and tumbled alongside down the rapids they shot. A blizzard blinded them the second day and forced them to camp until it spent its fury, but then they continued, the swift, flowing water taking them downward beneath the solemn gray sky between dull white banks of ice.

Late on the fourth day, they reached the broad St. Lawrence. It was so swollen with ice that Kryn decided to camp rather than chance the remaining hours paddling in the dark. As the sun rose over the river on the fifth day, a warm blue sky greeted them, and a gentle wind ruffled the water where ice floes moved swiftly along.

Joseph Kryn walked out on the flat beach where they had camped, spread his arms, and sang to awaken the young ones:

"Up rise the birds from their perch in the trees,
Up burns the sun in the crimson sky,
Up stands my spirit to walk in the world,
Rise, take my hand, and walk bravely with me."

The boys came running from the tent and joined him at the river. He lifted his son Peter to the rising sun, and the twins danced and sang. Karitha kindled the fire and grilled loin cuts of caribou. They ate, struck camp, and soon were on the river among the ice floes that gulls and pigeons rode, squawking and complaining.

Ahead, the island of Montreal came into view. The rapids at La Chine were so treacherous with high water, they went ashore to portage along the trail, then put their canoes back into the water. Finally, they were on the river with the mission to the southeast. They saw its gray stockade and small cabins with smoke curling up and the chapel with its cross and simple belfry in the center.

Joseph Kryn and Peter steered their canoes to shore. Many of the villagers had returned from the hunt. A dozen canoes were inverted on the bank.

"Let us hope we are not too late," Kryn said. He stepped into the water and hauled the canoe up on the bank. He spread his arms in thanksgiving for safe transport, then left the twins and Karitha to unpack. He took Peter, and they climbed through the swale and crossed the flood plain. Anastasia was hurrying from the chapel toward her longhouse.

"Anastasia!" he called. "Where are you running? Is the demon chasing you?"

"Do not joke, Joseph Kryn!" she said curtly and continued on.

"Wait! Why do you hurry?"

She stopped and turned. Tears were flowing down the lines of her weathered face. "We are losing her! Kateri!"

2.

Kryn and Peter ran with Anastasia to her home. All the mission's parishioners had formed a line that led up to the door, waiting to go inside.

"Father Claude just brought communion," Anastasia explained. "She was too weak to attend mass. He brought the Holy Eucharist out of the tabernacle, out of the chapel, and into a longhouse. Everyone marvels that he made an exception for her. She is so weak that he sent me for the holy chrism to anoint her." She showed him the golden disk in her hand.

They moved through the crowd and into the dim longhouse. The poles and beams of the ceiling were depleted of dried corn. The fire was burning brightly, and it cast a flickering light on six or seven forms that surrounded Kateri's sleeping place. Many more stood in the shadows, looking on. Muffled sobs filled the cabin. Father Chauchetière was kneeling by her head, speaking in soft, comforting tones, about to give her communion.

"Wait!" she whispered hoarsely, raising her hand in the air. "I sense . . . Father, I sense Joseph Kryn has arrived."

Chauchetière turned from the pallet and saw Kryn's large buck-skinned form in the firelight.

"Hello, Father!"

"She has been asking for you all morning," the priest said. His face was twisted with grief, and tears flowed freely down his cheeks. He was holding a host between his right thumb and forefinger.

"Come nearer," Kateri whispered. She was dressed in the white tunic Marie-Thérèse had lent her. "It is good you have come, Joseph Kryn, for I am about to leave you."

Anastasia wailed as she said this. Many of the women sent up the cries that were customary at the death of a child. The priest quieted them. "Please, please, she wishes to speak to us."

Kateri lay silently for a long moment, her lustrous eyes roaming about, looking at the chimney hole where the smoke was curling up into the open air.

"I must go, dear friends, Jesus is calling me . . ." Kateri closed her eyes and exhaled, appearing awestruck as if she were viewing a magnificent sunrise. She opened her eyes, surprised to find herself still in the dim cabin and the flickering firelight. She reached for Kryn's hand.

"Good Joseph Kryn."

He knelt by her bed of furs, opposite Father Claude, and held her hand. This seemed to strengthen her, and she smiled.

"Do not be sad, all of you that I love." She turned to the priest and nodded. She closed her eyes, opened her mouth, and extended her tongue to receive the host. Father Chauchetière trembled as he placed the host on her tongue. She closed her eyes, savored it, and then slowly swallowed. When she opened her eyes again, she had an expression of deep contentment.

Then suddenly, she shuddered and held out her hand to the priest.

"Protect our people, Father."

The sobbing grew louder.

"Please stop weeping," she whispered. "Where is Marie-Thérèse?"

"Here, my sister."

"I know what you did today to purchase an easier passage for me. Cease in this custom, sister. Promise me you will."

Marie-Thérèse was weeping inconsolably. "As you say."

Kateri tried to lift her head. Her eyes were unfocused as she looked around. "Do not be sad, all of you that I love. I go now to a place of glory. I will be with you always. I will be present at the death of each of you, and I will pray to God the Father and to Jesus and Mary for you."

The priest bowed and anointed her head with chrism. She gasped and lay her head back on the furs.

"If only you could see the beauty and the joy that await you," she murmured. "Take comfort. At the moment of your death, you too will see why you have lived."

The priest was weeping openly. This unnerved the villagers who had never seen such emotion from a blackrobe. Joseph Kryn placed a hand on the priest's shoulder. "Do not grieve, Father."

"I will be with you always," Kateri whispered hoarsely again, "but I must go now."

"No," Anastasia cried. "My beautiful Aurora!"

"Oh, my friends, pray always to Jesus and to Mary . . . to Jesus and . . . Mary . . ." A deep sigh broke from her lips, and she shivered imperceptibly and whispered, "Jesus . . . Mary . . . I love you." Then she closed her eyes and breathed her last.

"She is gone!" Father Chauchetière wailed. "Gone!" He dropped her hand and looked away, "Gone," he said, his fist at his lips. Anastasia and Marie-Thérèse began to wail again. The priest wrung his hands, then held them up in prayer, and he looked up to where the smoke from the fire curled along the ceiling poles and passed out into the light of the afternoon.

They all stood at her bedside, dumbstruck until a baritone lifted their hearts as Joseph Kryn intoned the *Te Deum*. One by one, the Christian People of the Longhouse took each other's hands and swayed back and forth singing. The priest who had taught them the hymn stood with them, held their hands, and sang reverently over the sunken, ravished flesh of the young Mohawk woman. And their song floated out on the fresh spring air, over the untilled fields, over the cross atop the chapel belfry, and farther out over the broad blue sweep of the river.

3.

A quarter of an hour passed. The villagers turned and threaded out of the cabin into the sun, leaving Father Claude alone in his vigil, kneeling by Kateri, murmuring prayers. In a few minutes, he looked up from his prayers and stared in shock and disbelief. He bent closely over Kateri's face, then he stood, and turned and ran out into the lanes of the village.

"Anastasia! Joseph Kryn! Marie-Thérèse! Come everyone! Come back!"

The villagers heard him and hurried into the lane. "She is still with us! Kateri! You must see!" He held the bearskin curtain open and led them back into the death chamber.

"What does it mean, Father?"

"It is a sign."

"She is so beautiful!" Marie-Thérèse said.

"Never have I seen anything like this," Anastasia said. Joseph Kryn simply folded his arms and smiled.

In the dim firelight, Kateri's face glowed with an unearthly radiance. All the scars and pockmarks that had marred her complexion had vanished. Her skin was now smooth, shining with divine light.

"She is entering heaven!" Anastasia whispered.

"Praise be to God," Marie-Thérèse said.

The curious eyes of other parishioners peered over their shoulders to witness this miracle. Father Chauchetière was on his knees praying over the small, starved form of the Mohawk maid now transfigured in celestial light. With all his doubt resolved, he stopped weeping and stood among them.

4.

The following morning two French *habitans* arrived at the mission for Holy Thursday services. By then, Marie-Thérèse and Anastasia had oiled and braided Kateri's hair, placed new moccasins on her feet, and tenderly laid her out in the borrowed white chemise on a robe of elk skin.

"Who is this beautiful girl who sleeps so peacefully?" one of the farmers asked Father Chauchetière, who had entered behind them.

"The fairest of our mission," the priest said. "Today will be her funeral."

"She is dead?" they asked, astonished, and they crossed themselves and knelt and prayed. After their prayers, they asked if they might make a coffin to bury her in the European way. Father Chauchetière gave them lumber, and while they set to work, he walked down to the riverbank in the bright spring morning.

"Hello, Father!" Joseph Kryn called. Father Chauchetière looked up and nodded. Despite the bright spring sun, his thoughts were dark. Kryn was skillfully repairing his canoe with greased cord, elm bark, and pine pitch. "After the Easter celebration, I will take our skins from the winter hunt to trade at Trois-Rivières."

"That is as it should be. Life goes on."

"You seem troubled, Father."

"She is gone," the priest looked at the ground. "A saint walked among us . . ."

"She is with us still, Father!" Kryn cried. He beat his massive fist on his breast. "We carry her in our hearts."

"Yes, we do. So simple. So perfect. So free from every vanity. She returned to God as pure as he created her. Yes, Joseph, we carry her in our hearts."

"Be of good cheer, then, Father. We helped her in her quest. I among our people and you in the paths of the faith. We had a purpose in her life, and her purpose in ours was to show us . . . perfection." He slapped the priest on the shoulder. "We all have purposes in each other's lives, eh, Father? That is what you instruct. And then when it is time, that purpose ceases, and we leave this world."

"But I miss her," the priest said and sadly began to turn away.

Kryn seized the priest in a firm embrace and lifted him, so they were face to face. "I knew Kateri from her birth. She urges us to follow where she has gone, to seek perfect love, Father, eternal, all-powerful love. Her memory unites us, and we must go forward with this knowledge." He put Father Claude back down.

"Good Joseph Kryn."

"Sunday, we will celebrate Easter, our risen Lord, Christ conquering death. Kateri is most surely in heaven with Him."

"It is as you say, Joseph." He looked at the big man. "Thank you."

"Thank you, Father, for your care and teaching."

As the priest walked away, along the river, he heard Joseph Kryn singing at his work.

5.

At sunset, Father Claude Chauchetière wore his purple stole and white surplice to lead a procession of people from many tribes and nations, along with two acolytes, and half a dozen French *habitans*. Father Cholonec swung the censer to perfume the air with incense through the village to the cemetery where

Joseph Kryn, Peter, and Paul had hewn a grave in the frozen ground.

As they walked through the village, they left the cover of the coffin open so all might see Kateri's face transfigured. When Joseph Kryn and the other pallbearers set down the coffin, Father Claude intoned the final prayers. With outstretched arms and a soaring voice, the priest commended Kateri's remains to the earth, and as the farmers and the native refugees from many nations bowed their heads, he closed the coffin lid. Some held hands, and some were sobbing as Father Claude sprinkled the pine coffin with holy water. Then they lowered their beloved Kateri into the earth. Together they joined hands and sang, and their sweet song echoed out over the broad blue river.

BOOK II
FATHER CLAUDE CHAUCHETIERE

She lived unknown, and few could know
When Lucy ceased to be;
But she is in her grave, and, oh,
The difference to me!

— William Wordsworth

CHAPTER TWENTY-TWO

THE LIGHT OF KATERI

I.

The day after Kateri's burial, Father Chauchetière scribbled remembrances of her in his notebook. He had a vague notion of writing a biography, but he was torn. His certainty that he had encountered a saint demanded him to bear witness, but he knew such an account about a native woman would draw skepticism, even scorn. Who could imagine this depth of piety and evidence of God's grace among the Iroquois? It was a matter of faith, of course, and faith was a private matter. Better to say nothing, do nothing.

At four in the morning on Easter Monday, the fifth day after Kateri's death, the same quiet, dark hour at which she used to enter the chapel, Father Claude was praying to her on his knees in his chamber. Suddenly a brightness flared up beyond his closed eyes as if someone had lit a torch. He opened his eyes, gasped, and fell back on his heels.

Hovering above him was his beloved Kateri, bathed in heavenly light. She held out to him a kettle filled with maize. Her face was radiant, free of all blemishes, and she was looking up to heaven in ecstasy. Her eyes, so dimmed and downcast in life, were open, bright, and filled with joy.

"You return!" he whispered.

She said nothing. She lifted the kettle of maize, offering it to him, and then within her circle of light, two smaller visions appeared to him. In the first apparition, on the right, the new mission church was upside-down. In the second, on the left, a torture victim was being burned on a stake.

"Are these prophesies?"

Kateri said nothing. She continued to look upward toward heaven, her face unspeakably beautiful, and her robes blazing in purest white. Nothing distracted her from her rapture as she looked toward heaven.

Father Claude sat back in contemplation. He lingered on her features, her long black braid, her deep brown eyes, her slender hands outstretched, her shining face of perfect innocence and purest love. He felt then a deep vibration—whether of light or sound he could not say—calming him, comforting him, assuring him that this vision was eternal, never to fade. Light streamed from Kateri as light from the sunrise, and a whispered voice said, "A vision even in daylight." Occasionally she looked down from her heavenly place. Once she looked directly into his eyes. Her look thanked him for his counsel during her life, and as he felt her gratitude, he knew with uncharacteristic certainty that he had fulfilled the purpose of his life.

For two hours, Kateri hovered in his cell, and then, as the first rays of the sun blushed in the eastern sky and the birds began to twitter in the trees, her image slowly dissolved. Claude was not saddened, though. This vision filled him with joy, courage, and a profound inner peace.

He told no one of the vision. Three days later, Anastasia sought him out.

"Father," she said excitedly, "Kateri came to me last night!"

Father Claude had never seen Anastasia so ecstatic.

"Everyone had gone to bed," Anastasia shivered with excitement. "I knelt praying by the fire until I grew tired and lay on my mat. I had hardly closed my eyes when I heard Kateri say: 'Mother, arise.' It was her voice, no mistaking it! I was not afraid. I sat up, and I saw her, Father! She was like the sun, beaming rays of holy light! And her face! Her face was clear and radiant, perfection itself. She looked at me with her eyes wide open, as if the damaged face she possessed during her earthly life had only been a mask, hiding her beauty that death uncovered. Her body was pure light up to the waist, and above, her face shone like the sun. She carried her cross in her hand, the most brilliant object I ever saw. From the cross came a light more intense and beautiful even than the sun.

"'Mother,' she said, 'look at this cross. How beautiful it is! This cross was my happiness during my life, and now I live always in its light. I ask that you make it yours as well.' She held up the cross, Father. Then the light streaming from that cross slowly hid Kateri, and the vision faded, leaving me alone in my dark cabin." Anastasia looked to the priest for guidance. "It was more real than anything I have ever seen! Are such things possible?"

"Yes," he said quietly. "She appeared to me as well."

"She is with us still!"

"And she always will be."

2.

As weeks and then months passed, Father Claude wrote more about her in his notebook. He tried to organize his memories and thoughts. He did not tell Father Cholonec about the vision, nor when Father Frémin returned from France did he confide in him. But he did not doubt that he had been a witness to Kateri's mystical union with God. He vowed to use his drawings and his writing to reveal this saint to the world, and he went about this task telling no one.

Father Claude spoke to Anastasia and Joseph Kryn to obtain

details of her life. He wrote about her life as an orphan in her uncle's home and her flight to the mission. He recorded all his observations and interactions with Kateri at the mission. He took great pleasure in making ink sketches of her portrait in the pages of his notebook.

Father Claude repeatedly requested of Father Cholonec that Kateri's remains be exhumed and carried into the chapel. Father Cholonec declined this honor because he felt it would set a bad precedent with the other Iroquois converts. But Chauchetière continued to advocate for special recognition, praying for a sign from heaven that would convince the more skeptical priest.

The following winter, a messenger summoned Father Claude to the home of a French farmer, Claude Caron, who could hardly breathe. A surgeon from Montreal told the family he would surely die and that he should be given the last rites since no earthly medicine could save him. On the way to Caron's farm, Father Claude stopped at Kateri's grave and prayed:

"O Lord, confirm for me the holiness of your handmaiden. In her name cure this man of his affliction. A cure will leave no doubt in what I have witnessed and will call others to pray to her as well."

Father Claude traveled to the Caron farm and found the forty-year-old father in his bed, gasping for breath.

"I started here to anoint you," Father Claude told him, "and to hear your last confession, but instead, I ask you to pray with me for the intercession of Kateri, the young Mohawk woman who died in our mission last spring. She may heal you."

Caron nodded, and holding his hand, Father Claude lifted his eyes and prayed: "Most beloved Kateri, this good man who is about to die asks for your intercession with the Lord. Help him recover and restore him to his family." He turned to the unkempt sick man. "Do you renounce your sins and invoke the intercession of Kateri Tekakwitha to be healed?"

The man nodded, his brown eyes looked out wide and frightened from a tangle of black hair, and his bearded mouth gasped out the words, "I do!"

Father Claude made the sign of the cross in front of him. "May you be restored to health, then, by the intercession of Kateri Tekakwitha."

The man's anxious wife and two elder daughters stood by, wringing their hands, and biting their lips. "Will you perform the last rites as well," the wife asked, "just in case the cure does not work?"

"We must have faith," Father Claude said, and he returned to the mission.

Shortly after Father Claude left, the wife and daughters sought to make Caron more comfortable, but he collapsed and fell on the floor as they raised him in the bed. Alarmed, they sent again for the priest and lifted him onto the bed. Caron lapsed into a deep sleep. An hour later, Father Claude revisited him, and as he prayed, Caron awoke, sat up, and looked about him in surprise.

"How do you feel?" Father Claude asked.

"As if a great stone has been lifted from my chest." Caron turned to his wife. "I am hungry, *mon cher*. Could I have something to eat?" The woman threw up her hands in amazement and rushed to the kitchen for a bowl of stew and a piece of bread.

"May Kateri be praised!" one of the daughters exclaimed.

On his way back to the mission, Father Claude stopped at Kateri's grave to pray in gratitude.

News of Caron's cure spread, and others asked for Kateri's help. Things she had touched became relics. Swatches of her clothing, and dirt from her gravesite effected cures for pneumonia and rheumatism, gout, and hearing loss. Soon the Mohawk virgin's intercession was regularly sought by women in childbirth.

René Cuillerier's wife had extreme difficulty delivering their first child, and they prayed to Kateri so mother and child would survive the ordeal. Together they promised to visit Kateri's grave. Soon after the successful delivery, they made a pilgrimage to offer their thanks.

A stable door fell on thirty-three-year-old Marguerite Picart, who was pregnant, and the infant was displaced in her womb. She prayed to Kateri, promising to have a mass said and make a novena, and she drank water into which earth from Kateri's grave and ashes from her clothing had been dipped. Two days later, the infant returned to the upper portion of her womb and was delivered without a problem when she came to term.

Marie-Magdeleine Fortin struggled in labor. No skill of a midwife could help her, and it was feared she and the child would both die. A neighbor brought a bag of earth from the grave and ashes from Kateri's garment, dipped it in water, and after the young mother promised to make a pilgrimage to Kateri's grave, her baby was born without difficulty.

News of these cures was accepted in La Chine and among the French more readily than among the Iroquois at La Prairie. Father Pierre Rémy of the Sulpician order was initially a skeptic who considered Kateri a creation of the Jesuits to draw attention to their conversion effort. But when at last he prayed to her, he was cured of an ear infection. This cure convinced him of her healing powers, and he applied to the Jesuits of Kanawaka for a supply of earth from her grave and ashes from her clothing. To effect cures, he dipped the earth and ashes in water, and he also made an unguent to apply to the skin. When the ill came to him for relief, he gave them tea made from the earth and ashes and applied the ointment. He counseled the sick to make a novena of an *Ave Maria* each day for nine days. Bolstered by the masses Father Rémy said, cures ensued.

Kateri appeared twice more to Father Claude on September 1, 1681, and then on April 21, 1682. Instead of appearing as the sunrise, her light now streamed from above, like the light of a noonday sun. She gave him a mandate: "Paint a favorable likeness of me." By now, Father Claude had made several drawings of Kateri as he remembered her, and he used these drawings to instruct children. He longed to paint her on canvas with oil paint, but when the materials arrived from France in the fall, he hesitated, doubting he could capture her essence. He wrote a long letter to his superior about her, detailing events at the mission:

"Iroquois mission of Sault St. François Xavier,
this 14th of October, 1682.

"My Reverend Father,
Pax Christi.

"In answer to Your Reverence's letter respecting what you have asked me, I will say that we are in a part of the country where the climate is not as good as in France, although, thanks be to God, I am in quite good health. We are in a very high and beautiful location, with a fine view, 60 leagues Distant from Quebec—which is called "the Iroquois mission." It is the finest mission in Canada, and, as regards piety and devotion, resembles one of the best churches in France.

"The river St. Lawrence here forms a lake two leagues wide; and the place where we are is so high that the waters of this great river fall here with a loud roar, and roll over many cascades, which frighten one to look at. The water foams as you see it do under a millwheel. We nevertheless readily pass over it every day in our Bark Canoes; and I cannot help saying that one must be crazy to run the rapids as we do, without any fear of being drowned. In truth, one must always be prepared for death in this country. You may Judge by this how much I need your prayers, obliged to be continually on the water, going and coming alone in a canoe. . . .

"Our village grows larger every year, while the Lorette mission, where Father Chaumont is, steadily diminishes. That of the mountain does not decrease, neither does it increase much; but ours grows continually. We think that in two or three years all the Agniez (Canienga/Mohawks) will be in this place. More than eighty have settled here recently, we have a chapel 25 feet Wide, and nearly 60 feet Long. We have three bells, with which we produce a very agreeable Carillon; and the natives will soon have another bell, weighing two hundred livres, to complete the harmony.

"The usual exercises of our mission are as follows: In the early morning, the bell is rung at 4 o'clock, which is the hour at which we rise, as in our houses in France. Many of our natives, through a spirit of devotion, come at once to the church, to adore the Blessed Sacrament; and they remain there until the first mass, which is said in winter at a quarter to 7, and in mid-Summer at 5 o'clock. While they are saying their prayers, I withdraw to my chamber, which is 6 feet Long and 5 feet wide, to say my orison; after this, I say the first mass, at which many are present although the bell is not rung for it. The 2nd, which is the mass for the natives, is said at half-past 5. I am present at it; the whole village also attends it every day, without a single person being absent; and the prayers are said aloud. Afterward the 3rd mass, which is for the children, begins, at which also I am present. We make them pray all together, after which I give them a short instruction on the Catechism. Such is my daily occupation.

"In addition to this, the natives come frequently during the day to visit the Blessed Sacrament, when they go to the fields and when they return from them. From eight o'clock until eleven, which is the hour for our repast, my occupation consists in visiting the natives, or in working to make books for them (because, as their nature is very fickle—of which They themselves complain—they must be often visited, either to give them suitable encouragement, or to prevent and appease their disputes, or to prepare the new-comers for receiving the sacraments). There are sixty Cabins—that is to say, from one hundred and twenty to 150 families, as there are at least two in each Cabin. To perform these visits with profit demands all the time of one missionary; another would be required for the children, and one for those who are more advanced, who need to be instructed in virtue.

"My work is made easier in this way: I sketch on paper the truths of the Gospel and the practices of virtue invented by Monsieur de Nobletz. Another Book contains colored pictures of the ceremonies of the mass applied to the passion of our Lord; another contains pictures showing the torments of hell; another the creation of the world. The natives view these with pleasure and profit, and these Books are their mute teachers. One of our catechists, with the assistance of these books, preaches long sermons; and I experienced much pleasure yesterday when I found a band of natives at the door of a cabin, learning to read in books of this kind.

"To return to the manner in which our time is employed, and to our usual occupations: at eleven o'clock the bell rings for our examination of conscience, and, at the same time, the Angelus is rung, which the natives recite with great devotion. Our afternoon is spent in teaching in the cabins. For my part, I visit the sick who would keep one man occupied. I have also charge of a Curé, consisting of a hundred French houses. With regard to Father Bruyas—who is the superior of the entire mission, and with whom I remained alone here during the whole of last year—he attends to the temporal and spiritual wants of the natives, and he is a father to them for both their bodies and their souls.

"You will be pleased to hear from me respecting the austerities practiced by certain native women—although there may be some indiscretion in their doing so; but it will show you their fervor. More than 5 years ago some of them learned, I know not how, of the pious practices followed by the nuns in Montreal who are hospital sisters. They heard of disciplines, of iron girdles, and of hair shirts. This religious life began to please them very much, and three of them formed an association, in order to commence a sort of convent; but we stopped them, because we did not think that the time had yet come for this. However, even if they were not cloistered, they at least observed Chastity; and one of them died with the reputation of sanctity, 3 years ago next spring. They, and some others who imitated them, would be admired in France, if what they do were known there.

"The first who began made her first attempt (Marie) about Christmas in the year 1676, when she divested herself of her clothing, and exposed herself to the air at the foot of a large cross that stands beside our Cemetery. She did so at a time when the snow was falling, although she was pregnant; and the snow that fell on her back caused her so much suffering that she nearly died from it—as well as her child, whom the cold chilled in its mother's womb. It was her own idea to do this—to do penance for her sins, she said. She has had four companions in her fervor, who have since imitated her. Two of them made a hole in the ice, in the depth of winter, and threw themselves into the water, where they remained during the time that it would take to say a Rosary slowly and sedately.

"One of the two who feared that she would be found out, did not venture to warm herself when she returned to her cabin, but lay down on her mat with lumps of ice adhering to her shoulders. There have been several other inventions of similar mortifications, which men and women have discovered for the purpose of tormenting themselves, and which constitute their usual exercises of penance. But we have made them give up whatever was excessive.

"During the past two years, their fervor has greatly augmented since God has removed from this world one of these devout native women who live like Nuns, and she died with the reputation of sanctity. We cease not to say masses to thank God for the graces that we believe we receive, every day, through her Intercession. Journeys are continually made to her tomb; and the natives, following her example, have become better Christians than they were. We daily see wonders worked through her Intercession. Her name was Kateri Tegaskouita. During her lifetime, she had made an agreement with a friend to make each other suffer, because she was too weak to do so by herself, owing to her continual illness. She had begged her companion to do her the charity of severely chastising her with blows from a whip. This they did for a year, without anyone knowing it, and for that purpose they withdrew, every Sunday, into a cabin in the middle of the cemetery; and there, taking in their hands willow shoots, they mingled prayers with penance.

"Finally, when one of the two saw that her companion had fallen sick at the end of the year, she was pressed by scruples to reveal the matter, and to ask whether she had not sinned in what she had done. At that time, people here used only willow shoots, or thorns, which here are very long; but since they have heard of disciplines, of iron girdles, and of similar instruments of penance, the use of this daily becomes more general. And, as the men have found that the women use them, they will not let themselves be outdone, and ask us to permit them to use these every day; but we will not do it. The women, to the number of 8 or 10, began the practice; and the wife of the *dogique*—that is to say, of him who leads the singing and says the prayers—is among the number. She it is who, in her husband's absence, also causes the prayers to be said aloud, and leads the singing; and in this capacity she assembles the devout women of whom we have spoken, who call themselves sisters. They tell one another their faults and deliberate together on what must be done for the relief of the poor in the village—whose number is so great that there are almost as many poor as there are natives.

"The sort of monastery that they maintain here has its rules. They have promised God never to put on their gala-dress (for the native women have some taste and take pride in adorning themselves with porcelain beads; with vermilion, which they apply to their cheeks; and with earrings and bracelets). They assist one another in the fields; they meet to incite one another to virtue . . .

"When they pray or sing in the church, they do so with so much devotion that all the French settlers here who see them are impressed by it and say that they are more devout than we allege. I was forgetting to tell you that, when they are in the woods, they have the Sundays and feast-days marked by small lines to the number of seven, one for each Day of the week; we mark crosses on the lines that indicate the feast-days and the Sundays, and they observe these very exactly. . . .

"If you wish me to tell you something about the manner in which the natives dress—although, had I time, I would have preferred painting some for you—you must know that it is not wanting in taste, especially on feast-days. The women have no other head-dress than their hair, which they part over the middle of the head, and then tie behind with a sort of ribbon, which they make out of eel-skin painted a bright red. I myself have often been deceived and have taken it for a real ribbon. They grease their hair, which thereby becomes as black as jet. . . .

"I would like to give you a more exact description of their consciences, of which you may have a fair idea from what I have said. But, besides the fact that it would take too long, and that I shall send something about it to one of my brothers, I would fear that it might perhaps be thought somewhat exaggerated.

"The native women sometimes propound to us doubts in spiritual matters as difficult as those that might be advanced by the most cultured persons in France. The knowledge of the cases of conscience often renders us good service here; without it we would be in danger of making many mistakes respecting proximate occasions, the baptism of adults, and marriages. In truth, the working of the Holy Ghost seems admirable in these minds, which have been trained amid the forests and the woods.

"When I read them your letter one Sunday, as I preached to them, they wept while listening to me; and the *dogique* then spoke to them in a very pathetic manner. They often ask me whether any prayers are said for them in France, and I assure them that there are. From time to time, they deplore the misfortunes of their birth; and, after they become Christians, they live like angels, fearing to fall into the evil ways from which faith and Christianity have withdrawn them."

Father Claude's letter noted that the healing cult dedicated to Kateri was growing, particularly among the poor white *habitans*.

3.

The prophecy of the overturned church from Kateri's first visitation to Father Claude came to pass in August of 1683. A violent thunderstorm struck the mission. Winds lifted the chapel and hurled it sixty feet off its foundation. All three priests were inside. Father Frémin was in the chancel and Father Cholonec in the sacristy. Father Claude was pulling the bell rope to sound the alarm. The two priests in the church were lifted and thrown aside along with sections of the building, and Father Claude had the bell rope pulled from his hand. But none of the priests was hurt. Due to this, Father Claude had a compelling argument for convincing Father Cholonec to move Kateri's remains into the church.

The following year, Father Cholonec finally agreed. In a ceremony as solemn as her funeral, they disinterred her bones and enshrined them in a sarcophagus in the rebuilt mission chapel. All the villagers were in attendance. Now the devout of the mission and pilgrims from afar might kneel and unburden their hearts as they prayed for miracles from the holy virgin.

CHAPTER TWENTY-THREE
MARQUIS DENONVILLE

I n the splendors of Versailles, King Louis XIV was concerned with the much larger spheres of global, imperial politics. The king had become alarmed at the incursions of the English who employed the Iroquois, particularly the Mohawks, as their war club. The English monopolized the fur trade from all five of the Iroquois nations, which undermined the economic basis of the king's colony. As in the days of de Tracy, the Iroquois needed to be chastised. The king appointed as governor an old veteran, Marquis Denonville, a pious colonel of dragoons who was as much at home in a battlefield tent as he someday would be in the Hall of Mirrors.

Denonville landed in Quebec in the summer of 1685 with five hundred soldiers. As the soldiers climbed the rock of Quebec, half of them collapsed from illness. They were carried into the halls, the church, the granary, and even the henhouse of the Hôtel-Dieu. As nuns nursed the men back to health, the new governor journeyed upriver to assess the land and the fortifications and consider how best to proceed to win his undeclared war with England.

In October, Father de Saint-Vallier, Bishop Laval's vicar-general, escorted the governor and his wife to the Mission of St.

Francis Xavier at the Sault. The governor was dressed in a long coat and breeches of golden brocade and wore a massive leonine periwig. His wife wore a well-cut gown of golden damask, and her hair was primped and curled into a towering coiffure in which jewels had been braided. They had come upriver on a barge with thirty soldiers to assist them in portaging around the rapids and in camping each night. Fathers Chauchetière and Cholonec escorted the governor and his wife to the tomb of Kateri Tekakwitha in the wooden chapel. Father Claude explained:

"This Mohawk maiden died a virgin in the odor of sanctity, and since her death, she has effected many cures. Native people and French alike come to pray at her tomb, and she answers many of their prayers."

"Indeed," the bishop's prelate said, "we consider her the Geneviève of Canada, our patroness in the court of the Almighty."

"Intriguing," the governor said, passing a scented handkerchief under his nose. "Not a century old, and Canada has its own saint. Quick work, Father."

Father Claude bowed, but the sarcasm stung.

"Father Chauchetière is writing her biography," Father Cholonec said.

The governor nodded with approval. "You must publish news of this native girl to all of Christendom. I'm sure she can teach us much about humility." There was a twinkle in his eye, and his wife snickered.

Again, Father Claude bowed, but he wanted desperately to escape from the governor's condescending mockery.

Ten months later, on August 1, 1686, Denonville returned to the mission, this time calling for full military honors. Montreal sent its garrison of bluecoats, and Joseph Kryn turned out his warriors in war paint and regalia. When the governor disembarked from his barge, the soldiers fired cannon and muskets to welcome him. Arrayed in his golden robes and huge periwig,

Denonville left little doubt who was in command. The soldiers marched beside him to the chapel, where he knelt and prayed before the Blessed Sacrament displayed for adoration. After kissing the monstrance, the general arose from the *prie-dieu* and turned to Father Claude.

"I wish to meet the one they call the Great Mohawk."

"We call him by his Christian name, Joseph Kryn."

"He has a reputation."

"It is well-deserved. He and his warriors await you in a long-house they have fitted out for your pleasure."

Chauchetière led the governor and his men through the village. The villagers gaped at the raiment of the governor. Reaching the longhouse, the priest held open the bearskin curtain for the governor to stoop and enter. The Iroquois had decorated the longhouse with branches, flowers, skins, and embroidered blankets. Father Claude served as interpreter.

"This is Joseph Kryn, your excellency, the one known as the Great Mohawk."

Kryn bowed. He wore a ceremonial breastplate and eagle feathers in his hair, but his face was clear of any war paint.

"Much is spoken about your bravery," the governor said. Denonville observed Kryn's height and massive shoulders and arms with approval. "It is told to me that you lead an exemplary life here at the mission. May I conclude from your fidelity to the one true God that you have a like fidelity to the king and to France?"

Kryn bowed. "My men and I are at your service, Onontio."

"Would you say the same if it involved a campaign against your relatives, the nations of Iroquois?"

"My people have been corrupted by the English. Their thinking is clouded by greed and by the rum the traders supply. Under the French king, I have found the greatest of all treasures. If my countrymen choose not to open their hearts, I must protect myself and my people, even by warfare if necessary."

"Could you raise a force if we asked you to?"

"I could raise two hundred warriors within a week."

"Let it be done then," Denonville said. "I shall return early next summer, and we shall embark on a campaign. In return for your service, I will be your protector."

"Who do we need to be protected from?" Kryn asked.

"The Seneca nation. It has threatened to attack the mission. The Seneca are traitors, and you must beware of them. Keep your fort here in good condition. I will send you *perriers* (small mortars) to help you hold your bastions and repel this cruel enemy. Send out scouts. Keep me informed. I will count on your vigilance as the guardian and defender of New France."

Joseph Kryn bowed. Then Father Chauchetière led them all to the chapel for benediction. The governor celebrated it on his knees, praying for guidance on his campaign against the Seneca next summer.

True to his word, Denonville sent the mortars upriver, and Kryn installed them in the fort's bastions. The marquis also sent a letter to Jesuit brothers in Iroquois country, Fathers Jacques and James Kateri's first confessor who still lived among the Mohawks at Onondaga. He asked for their help in peace talks about the fur trade which he planned for Fort Frontenac at the mouth of Lake Ontario. The priests carried his invitation to the Iroquois chiefs, and the chiefs deliberated this parley at their Onondaga council fire. They sent the younger priest, James, to Denonville to announce that they would attend the council and bring Jacques de Lamberville with them. In other words, Jacques would be their hostage.

While pretending his objectives were peaceful, Denonville transported two thousand soldiers up from Quebec in flat bottomed boats early the following spring. Father James de Lamberville met them with the message from the Onondaga council fire. The marquis collected another hundred men from La Chine and Ville-Marie, and his army left Montreal on June 13, 1687, crossing the river to rendezvous at the mission.

Joseph Kryn had raised a force of more than three hundred

Christian warriors—Iroquois, Algonquin, Huron, Abenaki—who camped in their battle dress and warpaint on the riverbank. All through the night of June 14, they danced their war dance and gorged on grilled meat. To assure loyalty, Denonville's men rooted out four natives, accused them of spying, and summarily hanged them.

On the morning of June 16, the enormous force boarded three hundred flatboats and swept across Lake St. Louis with bellied sails. The Iroquois paddled along in canoes to the front and the rear of Denonville's army. They easily proceeded around rapids and across other "lakes" in the river. Joseph Kryn's men were invaluable in helping the soldiers scrape their boats up the portages.

On June 19, the army captured two Cayuga chiefs and two warriors and their wives and sons, who were on a fishing expedition. To prevent their escape and possibly an attempt to warn the Seneca, Denonville took them as prisoners. On June 24, Denonville ordered Joseph Kryn's Christian warriors to capture a large group of Iroquois fishing near Otoniata Island. When Kryn's men reached the island, though, the Iroquois had fled. Because the Christian Iroquois balked at taking their kinsmen prisoners, Denonville's lieutenants accused them of warning the Iroquois, and this caused a hundred of Kryn's volunteers to desert. Joseph Kryn remained firm in his conviction to help.

On reaching Fort Frontenac, Denonville ordered his men to stake all Iroquois prisoners in the fort's yard, men, women, and children. He had their arms severely pinioned with leather thongs so they could not even swat the mosquitos and flies that tormented them. When Joseph Kryn entered the fort and saw this, he dashed to the first soldier guarding the prisoners and thrashed him soundly. He tried to meet with Denonville to obtain the release of these innocent prisoners, but the governor's man claimed he was in a council of war not to be disturbed.

One of the prisoners struggled free, and he leaped the wall of the fort and raced overland to Onondaga where the chiefs were discussing their rendezvous with Denonville. Learning of the trap, the chiefs refused to go north, but they did not kill Father Jacques de Lamberville for inviting them to an ambush. Ancient Garacontie called the priest to the council fire:

"We know you too well, Blackrobe, to think you would betray us. We believe you have been deceived as well. We will not punish you for the crimes of others, but we cannot afford to let you remain here because of this treachery. The younger warriors, whose blood is hot for vengeance, will want to burn you, so we order you to depart."

Father de Lamberville wasted no time in closing his chapel and leaving Onondaga. He soon joined Denonville, reporting that the Onondaga council was warned and would not attend. The invitation for the peace parley was still out to other nations, however, and when the appointed day arrived, fifty-one chiefs from clans of the Cayuga and Seneca arrived for the promised feast. Denonville sprang his trap. His soldiers seized the Iroquois chiefs as they entered the gate, bound them, and threw them into the fort's dungeon. He quickly readied a small fleet of flat-boats and the next morning shipped these chiefs and the other prisoners, men, women, and children, down to Quebec in chains to be transported across the sea to serve as slaves in the king's galley ships.

Meanwhile, the plains around Fort Frontenac bristled with tents and wigwams. A canoe arrived from Niagara with news that a large body of allies was at the falls. This force from Illinois and Michilimackinac (Michigan) had intercepted two parties of English traders and now waited below the great cataract for Denonville's signal. They had a hundred and eighty *coureurs de bois* and four hundred native men to join his force. Soon they saw a canoe flying across the water, summoning them to join the attack on the Seneca.

Hundreds of sails of Denonville's fleet billowed west from the shore of Fort Frontenac. The flotilla of La Durantaye, Tonty, Duluth, and the Ottawas of Michilimackinac moved across the face of the water from the northwest, and three thousand soldiers soon bivouacked on a sand bar separating Irondequoit Bay from Lake Ontario.

Fortune had smiled kindly on the marquis so far, but his excesses troubled the native warriors, particularly the seizure and enslavement of innocent chiefs. No stranger to the harsh realities of war, Kryn accepted this brutality as necessary and remained loyal. As the sun set and a soft summer night breathed cool darkness up from the lake, the men of many nations— streaked with war paint, naked or nearly so, iron earrings hanging below their headdresses of bison, elk, and deer—danced in the ruddy light of fires, miming attacks with their antler head-dresses as the spitting pine knots sent up showers of sparks. When a Seneca scout called from the bushes to ask why they were dancing the war dance, a reply came from a dozen throats: "To attack you!" The scout immediately ran to warn his people.

On July 12, Denonville gave his order to march, and blue flags with golden *fleur de lis* were unfurled. The marquis left four hundred men behind to guard the *bateaux* and canoes. The others shouldered their packs and followed a broad trail the Seneca had long ago worn between the lake and their village, eight leagues away. The soldiers hiked three leagues the first day and camped for the night. In the morning, while heat pulsed pitilessly from the sky, they waded waist-deep through an insect-infested swamp.

La Durantaye, and Tonty and Duluth, the officers from the northwest, led the advance force of *coureurs de bois*, French fron-tiersmen in buckskin who ranged through swampy forests without rank or file. To the left were Kryn and his fellow Chris-tians from the missions of St. Francis and Ville-Marie, reluc-tantly marching against their own countrymen, and on the right were the native warriors from the upper lakes. Behind this force of eight or nine hundred marched Denonville's main body, four battalions of regulars in light armor and a battalion of Canadians in homespun cloth and buckskin. The marquis struggled through the humidity in a shirt that hung, soaked with sweat and swamp water, from his large frame.

Scouts reported they had reached the clearings around the first Seneca village and found only a few women in the field. Thinking they could surprise the next village, the vanguard left the main body behind and pushed quickly forward through the forest into a swampy narrows. Dense woods hemmed them in on the left, and in front and to the right was a foul marsh. Suddenly the air exploded with war whoops, and muskets fired from alder thickets where the Seneca lay in ambush. The first volley hit Hot Cinders and seriously wounded the chaplain Father Enjarlan.

Naked Senecas in war paint sprang screaming from the brush and attacked with hatchets and swords. Joseph Kryn drew up his men behind the fallen chief.

"Stand your ground!" Kryn commanded, and his Christian warriors met the attack of their fellow Iroquois with muskets, hatchets, and knives.

Believing this was the entire invading force, the Seneca closed the trap, hoping to massacre all while they were bogged down in the mire. But soon, Denonville marched on the ambush from behind with his remaining force of sixteen hundred. The din of muskets and the war-whoops of the native warriors on both sides echoed in the trees. Many white soldiers, accustomed to fighting in battle lines on a broad plain, fell to the ground in panic. Kryn rallied his men, and they cut through the Seneca line with hatchets and war clubs, then turned and hacked their way back to meet Denonville's advancing bluecoats. When they saw the French swarming out of the woods, the Seneca fled. Denonville did not press on but gave the order, in view of the heat, to camp for the night.

The following day, his troops advanced through the marsh and emerged into a clearing. On a hill above rose the black remnants of a large town. The Seneca had torched the tall palisade and the bark longhouses. A few sizeable bins of the last year's corn harvest remained unburned and had attracted roaming swine. Denonville's men caught the hogs and butchered and ate them as they paused again for the night.

The following morning the vast army marched half a league to the next Seneca village. Since it had not been burned, they fired it, as well as the surrounding cornfields. In the next days, the army burned three more villages, but not a single Seneca was found. The French got sick from gorging on green corn and fresh pork, and their native allies deserted in droves.

On July 24, Denonville marched back to the lake and sailed to a post in Irondequoit Bay and then to Niagara. He built a fort on the site of a ruin used by LaSalle nine years before, and there he left a garrison of a hundred men under Chevalier de Troyes. Taking the rest of his army, he descended the river in triumph to Montreal. When he tallied the effect of his western campaign, Denonville noted he had captured and stopped two flotillas of English. He had burned all the Seneca villages, proving to them that any consorting with the English would be met with reprisals. But the Senecas had fled eastward to the Cayuga, where they were sheltered and fed until they rebuilt their villages and all nations of the Iroquois League now seethed for revenge.

During a rare opportunity to speak with the governor, Joseph Kryn responded to Denonville's self-satisfied rhetorical question:

"Do you think, Great Chief, the Seneca have been sufficiently chastised?"

"There's an old saying among my people, Onontio, that if you kick over a wasp's nest you better kill every one because the survivors will sting you blind."

"What is that supposed to mean?"

"You left many wasps alive."

CHAPTER TWENTY-FOUR
ONCE MORE, PEACE TALKS

I.

Claude Chauchetière had asked to serve as chaplain to the expedition, but Denonville selected a priest from Montreal, leaving Father Claude to tend to the souls of his mission. Claude spent his leisure time writing and painting. He was in his cabin, quill in hand, when the shout went up that the expedition was returning. He immediately walked to the riverbank in time to see the canoe of Joseph Kryn bravely shooting the rapids. Others followed. Kryn backpaddled and glided to the bank, where the villagers greeted him as their conquering hero.

The Great Mohawk rose from his canoe, waded ashore, and walked among the villagers, clasping their hands, embracing them warmly. When he came to Father Claude, he genuflected to receive a blessing. After the priest had made the sign of the cross over him, Kryn stood and held up his hands for silence.

"Let me report to all that our great chief Hot Cinders died heroically in a Seneca ambush."

The assembled bowed their heads and crossed themselves as Father Claude uttered a blessing. "May he rest in peace."

"I witnessed his death. A musket ball hit him in the first

volley. He dragged himself to the chaplain and told him calmly, 'I am dying, Father. God wills it. I praise Him with all my heart. I do not regret losing my life because Jesus Christ gave His life for me.' Then he fell at the feet of the priest, and with names of Jesus and Mary on his lips, he breathed his last."

"Lord have mercy on his soul," Father Claude said.

The villagers were deeply affected by this report, and Joseph Kryn continued: "War serves no one. We must work to end these disputes so everyone in this land may live in peace and harmony."

Joseph Kryn went to Karitha and Peter, and together they went home. After settling into his new lodge, he walked down the lane to visit Father Chauchetière.

"I am greatly troubled, Father," Kryn said when they were seated.

"Tell me, Joseph."

"When I pledged to lead a company of warriors from the mission, I understood that the governor would wage an honorable war. I am no stranger to campaigns, and I felled and scalped many an enemy before I embraced the faith. I know of the English infidels and how they use rum to destroy my people and cheat them of furs, and I know the importance of the great Sun King to keep the missions thriving and the faith strong. Still, the governor showed no restraint.

"He captured innocent Iroquois who were only fishing, and he tormented them in the fort. He used trickery to capture the chiefs of the Seneca and Cayuga by pretending to invite them to a feast. He communicated this ruse through Father de Lamberville, the brother of the dear friend who sent us Kateri, and thereby exposed that good priest to torture and burning. Some declined, but many chiefs appeared for the parley, and he threw them in chains and deported them across the sea, laughing that they will row the Sun King's ships as slaves until they die. Onontio is so blinded by his pride that he does not see these cruelties will be cruelly revenged."

"Do you know when or how?"

"I no longer hear from the Mohawk villages, but I know my people. These are not the days of de Tracy. The Seneca will not allow this attack to stand. I fear since I drew a large force from our people here that Mohawks or Senecas will massacre us and burn our mission."

The priest rose from his chair and reached for Kryn's hand. "Pray with me, Joseph. Let us pray to Kateri that she may help us achieve peace."

They knelt together on the floor. Father Claude spread his arms:

"Beloved Kateri, we who knew you and loved you in life now ask for your intercession with our Lord Jesus Christ and his mother, Holy Virgin Mary. Petition them and God the Father that He will cause all men to see the foolishness of war and sit down to negotiate a lasting peace. You loved this mission above all. Protect us in our vulnerable location and allow the Mohawks and the other Iroquois to see at last the advantages flowing from peace and prayer."

"Amen," the Great Mohawk said, and as they stood, "but we must do more than pray."

"What would you do?"

"Travel among my people, down to the river where I was born, sit in council with them, urge them away from revenge."

"That would be noble, Great Chief, but you must get permission from the governor before you do anything."

"Onontio does not understand my people and shows little desire to do so. I need no permission to act on behalf of the mission."

"And yet the governor calls you to Montreal," Father Claude held up a letter. "He asks that I bring you to him."

2.

Joseph Kryn and five Christian converts paddled across the

river with Father Claude the next day, and the delegation met with Marquis Denonville inside the fort at Ville-Marie. A change had now come over the marquis. He had fought in Europe and Asia for thirty years and always displayed vigor and courage before his men. This campaign, though, with its complex diplomacy among warring tribes and the insolence of English governor Thomas Dongan riling up the Seneca, had taken its toll on Denonville and aged him severely. His periwig was long gone, and he dressed no more in brocade but in a white cotton blouse.

"Your service on the late campaign was exemplary, Chief," the governor began. "Your loyalty and skill have been tested and battle-hardened."

Kryn bowed, though Father Claude knew the feelings were not mutual.

"I need to learn the temper of your people, the Mohawks, and the people of our unfortunate Hot Cinders, the Oneida, as well as the Onondaga. I would like you to serve as our ambassador."

Kryn bowed again.

"Go among your countrymen. Ask that they come to see us and seek lasting peace. Tell them if they pledge to remain neutral, I will release the two Onondaga and one Oneida captive we still hold."

Kryn accepted the task and left immediately with his nephews. Time was of the essence while opinions were still forming about Denonville's raid and how to respond. While paddling south on Lake Champlain, he saw a party of sixty warriors encamped on an island who were heading north to attack. Kryn entered the small bay where they camped.

"What is your nation?" Joseph Kryn asked from the water.

"Oneida," answered Gray Wolf, chief of the war party.

"Are there any Seneca with you?"

"No."

Kryn and his two nephews neared the shore. "I am Joseph

Kryn, called in times past 'The Great Mohawk.' I come from Onontio and wish to parley."

"Join us."

Gray Wolf welcomed him at the campfire where they were roasting a deer on a spit over a fire of hissing coals. They traded greetings. Kryn and his nephews were invited to eat and share their camp for the night. In the morning, Joseph Kryn acquainted Gray Wolf with the governor's invitation. Gray Wolf's companion, a hot-headed young man named Jannitie, asked why the Great Mohawk did not return to live in his former village.

"I have embraced the Prayer," Kryn answered. "I will not return to the lands of the People of Flint as long as they drink the English rum. Perhaps someday, if a blackrobe were welcomed at Saratoga where the sacred waters flow, many of our people who have accepted the Prayer would build a mission there."

After the meeting, Joseph Kryn went among the sixty warriors, greeting some old friends and relatives of Hot Cinders. He then exhorted them to abandon their raid of retaliation on French settlements. He invoked the memory of the Mohawk maiden Tekakwitha, urging that they work for peace and forgiveness instead of vengeance. Joseph Kryn then sent one nephew to the Mohawks and the Oneida, the other to the Onondagas, informing those nations that Onontio felt no anger for them, only the Seneca. With his mission accomplished, Kryn turned homeward. His speech had been so powerful that four of the party followed him to the mission to convert.

In gratitude for Kryn's great service to the French crown, Denonville gave him and his Iroquois soldiers clothes and food stores. "I cannot praise too highly the assistance we received from the Great Mohawk," the governor-general wrote, "and from his warriors in the village of Sault Saint Louis." But to the villagers, the gifts felt like guilt offerings for a dishonorable campaign against their relatives.

3.

After his many missteps, Denonville now sought peace. He feared retaliation. Scurvy and malaria had reduced the garrison at Fort Niagara from a hundred men to twelve, so Denonville dismantled it. Shamed at last by his precipitous act in kidnapping the chiefs, Denonville agreed to return the prisoners if any still lived. Of the fifty-one seized only last year, just thirteen survived. These men were returned, and Denonville sent them back to their families. Finally, his request for additional troops from the king fell on deaf ears.

Still smarting from Denonville's attack, an Iroquois chief named Big Mouth raised an army of twelve hundred. In October, he presented himself to be escorted from Fort Frontenac down the St. Lawrence to Montreal. Justifiably worried with Big Mouth's army poised to attack, the French officers presented him to the governor.

"We come to Onontio as a free and independent people," Big Mouth began. "We are subjects of neither the French nor the English king. We wish to be friends with both. We hold our lands by a right descended from the Great Spirit, and we have never been conquered in war. Just now, I have at my beck and call twelve hundred warriors. At a moment's notice, we could burn all the houses and barns of Canada, kill all your cattle, and burn your grain as de Tracy did to the Mohawks and you have done to the Seneca. Our people want to put this plan into motion, but I temporarily restrain them to offer peace. I have four days to return. Give me a favorable answer, let us sign a neutrality agreement, and a larger delegation from the confederacy will travel here to conclude a general peace."

With his back to the wall, Denonville accepted Big Mouth's offer. The French wrote out terms on a large parchment, and Big Mouth and his ambassadors signed with pictographs of birds and beasts.

As he promised, Big Mouth returned to the council fire at

Onondaga, and the terms were accepted. A delegation was sent north to Montreal to finalize the terms of peace, but they never arrived. On the way, they were ambushed by a wily Huron called "the Rat."

4.

From his quiet post at the mission, Father Claude Chauchetière watched the war and diplomatic disasters with a sinking heart. Marquis Denonville, who began with such a stirring campaign to bring all peoples under the reign of his glorious Sun King, had been caught in a web of tangled alliances fueled by liquor and greed for the lucrative fur trade. Armies and envoys had traveled back and forth, west and east, north and south, on dire missions to defend and rescue and attack, but still, the snow howled out of the sky, and the swollen breast of the river carried away farmhouses and chicken coops in the spring thaw. The only real treasure anyone attained in this land, incapable of being stolen or destroyed, was the saintliness of Kateri Tekakwitha. For Claude Chauchetière, this quiet, humble little woman with a retiring manner, a will of iron, and a love of God radiating from her like the sun, lit his path to salvation. Just as St. Geneviève saved Paris from Attila the Hun, Claude prayed Kateri would banish warfare from New France forever.

Locally, he promoted her cause, urging priests and medical people to turn to her for signs and cures. As war clouds rolled in and out, he embedded her image in his heart, a distillation of feminine purity, more sacred to him because of its humble origin among the rivers and forests of this wild continent. As he reviewed his life in self-reflection on retreat, he marked its turning point as April 17, 1680, the day of Kateri's death. It was from that date that he measured his new, tranquil life, confident in his faith. Though he still shied from publishing his sacred tract to the world, he continued to work on it.

CHAPTER TWENTY-FIVE
THE MASSACRE AT LACHINE

"The Rat" was aptly named. Like the ancient Onondaga chief Atotarho, whose hair was a mass of writhing snakes, the Rat possessed subtle political skills and a unique ability to lie. A master of intrigue, he had the strength of will to seize advantage out of loss, to turn chief on chief and reap destruction in the winds of change. The Rat was a Huron chief from Michilimackinac, the sworn enemy of all Iroquois who continually attacked and massacred his people. The French admired him, courted him, and employed him, and he pledged that so long as they fought the Iroquois, he would fight with them. But now the French were making peace with his enemies! He could not allow that.

During the summer of 1688, the Rat raised a raiding party of forty warriors and traveled down the rivers and lakes to attack the Iroquois. At Fort Frontenac, he heard that the deputies from Onondaga promised by Big Mouth would soon travel to Montreal to parley with Onontio. This served his purpose. He led his band to a camping place where he knew the Onondaga deputies would soon land. He hid in ambush until, as expected, he saw the Onondaga deputation gliding across the lake. As soon as it landed, the Rat ordered his men to fire, killing one of the chiefs and wounding many others. The Rat took all of them prisoner except one who escaped with a broken arm.

"I am in the service of Onontio, the great Denonville," he lied to the shocked Iroquois chiefs who trusted peace would soon prevail. "You are my prisoners."

"But that is not possible," one of them said. "We are journeying to Montreal as envoys of peace to sit in council with him."

The Rat exploded in rage: "Did Onontio not summon your brothers to a feast last summer and cast them in chains to be slaves of his king? Why did you believe him then? Why did I? These French will never stop until they destroy our people and seize our land! Because of their treachery I refuse to be an agent of Onontio's plots. I was told you were a raiding party and that I should kill you and not take any prisoners. I will disobey my orders, brothers. I will send you home to rouse your five nations and take a just vengeance on the French."

The Rat kept one warrior hostage, ostensibly for his own safe passage. But he had another purpose in mind when he handed the hostage over to the French garrison. The French soldiers had heard nothing of a proposed peace so when the young Oneida warrior protested that he had been on his way to finalize a treaty, the Rat mocked him: "How shamelessly he lies to save his life!" At this, the French soldiers marched the hostage before a firing squad and executed him. The Rat then sent for an old Iroquois, a prisoner for years among the Huron.

"Look at how these French treat your people! I gave them a young Oneida warrior to hold as you have been held these long years, and they killed him. In response to this, you shall have your freedom. Go back to your people and tell them of the injustice and cruelty of the French."

Meanwhile, the Iroquois youth who escaped the Rat with a broken arm finally reached Fort Frontenac and told the garrison of the Rat's treachery. The commander sent him downriver to Denonville, who flattered him and gave him gifts, then released him to return to Onondaga with explanations and apologies, instructing him to blame the Rat for all the treachery.

On the surface the chiefs seemed satisfied with Denonville's explanation, but after all that had transpired, they decided it was time to teach the French a lesson.

On the stormy night of August 4-5, 1689, as hailstones pelted the seventy-seven small structures clustered along the rapids at La Chine, a vast and silent horde of Iroquois, fifteen hundred strong, landed upriver and crept quietly into the village. They surrounded every house and waited. Suddenly a war-whoop gave the signal, and the Iroquois unleashed the fury of hell on seventy French families asleep in their homes. The Iroquois hacked through doors and windows with their hatchets and pulled men, women, and children out of their beds, tomahawking their skulls, slicing off scalps, and collecting prisoners to be tortured and burned. In two hours, the Iroquois killed twenty-four and hauled away seventy prisoners, setting fire to the village as they left.

One villager escaped and ran the three miles to the garrison of Fort Rémy. The captain of the garrison, Daniel d'Auger de Subercase, sent word immediately to Forts Rolland and La Présentation, and soon two hundred soldiers and a hundred civilians were in hot pursuit, seeking to free the prisoners the Iroquois still held.

Denonville and his force of seven hundred were bivouacked nearby in the fort of Ville-Marie, merely two leagues from the massacre, but he declined to respond. His true reason was fear, but his excuse was that punishing the Iroquois would succeed only in rousing them to new fury. Not only did he remain with his seven hundred safely behind the stockade wall, but he also ordered Captain Subercase to return immediately to his garrison and desist from following the Iroquois.

At sunrise, the Iroquois ferried their seventy prisoners across Lake St. Louis, just above the rapids and the mission. Father

Claude and Joseph Kryn watched black smoke billow from the burning settlement up into the rainy sky.

As soon as they reached the shore, the Iroquois planted poles in the ground, built bonfires around them, tortured, burned, and ate many prisoners, holding the rest hostage. They adopted three parentless children into their families. Some of the survivors, traded later in peace parleys, told how the Iroquois had forced parents to throw their own children into the flames.

As the members of the mission of St. Francis Xavier at Sault St. Louis lined the riverbank, Joseph Kryn spoke to Father Claude:

"Let us go there and see if we can be of service. I will protect you since I know some of the warriors. You might be able to administer confession or the last rites."

"Good Joseph Kryn," the priest said. He went to the rectory for his stole and his chrism, and they were soon paddling across the river.

They landed just below the rapids at La Chine and climbed the boulder-strewn pathway onto the grassy plain. Nearby, barns and houses were smoldering. Cows and pigs had been hacked apart by war hatchets, and loud crows filled the sky. As Kryn and Father Claude entered the village, they saw corpses of farmers and their wives and children strewn on the ground, hanging in and out of windows, slumped from stakes in the village green where they had been tied and tortured, laying in the lanes staring at the sky. Skulls were crushed from the blows of tomahawks. Crows and dogs and vultures were feasting on the dead, and a low acrid smoke hung over the village.

Kryn located a young woman whose left arm and scalp had been hacked off. Her skin was still warm, but nothing registered in her vacant eyes. Father Claude knelt beside her, kissed his stole, and draped it over his neck, then anointed her forehead and her remaining hand with chrism. When he finished giving her the last rites, the priest closed her eyes and laid a blanket over her.

"She is near Kateri's age when she entered heaven," Father Claude said, and he bowed his head and wept.

The two of them walked through the charred ruins, unconcerned about roving bands of Iroquois who even then were across the river, drunk on the settlers' brandy, torturing, and burning their prisoners.

As they paddled back to the mission, Father Claude said to Kryn: "Kateri foretold this massacre when she appeared to me. She showed the destruction of our chapel, and that soon came to pass. I did not know the meaning of the young man burning at a stake, but now I see. She was predicting the raid on La Chine, promising to protect the mission she loved."

"She saved us, Father. Far better than any army I could raise."

"What other explanation can there be? Your attack on the Seneca is well-known. Your attempt to negotiate a lasting peace, your rejection of the old ways, your embracing the Prayer, all these make you a prime target for revenge. Our mission too. Yet so near at hand, they spared us. Imagine the lanes of our mission smoldering like La Chine, all our good people dying."

"Kateri hated war," Joseph Kryn said. "I find war necessary to protect my family and my mission, so I will continue to wage it."

"And yet, you did not protect us this time, Joseph, she did." The men looked at each other. "Her love is a far greater weapon than any prowess with muskets and war hatchets. Jesus Himself taught us that. There will be no lasting peace until men follow her example and learn to live in harmony."

"There will be no lasting peace until the English are gone."

Father Claude mused on their different interpretations, while Kryn, always the man of action, tried to anticipate the next campaign.

CHAPTER TWENTY-SIX
DEATH OF A WARRIOR

I mmediately after his cowardly response to the massacre at La Chine, the vainglorious Marquis Denonville was recalled to France. Reports circulated that the recall had nothing to do with his rash attack on the Seneca, his brutal kidnapping of the fifty-one Iroquois sachems or his bungling of peace negotiations, or even his cowardice during the attack on La Chine. But everyone knew those were ample causes. As Denonville's replacement, the king re-appointed blustery old Count Frontenac to return and establish a lasting peace with musket and sword.

Frontenac formed a bold plan of falling on the British in New York and Albany, thereby seizing the English colony for France. Still, his lack of a navy and land troops substantially reduced his chance of success. Undeterred, he outlined three campaigns, one into Maine, one into Massachusetts, and one into New York. He sent his first raiding party down through the lakes into New York in January 1690. The men were ill-prepared, scantily provisioned, and deprived of a specific target. The raiding party included Iroquois soldiers led by Joseph Kryn. When the food supply ran low, Kryn demanded the French leader tell him the attack's strategic object. He feared they were being asked to attack their relatives still residing at Kanawaka.

"We are going to Albany," the French commander said.

"Since when are the French brave enough to attack the English?"

"We must regain the honor we have lost, and this requires a bold stroke."

"Bold? It is impossible. Albany's garrison will put us to flight!"

A thaw had melted the ice, so the army had to struggle through muddy swamps. The men were hungry, cold, and tired. When they approached the fork in the road, one leading to Albany, the other to Schenectady, they took the shorter route toward Schenectady to obtain food and shelter. Soon they came upon a cabin where four native women offered them a fireside and a kettle of food. Many men crammed into the little space to get warm. While they were together within, Joseph Kryn spoke:

"I urge you, my comrades in arms, to cleanse in blood all the wrongs done to us on behalf of the English who are the fathers of all warfare and bloodshed in this land. Let us fall on this fort and leave no building standing, no inhabitant alive! And may divine Providence guide and protect us!"

Cheers of battle lust met his exhortation. As the men departed from the cabin, it began to snow. Guided by the women, they soon reached the stockade, and the storm which grew into a heavy blizzard concealed them as they assembled at the east and west gates. Since the gates had been carelessly left open, they stealthily entered the stockade and surrounded each house. At a signal, the French and Joseph Kryn's men screamed and smashed open doors and windows with their tomahawks and war clubs. They knifed and shot and tomahawked the unsuspecting civilians rising from their beds.

For two hours, the massacre raged. Thirty-eight men and boys were killed, ten women and twelve children died, and nearly ninety prisoners were taken. When the violence ended, Joseph

Kryn stationed lookouts in all the lanes. He located rum in two taverns, and he stove in the barrels so his men could not drink it. Thirty Mohawks who had been visiting Schenectady were allowed to return home. Frontenac's lieutenant wanted to assure the Iroquois that Onontio harbored no ill-will toward them. He was only punishing the English.

The French army set fire to all the buildings and the stockade and collected forty horses. Then the army departed northward with twenty-seven men and boys, leaving sixty old men, women, and children behind. Swelled by victory, the army traveled more slowly, and when the hungry men required meat, they killed and roasted a horse. They returned to Montreal, having lost only nineteen men.

In May, Frontenac again called Joseph Kryn and his Christian Iroquois into service against the English. Reports came to him that the English were ranging in the territory around the Salmon River, stirring up the Mohicans. Leaving the mission by canoe, Kryn's force paddled to Sorel, and on May 18, they marched through the swamps. On the fifth day of the expedition, Joseph Kryn's scouts heard gunshots. They came on two temporary huts with fourteen Iroquois inside who, on questioning, revealed that the English had supplied weapons to the Mohicans so they would attack New France. An army of seven hundred was a day and a half away.

Badly outnumbered, Kryn thought it prudent to retreat to Montreal. He followed the Salmon River back toward Lake Champlain and paused with his men to build new canoes on the shore. That night, as they slept, a band of Algonquins from Trois-Rivières, loyal French allies, mistook them for non-Christian Iroquois. The Algonquins surrounded the camp and, before dawn, charged the sleeping Christian Iroquois. Joseph Kryn, the first to rise to defend his men, was also the first to fall. So long invincible to enemy attacks, Joseph Kryn died from friendly fire.

News of Kryn's death deeply saddened Father Claude, who

held a funeral service at the mission chapel and delivered a eulogy about his courage, loyalty, and unswerving faith.

"We have lost our protector, a giant among his people, among all peoples of the earth. He fell defending our king and defending his faith, and now Joseph Kryn is happy at last, in heaven with our beloved Kateri."

Sobbing filled the chapel. Father Claude struggled to maintain his composure as he turned back to the mass and held the host high above them, *"Hoc est enim corpus meum."*

**Portrait of Kateri Tekakwitha painted after her death by
Father Claude Chauchetière, circa 1692.**

CHAPTER TWENTY-SEVEN
RETIREMENT AT VILLE-MARIE

I.

The loss of Joseph Kryn was incalculable to Father Claude. Since his happy years at the mission, he had witnessed the departure of saintly Kateri, and now, a decade later, the noble Kryn. They died as they had lived, she at peace in the odor of sanctity, and he by force of arms. What did this portend for him?

Father Claude now worked on Kateri's biography and a full-length portrait of her on canvas. From the stark, lonely pinnacle of his faith, he looked down on the passions that drove men—the rise to power, greed, and constant violence to protect advantages gained, or acquire more—and then the inevitable fall. He accepted war as inescapable. Didn't Michael the Archangel's constant battle with forces of darkness prove that evil will never be vanquished? Loyola was a soldier before he gave his life to Christ. His Jesuits still waged a constant war against the evil one. Wars were like storm clouds passing, Claude observed, they swelled into dark, monstrous shapes and shook the world with thunder and lightning, and then dissipated into vapor. It tired him, all this deep-thinking. He counted a single memory, the vision of a dying maiden, transfigured and radiant in death, to be the attainment of his life. No greater wisdom lay beyond that glorious moment, and it gave him great comfort to sit in the afternoon sun and remember.

Father Claude's health began to slip. In 1692 he suffered from severe headaches, and from St. Anthony's fire, a red skin eruption on his face. He contracted dysentery at Montreal, and scurvy while visiting Fort Frontenac. His eyes weakened, but he refused to wear spectacles, so he squinted to see, which made him look old, annoyed, and irritable to his fellow priests and his communicants.

When his sixteen-year assignment as a missionary ended, he went into semi-retirement. He wrote his surviving brother from his new post as a, lecturer in mathematics and a parish priest on the island of Montreal:

"To my Reverend Father, Father Jean Chauchetière, of the society of Jesus, at Limoges.
Villemarie, this 7th of August, 1694.

"My Reverend Father,
Pax Christi.

"I have admirable things to tell of the Sault mission. As regards our Natives, they have continued this year as fervent as they are accustomed to be. Kateri's band (I wrote you her life last year. I know not whether you have received it because one of our ships was lost while returning to France, and those papers were perhaps on it, and you do not speak of it. I had placed her portrait therein) continue in the practice of the most Christian virtues, and in the heroic exercises that they have undertaken. Last winter the most hardened were touched by God and performed an act that deserves to be written down. It was called *hotouongannandi*, that is to say, 'public penance,' because it was done in the name of all. The men, gathered according to the native custom—that is, at a feast—expressed their detestation of drunkenness, which mastered them.

"This was done as follows: after agreeing together as to what they could do to give satisfaction to God, they came to the conclusion that each should speak for himself in full meeting; and that they who on account of illness, or for any other reason, were unable to do so, should have someone speak in their names. This was done to prepare for the festival of Christmas. Each spoke as the spirit of penance moved him; and some did so more eloquently by the tears that flowed in abundance from their eyes, than by their voices broken by sobs.

"Words were followed by results; the women, whose demons were gaming, vanity, and voluptuousness, completely abandoned the first of these; for a year, we have heard no more about it. Confraternities are being founded among them, and especially among the young girls, with the object of mutually assisting one another to live as Christians, and to prepare themselves for the most heroic actions. . . .

"We see in these natives the fine remains of human nature which are entirely corrupted in civilized nations. Of all the 11 passions they experience only two; anger is the chief one, but they are not carried away to excess by it, even in war. Living in common, without disputes, content with little, guiltless of avarice, and assiduous at work, it is impossible to find people more patient, more hospitable, more affable, more liberal, more moderate in their language. All our fathers and the French who have lived with the natives consider that life flows on more gently among them than with us. The faith, finding all these predispositions, makes astonishing progress with them. They wish that they had never seen any but the black gowns; and they repeat this to the confusion of our French Christians!

"You inform us of the misery that prevails in France; but it is otherwise in this country. Grain is common; cider is made, instead of wine; and trees are successfully raised, becoming continually more numerous. Last year we had excellent melons; but this country is very unreliable for plants that require heat. However, it is asserted that wine will be made this year; for close by is a vineyard belonging to the Gentlemen, which yields French grapes. What the country can produce is not yet known, because we try to grow only wheat and hay. The wild apple-trees, and those that are raised from seeds, bear fine apples, and the branches are easily grafted. The peach-trees produce abundantly, but like the vine—that is, the fruit is all on the ground, because the tree has to be covered with straw or other protection until the month of April, lest it freeze. The pear-trees are more delicate; I saw one that blossomed twice last year—once in the spring, and once during the summer.

"Farewell, my dear Father, and dear brother; I never cease to remember you at the altar and elsewhere.
　　Claude Chauchetière,
　　of the Society of Jesus.

"Post Scriptum: I must preach, but I have no sermons."

2.

Father Claude had no sermons. He had seen and done wondrous things, but he saw little use in crafting lessons to share them. From Kateri he learned a truth that few ever did, but he also knew that men and women rarely heed the words of others. They learn only from experience, so sermons were a waste of time. He could try to tell others, but they would not grasp it. He had glimpsed eternity. Shining in Kateri's eyes, he had seen the infinite love of God, and at her death, witnessed her transfiguration. How could any words fully communicate that?

JACK CASEY

All in all, he concluded, it was a matter of faith. Those who believed accepted things on faith; those who did not let doubt and skepticism rule them. It was not his responsibility anymore to convince. He did feel duty-bound, however, to communicate the marvels he had witnessed, so he called on Kateri to guide him. And she returned to him, not in unearthly visions, but in memories. He pushed himself to complete her biography in his labored prose, just as he had painted her portrait as an untutored folk artist. He prayed to her nightly, and when he felt challenged in his faith—a feud with the new bishop, for example, nearly got him excommunicated—he simply recalled her transfiguration, and it calmed him. He finished Kateri's portrait circa 1692 and completed her biography circa 1695. In his introduction he apologized for having taken so long:

"The pressing reason for keeping silent so long on this matter was the reluctance I observed in the mind of the French to believe in such great miracles, that perhaps I measured too much by myself who had such difficulty in believing the things I saw every day, or perhaps for having believed the French who doubt there is faith among the Natives. The main reason was certain difficulties that the Reverend Father superior of Quebec made for believing things when he saw them set forth in a little notebook I kept during 1680 so I might give an exact account, and in order to discover what was of God and what could not be of God.

"The reason I have to speak now is a powerful summons to no longer hold back in the shadows and silence a truth worthy of being published all over the world, that God was first to put forth by ordinary signs that he uses to make known to the living the merit and glory of the dead, and not deprive the missionaries of the recompense that God has given for their labors in showing in extraordinary ways the virtue and faith of

274

the Christian natives who are so often attacked by slandering tongues."

Father Claude's finished portrait was displayed in the chapel at Kanawaka. His biography was circulated to mixed reviews. Father Cholonec felt obliged to set some of Father Claude's observations in perspective, and the following year he wrote his own account of Kateri's life. His work was less effusive and more direct. It focused less on her humanity and pleasant attitude and influence over others in their praying than it did on her chastity.

As the years passed, Kateri's influence was felt in wider circles—from the humble mission, thence to Montreal and Quebec, even across the sea to France. As these circles widened, Father Claude's narrowed. Never gregarious, he became a recluse, retiring to the Jesuit rectory in Ville-Marie, where the holy Father Jogues had lived and prayed until his martyrdom. In his meditation, Father Claude often went back in memory to envision Kateri at her prayers in the chapel, or in the longhouse working at her handicrafts, or gliding through the lanes of the village huddled in her shawl. He enjoyed such sojourns into the past, and they sent smiles flickering across his features as he napped in the afternoon sun.

Father Chauchetière had been retired from the mission for nearly two decades and was lapsing into old age. Each April 17 he celebrated the anniversary of Kateri's transfiguration and death. On the twenty-ninth anniversary, in the sacristy of hewn logs, he was donning vestments, white vestments in tribute to her purity, when he sensed he was not alone. He turned toward the chapel door and to his amazement he saw Kateri standing in the doorway.

She was unchanged, exactly as he remembered her thirty years before, not floating in rays of heavenly light nor looking up at the radiance of God, just a slight, frail presence standing apart, holding her precious cross, and looking away from him. She was dressed simply, as always, the shawl obscuring her face, the white tunic and doeskin moccasins as he first saw her when Joseph Kryn introduced them on the riverbank. The familiarity of her being here brought a smile to his face. How had she come to be in the sacristy on this particular day?

"Kateri?"

She lifted her veil, and her face was as radiant as the day she died. Heavenly light illuminated the room.

"Yes, Father."

"Are you here for the mass?"

"No." She reached out her hand. "I am here for you."

"Where are we going?"

She smiled sweetly. "You answered that long ago."

As their fingers touched, Father Claude felt an overpowering ecstasy flood through his body. He closed his eyes and surrendered to it.

"Come," she whispered, "the others are waiting. Can you hear them?"

Father Claude listened. Far away he heard a choir singing in harmony, and he recognized the voices of Joseph Kryn and Anastasia among the others.

"Have Joseph and Anastasia returned too?" He looked about the room. "Where are they? In the chapel?"

"No." She smiled and inclined her head. Brilliant light shone from her eyes. "It is time for you to join us."

Father Claude bowed his head, and when he looked up, his face was radiant with light and joy. Kateri took his hand ever so gently in hers, and looking deeply into his eyes, into his heart, into his very soul, she led him to a holy stream that flows into the river of light.

THE END

A NOTE TO THE READER

Dear Reader,
For more than sixty years the story of Kateri Tekakwitha has inspired me with its stoic simplicity. I hope you enjoyed my telling of it. If you have a moment, I would appreciate your feedback.

Please leave a review on **Amazon** or **Goodreads** so others may find and read this work.

Also, I enjoy staying in contact with my readers, so please add your name and address to my mailing list at https://jackcasey.com/news/ or follow me on Facebook.

JACK CASEY

ALSO BY JACK CASEY

Hamilton's Choice

The Trial of Bat Shea

Into the Heartland

ABOUT THE AUTHOR

Jack Casey studied literature at Yale, Edinburgh and Cambridge Universities. He writes novels about his native New York State and practices law in Troy, NY. Recently married, he and Victoria make their home in Troy and in Raleigh, NC.

Connect with Jack at JackCasey.com and on Facebook.

9 781734 366600